Family Circle

ANNUAL
recipes
2012

RIGATONI WITH CREAMY
PEPPER SAUCE,
PAGE 73

Meredith® Consumer Marketing
Des Moines, Iowa

VERY BERRY ICE
CREAM, PAGE 191

WELCOME TO A YEAR'S WORTH OF FABULOUS *FAMILY CIRCLE*® RECIPES!

This year, our magazine underwent a redesign. In that process, we kept what we felt was working and changed what we thought needed changing. The redesign is just one example of how we constantly strive to improve at our job—which is to help you make your life and the lives of those you love healthier, happier, simpler and more inspired. That applies to everything we do, from decorating ideas to fashion to relationship advice to food.

At *Family Circle,* we're always thinking of ways to make your life easier, and we know that one of the things you're always thinking about is how to feed your family delicious, healthy meals that are quick and easy to make—and affordable too. That's why we created *Family Circle*® *Annual Recipes 2012.* Our regular Meal Deals feature serves up fabulous ideas for fast, fresh, great-tasting meals that keep your grocery bill in check. We also know you're fans of the slow cooker. Each month, a collection of slow cooker recipes provides innovative recipes for delicious dinners that are ready to eat when you walk through the door.

That's the practical side of our job. The other goal we have is to inspire you to create something special in the kitchen, especially around the seasons and various holidays. For Valentine's Day, make them melt with rich, decadent Cocoa-Almond-Coco Cake (page 61). When grill season rolls around, try BBQ Bacon Pizzas (page 159) or Pork Chops with Bourbon-Blueberry Glaze (page 160). And when it's cold outside or life has got you down and you need comfort, try one of our 10 new ways to enjoy macaroni and cheese, including Buffalo Mac and Smoky Wild Mushroom Mac (story starts on page 20).

Food and family are interconnected. Our hope is that you can enjoy them both around the table every day.

Linda

Linda Fears, Editor in Chief
Family Circle® Magazine

Family Circle Annual Recipes 2012

Meredith Consumer Marketing
Vice President, Consumer Marketing: Janet Donnelly
Consumer Product Marketing Director: Heather Sorensen
Business Director: Ron Clingman
Consumer Marketing Product Manager: Wendy Merical
Senior Production Manager: Al Rodruck

Waterbury Publications, Inc.
Editorial Director: Lisa Kingsley
Associate Editor: Tricia Bergman
Creative Director: Ken Carlson
Associate Design Director: Doug Samuelson
Graphic Designer: Mindy Samuelson
Contributing Copy Editors: Terri Fredrickson, Gretchen Kauffman
Contributing Indexer: Elizabeth T. Parson

Family Circle Magazine
Editor in Chief: Linda Fears
Creative Director: Karmen Lizzul
Food Director: Regina Ragone, M.S., R.D.
Senior Food Editor: Julie Miltenberger
Associate Food Editor: Michael Tyrrell
Assistant Food Editor: Melissa Knific
Editorial Assistant: Megan Bingham

Meredith National Media Group
President: Tom Harty

Meredith Corporation
Chairman and Chief Executive Officer: Stephen M. Lacy

In Memoriam: E.T. Meredith III (1933–2003)

Copyright © 2012
Meredith Corporation.
Des Moines, Iowa.
First Edition.
Printed in the United States of America.
ISSN: 1942-7476
ISBN: 978-0-696-30135-3

All of us at Meredith Consumer Marketing
are dedicated to providing you with
information and ideas to enhance your
home. We welcome your comments and
suggestions. Write to us at: Meredith
Consumer Marketing, 1716 Locust St.,
Des Moines, IA 50309-3023.

LET'S EAT! Sitting down at your own table at the end of a long day to enjoy a fresh, flavorful home-cooked meal soothes away the day's stresses and satisfies on so many levels. This compilation of recipes from the 2012 issues of *Family Circle*® Magazine makes it simpler than ever to serve up delicious food you cook yourself—whether it's a quick weeknight dinner or a special evening with friends. Recipes are organized by month to take advantage of what's in season and to make it easy to find just the right recipe for any occasion.

Mini Meatball Lasagna (shown below; recipe on page 231) is part of the Pasta Perfect feature in September. Itty-bitty meatballs are layered with sauce and cheese between ruffled layers of lasagna noodles. Pasta Perfect presents fresh and fun takes on everyone's favorite carb, including Spaghetti Carbonara Pie, Shrimp & Crab al Forno, Baked Pumpkin & Sausage Rigatoni, and hearty Beef Stroganoff Casserole.

FLANK STEAK WITH
TOMATO, CUCUMBER
& WATERMELON
SALAD, PAGE 201

CONTENTS

THREE-CHEESE BAKED MAC,
PAGE 28

JANUARY

11

18

23

MEAL DEALS
Great-tasting, affordable dinners.

Wine-Braised Beef with Celery Root Puree

MAKES 4 servings **PREP** 20 minutes **BRAISE** at 350° for 1½ hours **COOK** 38 minutes

WINE-BRAISED BEEF

- 1¼ **pounds beef chuck, cut into 2-inch cubes**
- ¼ **teaspoon salt**
- ¼ **teaspoon pepper**
- 1 **tablespoon vegetable oil**
- 3 **large carrots (about ½ pound), peeled and cut into 1-inch pieces**
- 8 **ounces frozen pearl onions (1¼ cups), thawed**
- 2 **garlic cloves, chopped**
- 2 **tablespoons flour**
- 2 **cups hearty red wine**
- 1 **cup low-sodium beef stock**
- 1 **tablespoon tomato paste**
- 1 **sprig fresh rosemary**
  Fresh parsley (optional)

CELERY ROOT PUREE

- 1 **celery root (about 1 pound), peeled and cut into 2-inch pieces**
- 2 **baking potatoes, peeled and cut into 2-inch pieces**
- 1 **garlic clove, smashed**
- ½ **cup 2% milk**
- ½ **teaspoon salt**

• **Wine-Braised Beef.** Heat oven to 350°. Season beef with salt and pepper. Heat oil in a Dutch oven on high; brown beef on all sides, about 3 to 5 minutes. Reduce heat to medium-high, add carrots, onions and garlic; cook for 2 minutes. Stir in flour and cook 1 minute. Add wine, stock, tomato paste and rosemary and bring to a boil. Cover, place in oven and braise at 350° for 1½ hours or until meat is knife-tender and sauce thickens.

• **Celery Root Puree.** Meanwhile, place celery root, potatoes and garlic in a lidded pot, covering with cold water. Bring to a boil, reduce heat to medium and simmer, covered, until vegetables are tender, 25 to 30 minutes. Drain; puree in blender or processor with milk until smooth. (Add more milk if necessary.) Season with salt.

• Serve braised beef and sauce on top of the celery root puree. Garnish with chopped parsley, if desired.

PER SERVING 588 **CAL**; 12 g **FAT** (4 g **SAT**); 41 g **PRO**; 58 g **CARB**; 6 g **FIBER**; 777 mg **SODIUM**; 67 mg **CHOL**

CHEAP TRICKS

Don't fall into the trap of associating wine with extravagance. Sure, pricey bottles abound but so do good-quality steals. For this recipe, we chose a bottle by Frunza, a brand sold nationwide at Sam's Club. The merlot features notes of blueberry and blackberry and costs a mere $5! It's perfect for braising red meat—or just sipping.

RING IN THE NEW

Start off the year on a healthy note with these deliciously good-for-you meals.

BEEF & BROCCOLI
LO MEIN, PAGE 19

TILAPIA VERACRUZ,
PAGE 19

CHICKEN, SWEET POTATO & CAULIFLOWER VINDALOO

Chicken, Sweet Potato & Cauliflower Vindaloo

MAKES 4 servings **PREP** 20 minutes
COOK 22 minutes

2	tablespoons vegetable oil
1	pound boneless, skinless chicken thighs
½	teaspoon salt
1	pound sweet potatoes, peeled and cut into ½-inch cubes
1	large onion, chopped
1	medium cauliflower, cut into florets
2	teaspoons curry powder
½	teaspoon cayenne pepper
1	can (14½ ounces) reduced-sodium chicken broth
1	can (14½ ounces) diced tomatoes
½	cup mint, coarsely chopped
2	cups cooked quinoa

• Heat 1 tablespoon of the oil in a large nonstick skillet over medium-high heat. Season chicken with ¼ teaspoon of the salt. Cook for 7 to 8 minutes. Remove to a plate.

• Add 1 remaining tablespoon of oil, sweet potatoes and onion to skillet and stir-fry for 5 minutes. Add cauliflower and cook 3 minutes. Stir in curry powder, cayenne and the remaining ¼ teaspoon salt; cook 1 minute. Add broth and tomatoes; cook 5 minutes, covered, stirring occasionally.

• Add chicken and heat through. Stir in mint and serve over cooked quinoa.

PER SERVING 458 **CAL**; 16 g **FAT** (3 g **SAT**); 31 g **PRO**; 50 g **CARB**; 7 g **FIBER**; 762 mg **SODIUM**; 110 mg **CHOL**

Kid Tweak For a less spicy version, cut cayenne down to a pinch.

Meatless Variation Eliminate chicken in the first step; replace with diced broiled tofu.

Roasted Salmon & Easy Romesco Sauce

MAKES 4 servings **PREP** 20 minutes **BAKE** at 450° for 30 minutes

ROMESCO SAUCE

1	cup roasted red peppers
2	tablespoons slivered almonds
1	tablespoon red wine vinegar
2	teaspoons olive oil
1	clove garlic, chopped
⅛	teaspoon salt
⅛	teaspoon black pepper

SALMON & VEGETABLES

1	pound Brussels sprouts, halved
1	pound carrots, cut into 1-inch pieces
1	tablespoon olive oil
¼	teaspoon salt
¼	teaspoon black pepper
4	salmon fillets, 4 ounces each
2	cups cooked whole-wheat couscous

• Heat oven to 450°. Coat two rimmed baking pans with nonstick cooking spray.

• **Romesco Sauce.** In a blender, process red peppers, almonds, vinegar, olive oil, garlic, salt and pepper until smooth.

• **Salmon & Vegetables.** Place Brussels sprouts and carrots in one of the prepared baking pans, toss with oil and season with ⅛ teaspoon each of the salt and pepper. Roast at 450° for 30 minutes or until tender.

• Meanwhile, season salmon with the remaining ⅛ teaspoon each salt and pepper. Place in the second prepared baking pan and roast at 450° for 15 minutes.

• Serve salmon, couscous and vegetables with romesco sauce on the side.

PER SERVING 471 **CAL**; 18 g **FAT** (2 g **SAT**); 35 g **PRO**; 45 g **CARB**; 10 g **FIBER**; 650 mg **SODIUM**; 72 mg **CHOL**

Spinach & Three-Bean Enchiladas

MAKES 6 servings PREP 15 minutes
COOK 9 minutes BAKE at 350° for 30 minutes

1	tablespoon vegetable oil
½	large onion, chopped
4	cloves garlic, chopped
1	can (15 ounces) kidney beans, drained and rinsed
1	can (15 ounces) black beans, drained and rinsed
1	can (15 ounces) pinto beans, drained and rinsed
1	can (8 ounces) no-salt-added tomato sauce
1	tablespoon chili powder
1	teaspoon ground cumin
1	bag (6 ounces) baby spinach
½	cup cilantro, chopped
6	whole-wheat fajita-size tortillas
1½	cups shredded reduced-fat Mexican-blend cheese
	Tossed salad, optional

• Heat oven to 350°. Coat a 13 x 9 x 2-inch baking dish with nonstick cooking spray.

• Heat oil in a large nonstick skillet over medium-high heat. Add onion and garlic and cook 3 minutes, stirring occasionally. Stir in beans, tomato sauce, chili powder and cumin; simmer 3 minutes, stirring occasionally.

• Gradually stir in spinach until wilted, about 3 minutes. Stir in cilantro and lightly mash bean mixture with a potato masher. Spoon about ¾ cup of the bean mixture down center of each tortilla and tightly roll up; place seam side down in prepared dish.

• Sprinkle cheese over enchiladas; cover and bake at 350° for 30 minutes. Serve warm with tossed salad, if desired.

PER SERVING 373 CAL; 11 g FAT (3 g SAT); 23 g PRO; 52 g CARB; 19 g FIBER; 757 mg SODIUM; 20 mg CHOL

Broccoli & Mushroom Lasagna

MAKES 8 servings PREP 30 minutes COOK 17 minutes BAKE at 350° for 45 minutes
LET STAND 10 minutes

⅓	cup all-purpose flour
3½	cups low-fat (1%) milk
1	teaspoon salt
¼	teaspoon black pepper
⅛	teaspoon nutmeg
¾	cup grated Parmesan cheese
2	heads broccoli, cut into florets
10	ounces sliced mixed mushrooms
12	traditional lasagna noodles (from a 16-ounce package)
1	container (15 ounces) reduced-fat ricotta cheese, mixed with 1 egg
2	cups shredded reduced-fat mozzarella cheese

• Heat oven to 350°. Coat a 13 x 9 x 2-inch baking dish with nonstick cooking spray.

• In a medium saucepan, whisk flour and 1 cup of the milk until smooth. Stir in remaining 2½ cups milk and bring to a boil; boil for 3 minutes, whisking constantly, until thickened. Whisk in salt, pepper, nutmeg and ½ cup of the Parmesan. Set aside.

• Meanwhile, bring a large pot of lightly salted water to a boil. Add broccoli and cook 4 minutes; add mushrooms during last minute of cooking time. Using a slotted spoon, remove broccoli and mushrooms to a bowl. In the same pot, cook lasagna noodles following package directions, about 10 minutes. Drain.

• Assemble lasagna: Spread ½ cup of the cheese sauce in bottom of prepared dish. Place 3 noodles over sauce, evenly spread ricotta mixture over top and add another layer of noodles. Spoon on vegetables, 2 cups of the sauce and ½ cup of the mozzarella. Place another layer of noodles over vegetables and top with the remaining 1½ cups of cheese and remaining noodles. Evenly spread the remaining 1 cup of sauce over top and sprinkle with the remaining ¼ cup Parmesan cheese.

• Cover with nonstick foil and bake at 350° for 30 minutes; uncover and bake for an additional 15 minutes. Allow to stand 10 minutes before serving.

PER SERVING 394 CAL; 15 g FAT (9 g SAT); 29 g PRO; 39 g CARB; 3 g FIBER; 800 mg SODIUM; 78 mg CHOL

Baked Pears with Craisins & Walnuts

MAKES 6 servings **PREP** 10 minutes **BAKE** at 375° for 45 minutes

3	ripe Bosc pears, halved lengthwise and core removed
⅓	cup Ocean Spray blueberry juice–infused dried Craisins
¼	cup coarsely chopped walnuts
2	tablespoons brown sugar Juice and zest from 1 small lemon
¾	cup cranberry juice
1½	cups reduced-fat frozen yogurt

• Heat oven to 375°.

• Cut a thin slice from bottom of each pear half so that pears lie flat. Place in a 13 x 9 x 2-inch baking dish, cored side up.

• In small bowl, combine Craisins, walnuts, brown sugar, lemon juice and zest. Spoon an equal amount of the mixture into each pear half.

• Pour cranberry juice over pears and cover. Bake at 375° for 30 minutes. Uncover and bake for an additional 15 minutes or until tender.

• Serve warm with frozen yogurt.

PER SERVING 238 **CAL**; 6 g **FAT** (2 g **SAT**); 6 g **PRO**; 44 g **CARB**; 3 g **FIBER**; 31 mg **SODIUM**; 33 mg **CHOL**

Beef & Broccoli Lo Mein

MAKES 4 servings   **PREP** 20 minutes
COOK 15 minutes

- 1   cup reduced-sodium beef broth
- 3   tablespoons reduced-sodium soy sauce
- 3   tablespoons ketchup
- 1   tablespoon rice vinegar
- 1   tablespoon cornstarch
- ¼   teaspoon red pepper flakes
- 1   large head broccoli, cut into florets
- ½   pound whole-grain linguine (such as Barilla)
- 2   tablespoons vegetable oil
- ½   pound flank steak, sliced into ¼-inch-thick slices
- 1   large green bell pepper, cored, seeded and thinly sliced
- 1   can (8 ounces) chopped water chestnuts, drained

• In a small bowl, whisk broth, soy sauce, ketchup, vinegar, cornstarch and red pepper flakes. Set aside.

• Bring a large pot of water to a boil. Lightly salt and add broccoli. Bring back to a boil and cook for 3 minutes. Scoop out broccoli with a slotted spoon and reserve. In same pot, cook pasta for 6 minutes; drain and set aside.

• In a large nonstick skillet, heat oil over medium-high heat. Add steak and pepper and stir-fry for 3 minutes. Stir in sauce and simmer 1 minute until thickened. Add broccoli and water chestnuts; cook 2 minutes. Toss with pasta and serve immediately.

PER SERVING 453 **CAL**; 12 g **FAT** (3 g **SAT**); 26 g **PRO**; 63 g **CARB**; 7 g **FIBER**; 689 mg **SODIUM**; 19 mg **CHOL**

Meatless Variation Substitute soy crumbles for flank steak.

Tilapia Veracruz

MAKES 4 servings   **PREP** 15 minutes
COOK 16 minutes

- 2   tablespoons olive oil
- 3   large sweet red and green peppers, cored, seeded and thinly sliced
- 1   large onion, thinly sliced
- 1   large jalapeño pepper, seeded and chopped
- 4   cloves garlic, sliced
- 4   plum tomatoes, seeded and chopped
- 1   can (8 ounces) no-salt-added tomato sauce
- ¾   teaspoon salt
- ¼   teaspoon black pepper
- 4   tilapia fillets (about 4 ounces each)
- 1   cup cilantro leaves, chopped
- 3   cups cooked brown and wild rice blend (such as RiceSelect Royal Blend)
- 1   lemon, cut into wedges

• Heat oil in a large nonstick skillet over medium-high heat. Add peppers, onion, jalapeño and garlic. Cook for 10 minutes, stirring occasionally. Stir in tomatoes, tomato sauce, ½ cup water, ½ teaspoon of the salt and ⅛ teaspoon of the black pepper. Bring to a simmer.

• Season tilapia with remaining ¼ teaspoon salt and ⅛ teaspoon black pepper. Place fish in skillet and cover with sauce. Simmer, covered, for 6 minutes or until fish flakes easily. Sprinkle cilantro over top.

• Serve with cooked rice. Squeeze a few lemon wedges over each serving.

PER SERVING 455 **CAL**; 11 g **FAT** (2 g **SAT**); 38 g **PRO**; 51 g **CARB**; 7 g **FIBER**; 611 mg **SODIUM**; 82 mg **CHOL**

When using reduced-sodium products such as tomato sauce, punch up the flavor with add-ins like hot peppers, fresh herbs and lemon juice.

MACARONI. CHEESE.

10 faves. Enough said.

BUFFALO MAC,
PAGE 31

SMOKEY WILD
MUSHROOM MAC,
PAGE 28

PESTO ALFREDO MAC

Pesto Alfredo Mac

MAKES 8 servings **PREP** 15 minutes
COOK 15 minutes

- 1 **box (14.5 ounces) Barilla Plus farfalle**
- 2 **cups packed basil**
- ½ **cup pine nuts, toasted**
- 2 **garlic cloves, roughly chopped**
- ⅓ **cup olive oil**
- ⅔ **cup shredded Parmesan**
- ¼ **teaspoon salt**
- ⅛ **teaspoon pepper**
- 2 **tablespoons unsalted butter**
- 2 **tablespoons all-purpose flour**
- 2 **cups 2% milk**
- ⅛ **teaspoon nutmeg**
- 2 **cups shredded mozzarella**
- 1 **pint grape tomatoes, halved**

- Bring a large pot of lightly salted water to boiling. Add farfalle and cook 10 minutes; drain and set aside.

- Meanwhile, in a food processor, combine basil, ¼ cup of the pine nuts and the garlic. With machine running, slowly add oil in a thin stream until well combined. Remove to a small bowl and stir in ⅓ cup of the Parmesan, the salt and pepper. Set aside.

- In a large saucepan, melt butter on medium heat. Sprinkle in flour, whisking constantly for 2 minutes. Pour in milk, nutmeg and pesto, whisking until the liquid comes to a boil. Simmer until thickened, about 2 to 3 minutes. Remove from heat and stir in 1½ cups of the mozzarella and remaining ⅓ cup Parmesan. Mix until smooth.

- Stir in tomatoes and pasta. Fold remaining ½ cup mozzarella into mixture; pour into serving dish. Top with remaining ¼ cup pine nuts.

PER SERVING 527 **CAL**; 28 g **FAT** (8 g **SAT**); 24 g **PRO**; 47 g **CARB**; 5 g **FIBER**; 402 mg **SODIUM**; 36 mg **CHOL**

Cheddar-Apple Sausage Mac

MAKES 8 servings **PREP** 15 minutes **COOK** 22 minutes **BAKE** at 350° for 25 minutes
BROIL 3 minutes

- 1 **pound rigatoni**
- 1 **package (12 ounces) sweet apple-chicken sausage, sliced**
- 3 **tablespoons unsalted butter**
- 2 **Granny Smith apples, cored, peeled and sliced**
- ½ **small sweet onion, sliced**
- ⅛ **teaspoon each salt and pepper**
- 2 **tablespoons all-purpose flour**
- 1½ **cups 2% milk**
- 1 **tablespoon Dijon mustard**
- 3 **cups shredded extra-sharp cheddar cheese**
- ½ **cup panko bread crumbs**

- Heat oven to 350°. Coat a 13 x 9 x 2-inch broiler-safe baking dish with nonstick cooking spray. Bring a large pot of lightly salted water to boiling. Add rigatoni and cook for 13 minutes, or as per package directions. Drain and return to pot.

- Coat a large nonstick skillet with nonstick cooking spray and place over medium-high heat. Add sausage and cook 4 minutes, stirring until browned. Remove to a plate with a slotted spoon and keep warm.

- Stir 1 tablespoon of the butter into same skillet. Add apples and onion and cook 5 minutes over medium heat. Remove from heat and stir in sausage, salt and pepper. Add to pasta in pot.

- Meanwhile, melt remaining 2 tablespoons butter over medium heat in a medium saucepan. Whisk in flour and cook 1 minute. Pour in milk and mustard and bring to a simmer. Cook 3 minutes, whisking occasionally. Remove from heat and whisk in cheese. Stir into pasta mixture in pot.

- Pour pasta mixture into prepared dish. Top with panko. Bake at 350° for 25 minutes. Increase oven temperature to broil and broil dish for 3 minutes until lightly browned.

PER SERVING 570 **CAL**; 25 g **FAT** (14 g **SAT**); 26 g **PRO**; 59 g **CARB**; 3 g **FIBER**; 628 mg **SODIUM**; 91 mg **CHOL**

Chicken Parm Mac

MAKES 8 servings **PREP** 15 minutes
COOK 17 minutes **BAKE** at 425° for 12 minutes
BROIL 3 minutes

- **1 package (12 ounces) baked breaded Italian-style chicken breast cutlets (such as Perdue)**
- **1 pound ziti**
- **3 tablespoons unsalted butter**
- **2 cloves garlic, chopped**
- **3 tablespoons all-purpose flour**
- **2 cups 2% milk**
- **1 package (7 ounces) 2% Italian cheese blend**
- **½ cup shredded Parmesan**
- **1 can (14½ ounces) diced tomatoes with Italian seasoning, drained**
- **1 cup jarred marinara**

• Heat oven to 425°. Place cutlets on a baking sheet. Bake at 425° for 12 minutes, turning once. Remove from oven; cool and cut into bite-size pieces.

• Meanwhile, bring a large pot of lightly salted water to boiling. Add pasta and cook 12 minutes, or as per package directions. Drain.

• Increase oven temperature to broil. Melt butter in a medium saucepan over medium heat. Add garlic; cook 1 minute. Whisk in flour; cook 1 minute. Pour in milk, whisking. Bring to a simmer and cook 3 minutes. Remove from heat and whisk in 1¼ cups of the Italian-blend cheese and ¼ cup of the Parmesan.

• Stir cheese sauce and tomatoes into pasta. Fold in chicken. Pour into broiler-safe dish. Top with marinara and remaining ½ cup Italian-blend cheese and ¼ cup Parmesan. Broil 3 minutes until cheese is lightly browned.

PER SERVING 508 **CAL**; 18 g **FAT** (9 g **SAT**); 25 g **PRO**; 59 g **CARB**; 4 g **FIBER**; 907 mg **SODIUM**; 51 mg **CHOL**

Meat Lover's Mac

MAKES 8 servings **PREP** 15 minutes **COOK** 14 minutes

- **1 pound medium shell-shape pasta**
- **6 slices bacon, diced**
- **½ pound 90% lean ground beef, crumbled**
- **1 pouch pepperoni (from a 3.5-ounce package), about 26 slices, chopped**
- **3 scallions, trimmed and sliced**
- **2 tablespoons unsalted butter**
- **2 tablespoons all-purpose flour**
- **1½ cups 2% milk**
- **8 ounces Monterey Jack cheese, shredded**
- **4 ounces sharp white cheddar, shredded (about 1 cup)**

• Heat a large pot of lightly salted water to boiling. Add shells; cook 10 minutes, or as per package directions. Drain and return to pot.

• Meanwhile, combine bacon and ground beef in a medium saucepan over medium heat. Cook 5 minutes, stirring occasionally. Stir in pepperoni; cook another 5 minutes. Stir in two-thirds of the chopped scallions. Remove to a paper towel–lined plate with a slotted spoon. Discard drippings from pot.

• In same saucepan, melt butter over medium heat. Sprinkle with flour and cook, whisking, 1 minute. Whisk in milk and bring to a simmer, whisking frequently. Simmer 3 minutes, whisking until thickened. Remove from heat and add cheeses. Whisk until smooth. Stir in meat mixture and fold into pasta. Top with remaining scallions and serve.

PER SERVING 525 **CAL**; 25 g **FAT** (13 g **SAT**); 28 g **PRO**; 47 g **CARB**; 2 g **FIBER**; 496 mg **SODIUM**; 82 mg **CHOL**

CHICKEN PARM MAC

SPANISH MAC

Spanish Mac

MAKES 8 servings **PREP** 10 minutes
COOK 15 minutes

- 1 **pound elbow macaroni**
- 1 **tablespoon olive oil**
- 1 **cup (4 ounces) cured chorizo, casing removed, diced**
- 1 **poblano pepper, seeded and diced**
- 3 **cloves garlic, minced**
- 1 **tablespoon unsalted butter**
- 2 **tablespoons all-purpose flour**
- 2 **cups 2% milk**
- 8 **ounces Manchego or Pecorino Romano cheese, grated**
- ½ **cup pimento-stuffed green olives, sliced**

• Bring a large pot of lightly salted water to boiling. Add elbow macaroni and cook 7 minutes, or as per package directions; drain and transfer to a large bowl.

• Meanwhile, in a large saucepan, heat oil on medium-low heat. Add chorizo and cook 5 minutes. Increase heat to medium-high and add pepper; sauté for 3 minutes. Stir in garlic and cook another 1 to 2 minutes.

• Add butter to saucepan; when melted, sprinkle in flour, whisking constantly for 2 minutes. Pour in milk, whisking until the liquid comes to a boil. Simmer until thickened, about 3 minutes. Remove from heat and stir in cheese. Mix until smooth. Stir into cooked macaroni with olives.

PER SERVING 467 **CAL**; 21 g **FAT** (10 g **SAT**); 25 g **PRO**; 47 g **CARB**; 2 g **FIBER**; 959 mg **SODIUM**; 49 mg **CHOL**

Goat Cheese, Fig & Walnut Mac

MAKES 8 servings **PREP** 10 minutes **COOK** 30 minutes

- 2½ **cups 2% milk**
- 1 **sprig fresh rosemary**
- 1 **pound gemelli**
- 2 **tablespoons unsalted butter**
- 2 **tablespoons all-purpose flour**
- 2 **logs (4 ounces each) goat cheese**
- ½ **teaspoon salt**
- 1 **cup dried figs, sliced**
- 1 **cup chopped toasted walnuts**

• Add milk and rosemary to a small lidded saucepan over low heat. Cover for 20 to 25 minutes, allowing herb to infuse. Remove rosemary sprig.

• Meanwhile, bring a large pot of lightly salted water to boiling. Add gemelli. Cook 10 minutes, or as per package directions; drain and set aside.

• In a large saucepan, melt butter over medium heat. Sprinkle in flour, whisking constantly for 2 minutes. Pour in infused milk, whisking until it comes to a boil. Simmer until thickened, about 3 minutes. Crumble in goat cheese, piece by piece, stirring until smooth. Add salt, figs, walnuts and cooked gemelli. Serve immediately.

PER SERVING 499 **CAL**; 20 g **FAT** (8 g **SAT**); 19 g **PRO**; 66 g **CARB**; 5 g **FIBER**; 287 mg **SODIUM**; 27 mg **CHOL**

Smoky Wild Mushroom Mac

MAKES 8 servings PREP 15 minutes COOK 17 minutes BAKE at 350° for 20 minutes

- **1 pound campanelle**
- **2 tablespoons unsalted butter**
- **1 tablespoon olive oil**
- **½ cup diced shallots**
- **1½ pounds mixed wild mushrooms (cremini, shiitake and oyster), tough stems removed, sliced**
- **1 tablespoon chopped fresh thyme**
- **2 cloves garlic, minced**
- **3 tablespoons all-purpose flour**
- **3 cups 2% milk**
- **10 ounces smoked Gouda, shredded**
- **½ teaspoon salt**
- **¼ teaspoon pepper**

• Heat oven to 350°. Bring a large pot of lightly salted water to boiling. Add campanelle and cook 8 minutes, or about 1 to 2 minutes less than package directions. Drain and set aside.

• Meanwhile, in a large saucepan, heat 1 tablespoon of the butter and the oil over medium heat. Add shallots and cook 3 minutes. Stir in mushrooms and thyme; cook 5 to 7 minutes. Add garlic and cook another 1 to 2 minutes.

• Add remaining 1 tablespoon butter to saucepan; when melted, sprinkle in flour, whisking for 2 minutes. Pour in milk, whisking until liquid comes to a boil. Simmer until thickened, about 3 minutes. Remove from heat and stir in cheese, salt and pepper until smooth. Stir in cooked campanelle.

• Pour mixture into a 13 x 9 x 2-inch baking dish. Bake at 350° for 20 minutes, until lightly browned and bubbly.

PER SERVING 475 CAL; 19 g FAT (10 g SAT); 22 g PRO; 56 g CARB; 3 g FIBER; 421 mg SODIUM; 52 mg CHOL

Three-Cheese Baked Mac

MAKES 12 side-dish servings PREP 15 minutes
COOK 11 minutes BAKE at 350° for 20 minutes
BROIL 4 minutes

- **1 pound penne**
- **3 tablespoons unsalted butter**
- **3 tablespoons all-purpose flour**
- **2 cups 2% milk**
- **1 tablespoon onion flakes**
- **2 teaspoons mustard powder**
- **¼ teaspoon salt**
-   **Pinch of cayenne pepper**
- **1 bag (8 ounces) shredded Swiss cheese**
- **8 ounces sharp cheddar, shredded (2 cups)**
- **4 ounces Gouda, shredded (1 cup)**

• Heat oven to 350°. Coat a 2-quart broiler-safe dish with nonstick spray. Bring a large pot of lightly salted water to boiling. Add penne; cook 11 minutes, or as per package directions. Drain.

• Meanwhile, melt butter in a medium saucepan over medium heat. Sprinkle with flour and cook, whisking, 1 minute. Whisk in milk, onion flakes, mustard powder, salt and cayenne. Bring to a simmer over medium-high heat. Reduce heat and simmer, whisking, 3 minutes. Remove from heat.

• Toss cheeses together. Whisk 2½ cups of the cheese into milk mixture until smooth. Stir sauce into pasta. Spoon half into prepared baking dish. Top with half of the remaining cheese. Repeat layering, ending with cheese.

• Bake at 350° for 20 minutes. Increase heat to broil and broil 3 to 4 minutes until bubbly and browned.

PER SERVING 383 CAL; 19 g FAT (11 g SAT); 19 g PRO; 34 g CARB; 2 g FIBER; 298 mg SODIUM; 59 mg CHOL

THREE-CHEESE
BAKED MAC

ANTIPASTO MAC

Antipasto Mac

MAKES 8 servings **PREP** 15 minutes
LET STAND 5 minutes **COOK** 8 minutes

- ½   cup sun-dried tomatoes
- 1   pound cavatappi or cellentani
- 1   package (9 ounces) frozen artichoke hearts, thawed
- 2   tablespoons unsalted butter
- 2   tablespoons all-purpose flour
- 2   cups 2% milk
- ½   teaspoon dried oregano
- ¼   teaspoon each salt and pepper
- ½   pound Fontina cheese, grated (2 cups)
- ¼   pound Asiago cheese, shredded (1 cup)
- 1   jar (12 ounces) roasted red peppers, drained and diced

• Bring a large pot of lightly salted water to boiling. Carefully remove 1 cup of the boiling water and pour over sun-dried tomatoes in a medium bowl. Let stand for at least 5 minutes while making sauce. Add pasta to remaining water; cook 8 minutes, or as per package directions. Add artichoke hearts for the last 4 minutes. Drain and set aside.

• Meanwhile, melt butter in a medium saucepan over medium heat. Sprinkle with flour and cook, whisking, for 1 minute. Pour in milk, oregano, salt and pepper. Bring to a simmer. Cook, whisking, 3 minutes.

• Remove from heat and whisk in both cheeses. Drain and chop sun-dried tomatoes and stir into cheese sauce along with roasted peppers. Combine sauce with pasta-artichoke mixture and serve.

PER SERVING 492 **CAL**; 20 g **FAT** (11 g **SAT.**); 22 g **PRO**; 56 g **CARB**; 6 g **FIBER**; 606 mg **SODIUM**; 58 mg **CHOL**

Buffalo Mac

MAKES 8 servings **PREP** 10 minutes **COOK** 16 minutes **MICROWAVE** 30 seconds **BROIL** 3 minutes

- 1   pound fusilli or rotini
- 1   pound boneless, skinless chicken breasts, cut into 1-inch cubes
- 1   teaspoon celery seeds, crushed
- 2   teaspoons paprika
- ¼   teaspoon salt
- 1   tablespoon olive oil
- 2   celery ribs, diced
- 3   cloves garlic, minced
- 4   tablespoons unsalted butter
- 3   tablespoons all-purpose flour
- 2   teaspoons dry mustard
- 2½   cups 2% milk
- ½   cup Frank's RedHot Buffalo Wings Sauce
- 8   ounces sharp cheddar, shredded
- ¾   cup crumbled blue cheese
- ½   cup plain bread crumbs

• Heat broiler. Bring a large pot of lightly salted water to boiling. Add pasta and cook 8 minutes, or as per package directions; drain.

• Meanwhile, season chicken with ½ teaspoon of the celery seeds, 1 teaspoon of the paprika and the salt. In a large skillet, heat oil over medium-high heat. Brown chicken, 3 to 5 minutes, until cooked through; set aside. Lower heat to medium. Add celery to same skillet; sauté 4 minutes. Add garlic; cook 1 to 2 minutes. Set aside with chicken.

• In saucepan, melt 3 tablespoons of the butter over medium heat. Sprinkle in flour and mustard powder, whisking for 2 minutes. Pour in milk and sauce, whisking until it boils. Simmer 3 minutes. Remove from heat; stir in cheddar, ½ cup of the blue cheese and remaining teaspoon paprika.

• Add pasta, celery, garlic and chicken. Place in a broiler-safe dish.

• Microwave remaining 1 tablespoon butter for 30 seconds. Stir in bread crumbs and remaining ½ teaspoon celery seeds; sprinkle over dish with remaining ¼ cup blue cheese. Broil 2 to 3 minutes, or until browned.

PER SERVING 581 **CAL**; 24 g **FAT** (13 g **SAT**); 35 g **PRO**; 56 g **CARB**; 3 g **FIBER**; 987 mg **SODIUM**; 94 mg **CHOL**

CHIPOTLE BROWNIES,
PAGE 58

FEBRUARY

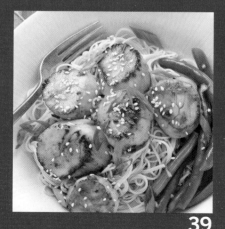

39

52

61

MEAL DEALS

Great-tasting, affordable dinners.

Pork with Apple-Fennel Compote

MAKES 4 servings **PREP** 15 minutes **COOK** 21 minutes **ROAST** at 400° for 20 minutes **LET REST** 5 minutes

PORK & APPLE-FENNEL COMPOTE

2	teaspoons cumin
½	teaspoon salt
¼	teaspoon cayenne pepper
1	pound pork tenderloin
1	teaspoon vegetable oil
⅓	cup cider vinegar
⅓	cup packed light-brown sugar
¼	teaspoon ground cloves
½	teaspoon cinnamon
½	fennel bulb, thinly sliced, fronds reserved for garnish
½	sweet onion, thinly sliced
2	apples, peeled, cored and thinly sliced
2	cloves garlic, minced

SPINACH

1½	tablespoons olive oil
2	cloves garlic, minced
2	teaspoons caraway seeds
18	ounces fresh spinach
¼	teaspoon salt

• **Pork.** Heat oven to 400°. Line a baking sheet with foil. Combine 1 teaspoon of the cumin, salt and cayenne. Trim pork and pat dry with paper towels, coat with vegetable oil and rub with spices. Place pork on prepared baking sheet. Roast at 400° for 20 minutes or until internal temperature registers 145°. Let rest 5 minutes.

• **Compote.** In a large sauté pan, combine vinegar, brown sugar, cloves, cinnamon and remaining 1 teaspoon cumin on medium-high heat until sugar dissolves, about 1 minute. Add fennel, onion, apples and garlic; cook 15 to 20 minutes or until apples have softened.

• Meanwhile, make **Spinach.** In another large sauté pan, heat olive oil over medium heat. Add garlic and caraway seeds; cook 1 minute. Add spinach and cook until wilted, about 3 minutes. Season with salt.

PER SERVING 381 **CAL**; 11 g **FAT** (2 g **SAT**); 28 g **PRO**; 47 g **CARB**; 9 g **FIBER**; 725 mg **SODIUM**; 74 mg **CHOL**

CHEAP TRICKS

Prepackaged, prewashed fresh baby spinach can cost a bundle. Keep in mind that large-leaf spinach typically costs less (and swapping it out won't make a difference when wilted so long as the tough stems are removed). Look for the long-stemmed bunches next to other greens like kale and romaine.

OFF THE HOOK

These quick, satisfying, heart-healthy seafood suppers are sure to reel in your crew.

CRISPY FISH STICKS
& CHILI DIPPING SAUCE, PAGE 43

SHRIMP ÉTOUFFÉE,
PAGE 43

HONEY-SESAME SCALLOPS

Honey-Sesame Scallops

MAKES 4 servings **PREP** 15 minutes
MARINATE 30 minutes **COOK** 7 minutes

- 3 tablespoons reduced-sodium soy sauce
- 2 tablespoons rice vinegar
- 2 tablespoons honey
- 2 tablespoons chopped ginger
- 2 teaspoons sesame oil
- 1½ pounds sea scallops
- 8 ounces angel hair pasta, cooked following package directions
- 2 scallions, thinly sliced
- 2 teaspoons toasted sesame seeds
  Garlic String Beans (optional)

• In a large bowl, whisk together soy sauce, vinegar, honey, ginger and sesame oil. Add scallops and toss to coat. Cover and refrigerate for 30 minutes.

• Heat a large nonstick skillet over medium-high heat. Add scallops, reserving marinade; cook scallops 3 minutes per side. Remove and place on a plate.

• Pour reserved marinade into same skillet and boil 1 minute. Return scallops to skillet and heat through, coating with sauce.

• Equally divide pasta among four plates and drizzle each with sauce from skillet. Place about 6 scallops over each serving and garnish with scallions and sesame seeds. Serve with Garlic String Beans (see recipe, below).

PER SERVING 495 **CAL**; 9 g **FAT** (1 g **SAT**);
38 g **PRO**; 63 g **CARB**; 4 g **FIBER**; 731 mg
SODIUM; 56 mg **CHOL**

Garlic String Beans

Bring a large pot of lightly salted water to boiling. Add 1 pound trimmed green beans and cook 4 minutes until crisp-tender; drain. In same pot, heat 1 tablespoon olive oil over medium-high heat. Add 3 cloves sliced garlic and cook 1 minute; stir in beans and toss to coat with oil. Cook 1 minute and season with ⅛ teaspoons each salt and black pepper.

Cornmeal-Crusted Catfish Po' Boys

MAKES 4 servings **PREP** 20 minutes **BROIL** 8 minutes

- 2 tablespoons reduced-fat mayonnaise
- 1 tablespoon lemon juice plus 1 teaspoon zest
- 1 teaspoon lime zest
- 1 clove garlic, finely chopped
  Dash of cayenne pepper
- ¼ cup cornmeal
- 1 tablespoon Old Bay seasoning
- 4 catfish or flounder fillets (about 4 ounces each)
- 4 soft hearty white rolls (about 3 ounces each), split in half lengthwise
- 1 ripe tomato, thinly sliced
- 4 pieces of Bibb lettuce

• Heat broiler. Coat a broiler pan with nonstick cooking spray.

• In a small bowl, stir together mayonnaise, lemon juice, zests, garlic and cayenne until smooth.

• In a shallow glass dish, whisk together cornmeal and Old Bay seasoning. Coat fillets with nonstick cooking spray and dredge in cornmeal. Place on prepared broiler pan and broil, 4 inches from heat, for 7 to 8 minutes or until fish flakes easily.

• To assemble, pull out some of the soft center of the rolls and discard. Cover both cut sides of the rolls with the mayonnaise mixture and fill with a fish fillet, tomato slices and lettuce.

PER SERVING 437 **CAL**; 15 g **FAT** (4 g **SAT**);
32 g **PRO**; 43 g **CARB**; 3 g **FIBER**; 757 mg
SODIUM; 70 mg **CHOL**

Grilled Tuna with Red Quinoa Risotto

MAKES 4 servings **PREP** 15 minutes **COOK** 23 minutes **GRILL** 6 minutes

- 1 tablespoon canola oil
- 1 cup chopped onion
- 1¼ cups red quinoa
- 1½ cups vegetable broth
- ¼ plus ⅛ teaspoon salt
- 1 package (7½ ounces) frozen asparagus, thawed and cut into 1-inch pieces
- ¼ cup grated Parmesan cheese
- 2 tablespoons unsalted butter
- 2 tuna fillets (about 10 ounces each, 1 inch thick)
- ½ teaspoon dried Italian seasoning
- ⅛ teaspoon black pepper

• In a medium-size saucepan, heat oil over medium heat; add onion and cook 5 minutes, stirring occasionally. Stir in quinoa, broth and ¼ teaspoon of the salt. Bring to boil; reduce heat to medium-low and simmer, covered, for 17 to 18 minutes until liquid is absorbed and quinoa is tender. Stir in asparagus during last 5 minutes of cooking time. Add an additional ¼ cup water if quinoa becomes too dry. Let stand, covered, 5 minutes.

• Just before serving, stir Parmesan and butter into quinoa.

• Meanwhile, heat a grill pan over medium-high heat; lightly grease. Season tuna with remaining ⅛ teaspoon salt, Italian seasoning and black pepper. Grill for 2 to 3 minutes per side for medium-rare.

• Cut each piece of tuna into 2 servings and serve over quinoa risotto.

PER SERVING 494 **CAL**; 16 g **FAT** (6 g **SAT**); 44 g **PRO**; 44 g **CARB**; 5 g **FIBER**; 770 mg **SODIUM**; 89 mg **CHOL**

Halibut Provençal

MAKES 4 servings **PREP** 15 minutes
COOK 30 minutes **BROIL** 6 minutes

SAUCE
- 1 tablespoon olive oil
- 1 large shallot, chopped
- 3 cloves garlic, chopped
- 1 sweet red pepper, seeds removed, chopped
- 1 orange pepper, seeds removed, chopped
- 2 cups grape tomatoes, halved
- ⅓ cup sliced pitted Kalamata olives
- 3 tablespoons red wine vinegar
- ½ cup basil leaves, torn
- ¼ teaspoon salt
- ⅛ teaspoon black pepper

BARLEY AND FISH
- 1 cup barley
- ½ teaspoon salt
- ¼ teaspoon black pepper
- 1¼ pounds halibut, skin on, cut into 4 equal-size pieces
- 2 teaspoons olive oil

• **Sauce.** In a large nonstick skillet, heat olive oil over medium heat. Add shallot and garlic; cook 2 minutes, stirring occasionally. Add peppers and tomatoes and cook 5 minutes, stirring occasionally. Stir in olives, vinegar, basil, salt and pepper.

• **Barley and Fish.** Meanwhile, bring 3 cups water to boiling over high heat. Add barley and cook 30 minutes. Drain and season with ¼ teaspoon of the salt and ⅛ teaspoon of the pepper.

• Heat broiler. Place fish on a greased broiler pan, skin-side down; brush with olive oil and season with remaining ¼ teaspoon salt and ⅛ teaspoon pepper. Broil for 6 minutes or until fish flakes easily.

• To serve, gently heat sauce and spoon over fish and barley.

PER SERVING 472 **CAL**; 13 g **FAT** (2 g **SAT**); 37 g **PRO**; 54 g **CARB**; 11 g **FIBER**; 710 mg **SODIUM**; 45 mg **CHOL**

Pecan Salmon & Smashed Potatoes

MAKES 4 servings   PREP 20 minutes   BAKE at 450° for 15 minutes   COOK 20 minutes

- ⅓ **cup chopped pecans**
- 3 **tablespoons brown sugar**
- 1 **tablespoon all-purpose flour**
- 4 **teaspoons lemon-pepper seasoning**
- 1 **teaspoon olive oil**
- 1 **pound salmon fillet, cut into 4 equal-size pieces**
- 1½ **pounds Yukon Gold potatoes, cut into ½-inch pieces**
- 2 **tablespoons Brummel & Brown yogurt spread**
- ¼ **cup reduced-sodium chicken broth**
- 2 **tablespoons chopped parsley Roasted Cauliflower (optional)**

● Heat oven to 450°. Coat a baking dish with nonstick cooking spray.

● Combine pecans, brown sugar, flour, 2 teaspoons of the lemon pepper and the oil. Place salmon, skin side down, in the prepared dish and coat with cooking spray. Sprinkle with the pecan mixture and spritz lightly with cooking spray. Cover and bake at 450° for 5 minutes; uncover and bake for 7 to 10 minutes more, or until fish flakes easily.

● Meanwhile, place potatoes in a medium-size saucepan and cover with lightly salted water. Simmer for 15 to 20 minutes or until tender; drain. Add remaining 2 teaspoons of the lemon pepper, the yogurt spread and broth.

Mash until smooth; stir in parsley.

● Serve salmon with potatoes and, if desired, Roasted Cauliflower (see recipe, below).

PER SERVING 471 CAL; 18 g FAT (2 g SAT); 31 g PRO; 48 g CARB; 5 g FIBER; 558 mg SODIUM; 72 mg CHOL

Roasted Cauliflower

Cut 1 small yellow and 1 small green cauliflower into florets. Place on a greased baking sheet and toss with 1 tablespoon olive oil. Season with ¼ teaspoon salt and ⅛ teaspoon black pepper. Roast at 450° for 25 minutes, turning once, or until tender.

Crispy Fish Sticks & Chili Dipping Sauce

MAKES 4 servings **PREP** 20 minutes
BAKE at 450° for 10 minutes

½ **cup unseasoned bread crumbs**
½ **cup corn flake crumbs**
¾ **teaspoon seasoned salt**
½ **cup all-purpose flour**
3 **egg whites, lightly beaten**
1 **pound tilapia fillets, cut into
    ½ x 3-inch strips**
½ **cup Thai Kitchen sweet red chili
    sauce**
1 **scallion, chopped**

• Heat oven to 450°. Place a wire rack on a baking sheet and coat with nonstick cooking spray.

• Whisk together bread crumbs, corn flake crumbs and seasoned salt in a shallow dish. Place flour in a second dish and egg whites in a third dish.

• Coat each fish strip with flour, dip in egg white and coat with bread crumb mixture. Place on prepared pan.

• Coat breaded fish sticks with cooking spray. Bake at 450° for 10 minutes or until lightly browned.

• Combine chili sauce and scallion. Serve fish sticks with the chili dipping sauce and Broccoli-Carrot Slaw (see recipe, above right).

PER SERVING 380 **CAL**; 5 g **FAT** (1 g **SAT**.); 31 g **PRO**; 52 g **CARB**; 5 g **FIBER**; 800 mg **SODIUM**; 59 mg **CHOL**

Broccoli-Carrot Slaw

In a large bowl, whisk together ¼ cup rice vinegar, 2 tablespoons reduced-fat mayonnaise and 1 teaspoon sugar. Add 1 bag (12 ounces) broccoli slaw, 1 cup petite baby carrots and 2 sliced scallions; toss and coat with dressing. Cover and refrigerate until ready to serve.

Shrimp Étouffée

MAKES 4 servings **PREP** 20 minutes
COOK 29 minutes

¼   **cup all-purpose flour**
¼   **cup vegetable oil**
1   **large onion, chopped**
1   **large green pepper, seeds
     removed, chopped**
1   **cup chopped celery**
3   **cloves garlic, chopped**
1   **can (8 ounces) no-salt-added
     tomato sauce**
3   **tablespoons reduced-sodium
     Worcestershire sauce**
2   **teaspoons Cajun seasoning (such
     as McCormick)**
1¾ **pounds large shrimp, cleaned and
     deveined**
½   **cup parsley, chopped**
3   **cups cooked brown rice**
     Lemon wedges
     Steamed squash (optional)

• In a large heavy-bottomed pot, whisk together flour and oil until combined. Bring to boiling; reduce heat to medium and cook for 5 minutes, whisking continuously, until reddish-brown in color.

• Add onion, green pepper, celery and garlic. Cook 5 minutes, stirring occasionally. Stir in tomato sauce, 1 cup water, Worcestershire sauce and Cajun seasoning; simmer 15 minutes.

• Add shrimp and simmer 4 minutes. Stir in parsley.

• Serve shrimp over brown rice. Squeeze lemon wedges over each plate. Serve with steamed squash, if desired.

PER SERVING 500 **CAL**; 17 g **FAT** (3 g **SAT**); 33 g **PRO**; 53 g **CARB**; 6 g **FIBER**; 660 mg **SODIUM**; 252 mg **CHOL**

A quick version of roux—a base of flour and fat that's cooked until it has a copper-penny color and nutty flavor—makes this étouffée doable any night.

LOVIN' SPOONFULS

A bowl of steaming soup or stew does wonders to take the edge off winter.

ROASTED CHERRY
TOMATO BISQUE,
PAGE 51

THAI TOM KHA GAI,
PAGE 55

SAUSAGE & ESCAROLE SOUP,
PAGE 52

PORK GOULASH

Pork Goulash

MAKES 6 servings **PREP** 15 minutes
COOK 1 hour, 10 minutes

3	pounds pork roast, cut into 1½-inch pieces
3	tablespoons all-purpose flour
2	tablespoons sweet Hungarian paprika
½	teaspoon salt
3	tablespoons vegetable oil
1	medium onion, chopped
1	sweet red pepper, cored and diced
3	tablespoons apple cider vinegar
1	teaspoon caraway seeds
1	can (14.5 ounces) diced tomatoes
1	cup beef broth
2	tablespoons tomato paste
	Chopped fresh parsley
	Cooked egg noodles (optional)

• In a large bowl, combine pork, 2 tablespoons of the flour, 1 tablespoon of the paprika and ¼ teaspoon salt. Heat 1½ tablespoons of the oil in a large Dutch oven over medium-high heat. Add half of the pork to the pot and brown on all sides, 5 minutes. Remove with a slotted spoon; repeat with remaining 1½ tablespoons oil and the rest of the pork.

• Reduce heat to medium and add onion. Cook 3 minutes. Stir in sweet red pepper. Cook 2 minutes. Sprinkle with remaining tablespoon each of flour and paprika. Cook 1 minute. Stir in vinegar; let simmer. Sprinkle with caraway seeds, then pour in tomatoes and broth, scraping up any brown bits from pan. Return pork to mixture. Cover and simmer over low heat for 1 hour. Stir in tomato paste and remaining ¼ teaspoon salt. Cook, uncovered, 10 minutes. Sprinkle with parsley and serve over egg noodles, if desired.

PER SERVING 441 **CAL**; 20 g **FAT** (5 g **SAT**); 52 g **PRO**; 12 g **CARB**; 2 g **FIBER**; 678 mg **SODIUM**; 125 mg **CHOL**

Split Pea with Bacon

MAKES 6 servings **PREP** 15 minutes **COOK** 53 minutes

6	slices bacon, diced
1	medium onion, peeled and diced
3	carrots, peeled and diced
2	ribs celery, trimmed and diced
2	cloves garlic, minced
1	bag (1 pound) green split peas
1	box (32 ounces, such as Swanson's certified organic) vegetable broth
2	teaspoons fresh rosemary, chopped
¾	teaspoon salt
¼	teaspoon pepper

• Cook bacon over medium heat in a large pot for 8 minutes. Remove half with a slotted spoon to a bowl. Add onion, carrots, celery and garlic to pot. Continue to cook 5 minutes.

• Stir in split peas, broth, 2 cups water and rosemary. Bring to a boil over medium-high heat. Reduce heat, cover and cook 40 minutes or until peas are soft. Season with salt and pepper.

• Ladle soup into bowls; top each with a little of the reserved bacon bits.

PER SERVING 362 **CAL**; 7 g **FAT** (2 g **SAT**); 22 g **PRO**; 54 g **CARB**; 21 g **FIBER**; 867 mg **SODIUM**; 11 mg **CHOL**

Chicken & Dumplings

MAKES 6 servings **PREP** 15 minutes **COOK** 50 minutes

STEW

- 2¼ **pounds bone-in chicken breasts**
- 2 **tablespoons olive oil**
- 2 **medium carrots, peeled and diced**
- 2 **ribs celery, trimmed and diced**
- 1 **leek, trimmed, cleaned and thinly sliced**
- 3 **tablespoons all-purpose flour**
- ¼ **teaspoon each salt and pepper**
- 4 **cups reduced-sodium chicken broth**
- 1 **cup frozen peas, thawed**
- 1 **tablespoon chopped fresh dill**

DUMPLINGS

- 2 **cups biscuit mix**
- ½ **cup milk**
- 1 **tablespoon chopped fresh dill**

● **Stew.** Heat a large, lidded nonstick skillet over medium-high heat. Add chicken, skin-side down, and cook until browned, 4 to 5 minutes. Add 4 cups water, cover and reduce heat to a simmer. Poach 20 minutes, or until cooked through. Remove chicken from liquid (save liquid) and let cool. When cool enough to handle, remove and discard skin and bones and cut chicken into bite-size pieces.

● Heat oil in a large pot over medium heat. Add carrots, celery and leek. Cook 5 minutes or until softened. Sprinkle with flour, salt and pepper. Cook 3 minutes, stirring. Add broth and 2 cups of the poaching liquid. Bring to a simmer; cook 5 minutes. Stir in chicken.

● Meanwhile, make **Dumplings.** In medium bowl, combine biscuit mix, milk and dill. Drop by tablespoonfuls into simmering liquid. Cover pot tightly; cook 10 minutes. Uncover and gently stir in peas and chopped dill.

PER SERVING 391 **CAL**; 11 g **FAT** (2 g **SAT**); 33 g **PRO**; 41 g **CARB**; 3 g **FIBER**; 941 mg **SODIUM**; 70 mg **CHOL**

Moroccan Beef Stew

MAKES 6 servings **PREP** 15 minutes
COOK 2 hours, 5 minutes

- 2 **tablespoons vegetable oil**
- 2 **pounds beef chuck for stew, cut into 1-inch pieces**
- 2 **tablespoons all-purpose flour**
- ¾ **teaspoon salt**
- ⅛ **teaspoon pepper**
- 1 **medium onion, diced**
- 1 **teaspoon ground cumin**
- ½ **teaspoon ground cinnamon**
- ¼ **teaspoon ground cloves**
- 1 **can (14.5 ounces) beef broth**
- 1 **cup pitted prunes, chopped**
- 1 **cup dried apricots, chopped**
- 3 **cups baby spinach, roughly chopped**
   Cooked pearl couscous (optional)

● Heat oil in a large pot over medium-high heat. In a bowl, toss beef cubes in flour, ¼ teaspoon of the salt and the pepper. Add half of beef to pot. Brown on all sides, about 4 minutes. Remove to a plate with a slotted spoon and repeat with remaining beef.

● Reduce heat to medium and add onion to pot. Cook 3 to 5 minutes to soften. Sprinkle with cumin, cinnamon and cloves. Cook 1 minute. Add a splash of the beef stock; cook 1 minute, scraping up any browned bits from bottom of pot.

● Add broth and bring to a boil. Return beef to pot along with any liquid. Cover and simmer 1½ hours over low heat.

● Uncover pot and stir in prunes and apricots. Cover and cook 15 minutes. Uncover and stir in spinach. Cook, uncovered, 5 minutes. Season with remaining ½ teaspoon salt. Serve stew over pearl couscous, if desired.

PER SERVING 392 **CAL**; 12 g **FAT** (3 g **SAT**); 35 g **PRO**; 36 g **CARB**; 4 g **FIBER**; 670 mg **SODIUM**; 64 mg **CHOL**

MOROCCAN BEEF STEW

FRENCH ONION SOUP

French Onion Soup

MAKES 6 servings PREP 15 minutes
COOK 31 minutes BROIL 5 minutes

- **3 tablespoons unsalted butter**
- **3 pounds onions, peeled and thinly sliced**
- **1 teaspoon sugar**
- **2 tablespoons all-purpose flour**
- **1 large box (32 ounces) reduced-sodium beef broth**
- **¼ cup red wine**
- **6 slices French bread**
- **6 ounces Gruyère cheese**

• Melt butter in a very large, deep pot over medium heat. Add onions and stir to coat. Cover; cook 15 minutes, stirring occasionally, until onions are very soft and begin to turn golden brown.

• Uncover; increase heat to medium-high. Add sugar and cook, uncovered, 10 minutes, stirring often. Sprinkle with flour; cook 1 minute. Stir in broth, wine and 1 cup water. Simmer, uncovered, for 5 minutes.

• Heat broiler. Spread bread slices on a baking sheet; toast under broiler for 1 to 2 minutes per side; set aside. Place six ovenproof bowls or crocks on a baking sheet. Divide soup evenly among bowls (about 1 cup in each).

• Use a vegetable peeler or cheese plane to thinly slice pieces of cheese. Place slice of toast on each serving of soup, top with cheese (divide evenly among bowls). Heat under broiler for 3 minutes or until cheese is melted and bubbly. Carefully remove from oven and serve warm.

PER SERVING 370 CAL; 16 g FAT (9 g SAT); 17 g PRO; 40 g CARB; 5 g FIBER; 590 mg SODIUM; 46 mg CHOL

Roasted Cherry Tomato Bisque

MAKES 4 servings PREP 10 minutes ROAST at 425° for 35 minutes COOK 13 minutes

- **2 pounds cherry tomatoes, halved**
- **6 cloves garlic, peeled**
- **3 tablespoons olive oil**
- **½ teaspoon salt**
- **½ teaspoon fresh thyme leaves, chopped**
- **¼ teaspoon black pepper**
- **1 can (14.5 ounces) chicken broth with roasted vegetables**
- **1½ cups half-and-half**
- **1 tablespoon balsamic vinegar**
  Focaccia (optional)

• Heat oven to 425°. In a large bowl, combine tomatoes, garlic, olive oil, salt, thyme and pepper. Spread onto a large rimmed baking sheet and roast at 425° for 30 to 35 minutes, stirring once.

• Spoon tomato mixture and any accumulated liquid into a large soup pot. Add chicken broth and 1 cup water. Bring to a simmer; cook 10 minutes. Transfer in batches to a blender and puree until smooth. Return to pot and stir in half-and-half and balsamic vinegar. Cook 3 minutes until heated through (do not boil). Serve with focaccia, if desired.

PER SERVING 268 CAL; 20 g FAT (7 g SAT); 6 g PRO; 14g CARB; 3 g FIBER; 770 mg SODIUM; 45 mg CHOL

Seafood Chowder

MAKES 6 servings **PREP** 20 minutes
COOK 24 minutes

- ½ **pound raw shell-on shrimp (thawed if frozen)**
- 2 **tablespoons olive oil**
- 2 **shallots, peeled and minced**
- 1 **sweet red pepper, cored, seeded and diced**
- ¾ **pound small new potatoes, diced**
- 1 **can (6.5 ounces) chopped clams in juice**
- ½ **pound tilapia fillet**
- 3 **tablespoons all-purpose flour**
- ½ **teaspoon salt**
- 2 **cups milk**
- 1 **can (10¾ ounces) condensed cream of shrimp soup**
- 1 **box (10 ounces) frozen corn kernels, thawed**
  Oyster crackers (optional)
  Snipped fresh chives (optional)

• Peel shrimp. Place shells in a medium saucepan. Add 2½ cups water, cover and bring to a simmer over medium heat. Cook 10 minutes.

• Meanwhile, heat oil in a large pot over medium heat. Add shallots and sweet red pepper. Cook 5 minutes to soften. Stir in potatoes and cook 1 minute. Strain clam juice into pot, reserving clams. Strain shrimp broth into pot; discard shrimp shells. Bring to a simmer; cook 10 minutes.

• While potato mixture cooks, cut shrimp and tilapia into bite-size pieces; whisk flour and salt into milk.

• Stir shrimp, tilapia, milk mixture, condensed soup, clams and corn into pot. Simmer 3 to 4 minutes, until shrimp is pink and fish is opaque. Top with crackers and chives, if desired.

PER SERVING 343 **CAL**; 12 g **FAT** (3 g **SAT**); 25 g **PRO**; 38 g **CARB**; 3 g **FIBER**; 875 mg **SODIUM**; 96 mg **CHOL**

Sausage & Escarole Soup

MAKES 6 servings **PREP** 20 minutes **COOK** 32 minutes

- ¾ **pound sweet Italian sausage, casings removed**
- ½ **large onion, diced**
- 3 **carrots, peeled and diced**
- 2 **cloves garlic, sliced**
- ¼ **teaspoon red pepper flakes**
- 1 **head escarole (about 1 pound), trimmed, chopped and rinsed**
- 48 **ounces light, fat-free chicken broth**
- 1 **can (15 ounces) cannellini beans, drained and rinsed**
  Parmesan cheese, for serving

• Heat a large pot (not nonstick) over medium-high heat. Crumble in sausage. Cook, stirring, 5 minutes, until browned, breaking apart large pieces with a wooden spoon. Remove to a plate with a slotted spoon.

• Reduce heat to medium. Add onion and carrots. Cook 5 minutes. Stir in garlic, red pepper flakes and escarole. Cook, stirring, 2 minutes.

• Pour in chicken broth and bring to a simmer over high heat. Reduce heat to retain simmer; cook 20 minutes. Return sausage to pot along with drained beans. Heat through. Serve sprinkled with Parmesan, if desired.

PER SERVING 204 **CAL**; 8 g **FAT** (3 g **SAT**); 13 g **PRO**; 19 g **CARB**; 6 g **FIBER**; 991 mg **SODIUM**; 16 mg **CHOL**

SEAFOOD CHOWDER

CURRIED SWEET POTATO SOUP

Curried Sweet Potato Soup

MAKES 8 servings **PREP** 20 minutes
COOK 21 minutes

SOUP

2	tablespoons unsalted butter
½	medium onion, chopped
2	teaspoons curry powder
½	teaspoon salt
¼	teaspoon black pepper
3	pounds sweet potatoes, peeled and cut up
2	medium carrots, peeled and cut up
4	cups vegetable broth
¼	cup packed brown sugar

ONIONS

½	medium onion, thinly sliced
2	tablespoons all-purpose flour
⅛	teaspoon curry powder
½	cup vegetable oil

• **Soup.** Heat butter in a large pot over medium heat. Add onion and cook 5 minutes. Sprinkle with curry, salt and pepper. Cook 1 minute.

• Stir sweet potatoes, carrots and broth into pot. Cover and bring to a boil. Reduce heat and simmer 15 minutes, until potatoes are soft.

• Meanwhile, make **Onions.** Toss sliced onion, flour and curry together in a medium bowl. Heat oil in a medium-size deep saucepan over medium-high heat. Test oil by dropping 1 onion into hot oil. It should turn light brown in about 3 minutes. Reduce heat if browning too quickly. Add half of the onion slices to the oil. Cook 4 minutes, turning, until golden. Transfer to paper towel-lined plate. Repeat with remaining onions.

• Once soup is done simmering, transfer in batches to a blender or use an immersion blender in pot. Puree until smooth. Stir in brown sugar and serve soup topped with some of the onion slices.

PER SERVING 273 **CAL**; 8 g **FAT** (3 g **SAT**);
3 g **PRO**; 49 g **CARB**; 6 g **FIBER**; 893 mg **SODIUM**;
10 mg **CHOL**

Thai Tom Kha Gai

MAKES 6 servings **PREP** 20 minutes **COOK** 15 minutes

4	cups low-sodium chicken broth
2	pieces (each about 4 inches long) lemongrass, root end crushed
1	piece fresh ginger (2 inches), peeled and sliced
3	cloves garlic, minced
1	package (8 ounces) mushrooms, sliced
2	teaspoons Sriracha (Thai garlic-chile sauce)
1	pound broccoli florets
¾	pound boneless, skinless chicken breasts, cut into ¾-inch pieces
1	sweet red pepper, cored, seeded and cut into matchsticks
1	can (14 ounces) coconut milk
¼	cup fresh lime juice
2	tablespoons fish sauce
	Sliced scallion (optional)

• Heat chicken broth in a large pot over medium-high heat. Add lemongrass and ginger. Simmer 5 minutes, until fragrant.

• Reduce heat to retain simmer; add garlic, mushrooms and chile sauce. Cover and cook 5 minutes.

• Stir in broccoli, chicken, sweet red pepper and coconut milk. Simmer 5 minutes, until chicken is cooked through. Remove from heat and stir in lime juice and fish sauce. Ladle into bowls and top with scallion, if using.

PER SERVING 240 **CAL**; 15 g **FAT** (12 g **SAT**);
19 g **PRO**; 10 g **CARB**; 4 g **FIBER**; 841 mg **SODIUM**;
33 mg **CHOL**

MELTING POINT

Nothing warms the heart like chocolate.

S'mores Pie

MAKES 12 servings PREP 10 minutes BAKE at 375° for 10 minutes; at 325° for 30 minutes BROIL 1 minute

CRUST

9	graham cracker boards
2	tablespoons packed light-brown sugar
¼	cup (½ stick) unsalted butter, melted

CHOCOLATE FILLING

2	eggs, at room temperature
¾	cup 2% milk
¾	cup heavy cream
2	tablespoons granulated sugar
⅛	teaspoon salt
½	teaspoon vanilla extract
8	ounces semisweet chocolate, chopped into small pieces
1	tablespoon unsweetened cocoa powder

MARSHMALLOW TOPPING

3	egg whites
3	tablespoons corn syrup
¾	cup granulated sugar
⅛	teaspoon salt
½	teaspoon vanilla extract

• **Crust.** Heat oven to 375°. Break graham crackers into food processor and run until fine crumbs are formed. Transfer crumbs to a bowl and mix in brown sugar and melted butter. Press mixture evenly into a 9-inch pie plate. Bake at 375° for 8 to 10 minutes or until crust is slightly brown. Cool 10 minutes.

• **Chocolate Filling.** Reduce oven to 325°. Beat eggs in a small bowl; set aside. Combine milk, cream, sugar and salt in a medium saucepan over medium heat until simmering. Remove from heat and add vanilla, chocolate and cocoa powder; stir until combined and smooth. Stir about ¾ cup of the chocolate mixture into the beaten eggs; stir chocolate-egg mixture back into saucepan. Pour filling into cooled crust. Bake at 325° for 25 to 30 minutes, or until the filling is set and glossy (do not overbake or it could bubble and crack). Cool completely on a wire rack.

• **Marshmallow Topping.** Bring 1 inch of water to a simmer in a medium saucepan. Combine egg whites, corn syrup, sugar and salt in a metal bowl large enough to sit on top of the saucepan. Whisk constantly in bowl over water until sugar is dissolved and eggs have reached 160°, about 3 to 5 minutes (do not overcook, as the eggs could scramble). Pour mixture and vanilla into the bowl of a stand mixer fitted with a whisk and beat on high speed until fluffy, about 5 minutes. Set aside.

• Heat broiler. Spoon Marshmallow Topping on cooled pie, leaving a 1-inch margin from edge. Broil until topping begins to brown, 1 minute.

PER SERVING 310 CAL; 18 g FAT (10 g SAT); 4 g PRO; 38 g CARB; 2 g FIBER; 154 mg SODIUM; 67 mg CHOL

Chipotle Brownies

MAKES 9 servings **PREP** 10 minutes **COOK** 4 minutes **BAKE** at 325° for 35 minutes
COOL 10 minutes

- **¼ cup all-purpose flour**
- **2 tablespoons unsweetened cocoa powder**
- **1 teaspoon baking powder**
- **½ teaspoon cinnamon**
- **¾ teaspoon chipotle powder**
- **½ teaspoon salt**
- **¼ cup (½ stick) unsalted butter, cut into small pieces**
- **2 ounces unsweetened chocolate, chopped**
- **3 ounces semisweet chocolate, chopped**
- **3 eggs**
- **¾ cup sugar**
- **½ teaspoon vanilla extract**
- **⅓ cup sour cream**
- **4 ounces (⅔ cup) chocolate chunks**

• Heat oven to 325°. Butter and flour an 8 x 8-inch baking pan. Combine flour, cocoa, baking powder, cinnamon, chipotle powder and salt in a medium bowl; set aside.

• In a medium saucepan, bring 1 inch of water to a simmer. Add butter, unsweetened chocolate and semisweet chocolate to a metal bowl large enough to sit on top of the saucepan. Melt ingredients, about 4 minutes. Remove from heat and stir until smooth.

• In the bowl of a stand mixer fitted with a whisk attachment, combine eggs, sugar and vanilla. Whisk on high speed until slightly thickened, 1 to 2 minutes. Pour in the melted chocolate mixture and whisk on medium for 30 seconds. Add the flour mixture and whisk on low for 30 seconds. Add sour cream and whisk on medium for 30 seconds. Stir in chocolate chunks by hand.

• Bake at 325° for 35 minutes, or until a toothpick inserted in the center comes out clean. Cool on wire rack 10 minutes.

PER SERVING 320 **CAL**; 19 g **FAT** (11 g **SAT**); 5 g **PRO**; 36 g **CARB**; 3 g **FIBER**; 205 mg **SODIUM**; 90 mg **CHOL**

Hot Fudge Sauce

MAKES 2 cups **PREP** 5 minutes

- **8 ounces unsweetened chocolate, chopped**
- **¼ cup (½ stick) unsalted butter, cut into chunks**
- **¼ teaspoon salt**
- **¾ cup sugar**
- **⅓ cup light corn syrup**
- **1 cup heavy cream**

• Combine ingredients in a medium heavy-bottomed saucepan over medium-low heat. Stir constantly until the ingredients have melted and the mixture is steaming and uniformly smooth. Do not boil. Serve over ice cream and Chipotle Brownies, if desired.

PER TABLESPOON 95 **CAL**; 8 g **FAT** (5 g **SAT**); 1 g **PRO**; 8 g **CARB**; 1 g **FIBER**; 25 mg **SODIUM**; 14 mg **CHOL**

Chocolate Pots de Crème with Sea Salt

MAKES 8 servings PREP 10 minutes
COOK 15 minutes LET STAND 3 minutes
CHILL at least 6 hours

- 5 egg yolks
- ¼ cup sugar
- ¾ cup heavy cream
- 1¼ cups whole milk
- ¼ teaspoon salt
- 8 ounces bittersweet chocolate, chopped into small pieces
- ½ teaspoon vanilla
  Sea salt flakes (such as Maldon) or coarse sea salt

• In a small bowl, whisk together yolks and sugar. In a medium saucepan over medium-low heat, combine cream, milk and salt; pour in yolk-sugar mixture. Stir continuously until the temperature registers 175° to 180° on an instant-read thermometer or it coats the back of a wooden spoon, about 15 minutes. (Do not overcook, as the eggs could scramble.)

• Immediately pour hot mixture over chocolate in a bowl. Cover with plastic wrap and let stand 3 minutes. Uncover, add vanilla and stir to completely combine.

• Pour into eight 4-ounce ramekins and let cool. When room temperature, cover each with plastic wrap, and refrigerate for at least 6 hours or overnight.

• Before serving, sprinkle with a pinch of sea salt flakes.

PER SERVING 277 CAL; 23 g FAT (12 g SAT); 4 g PRO; 21 g CARB; 2 g FIBER; 86 mg SODIUM; 159 mg CHOL

Black Forest Macarons

MAKES 24 sandwich cookies PREP 10 minutes BAKE at 350° for 18 minutes

- 1½ cups confectioners' sugar
- ¾ cup almond flour (such as Bob's Red Mill)
- 3 tablespoons unsweetened cocoa powder
- ⅛ teaspoon salt
- 3 egg whites
- ⅛ teaspoon cream of tartar
- 3 tablespoons granulated sugar
- ⅓ to ½ cup cherry jam

• Heat oven to 350°. Combine confectioners' sugar, almond flour, cocoa powder and salt in a food processor. Pulse until combined and the mixture reaches a fine texture, about 30 seconds.

• Add egg whites to the bowl of a stand mixer fitted with a whisk attachment. Beat on medium-high speed until foamy, about 30 seconds. Add cream of tartar and beat until soft peaks form, about 1 minute. Slowly add granulated sugar and beat until stiff peaks form and the mixture is shiny, 2 to 3 more minutes.

• Fold one-third of the almond flour mixture into the egg whites, being careful not to deflate them. Repeat two more times, then transfer to a pastry bag or resealable plastic bag and snip off corner. Pipe 1-inch circles of batter about 1 inch apart onto two baking sheets lined with parchment paper. Smooth out tops of piped batter.

• Bake at 350° for 15 to 18 minutes. Cool completely on baking sheet. When cool, spoon a scant teaspoon of the jam in the center of the flat side of a cookie; gently press another cookie on top to form the macaron. Repeat with remaining cookies and jam.

PER COOKIE 76 CAL; 2 g FAT (0 g SAT); 1 g PRO; 15 g CARB; 1 g FIBER; 21 mg SODIUM; 0 mg CHOL

Cocoa-Almond-Coco Cake

MAKES 18 servings   **PREP** 20 minutes   **BAKE** at 350° for 25 minutes   **LET STAND** 3 minutes

CAKE

3	cups cake flour (not self-rising), sifted
¾	cup unsweetened cocoa powder
1	teaspoon baking soda
½	teaspoon baking powder
¼	teaspoon salt
½	cup sour cream
1	can (13.5 ounces) light coconut milk
¾	cup (1½ sticks) unsalted butter, at room temperature
2½	cups packed light-brown sugar
4	eggs
1	teaspoon almond extract
1	teaspoon vanilla extract

CHOCOLATE GANACHE

¾	cup heavy cream
10	ounces semisweet chocolate, chopped into small pieces
1	teaspoon vanilla extract

FILLING

¾	cup (1½ sticks) unsalted butter, at room temperature
2¼	cups confectioners' sugar
1	teaspoon vanilla extract
1½	cups sweetened flaked coconut
½	cup sliced almonds, roughly chopped

GARNISH

⅓	cup sweetened flaked coconut
1	heaping tablespoon sliced almonds

• **Cake.** Heat oven to 350°. Butter and flour three 9-inch round cake pans. Line the bottom of each with a circle of wax paper.

• In a medium bowl, whisk together flour, cocoa, baking soda, baking powder and salt; set aside. In a second medium bowl, whisk together sour cream and coconut milk. In a large bowl, beat butter and brown sugar on medium speed until fluffy, about 2 to 3 minutes. Add eggs, one at time, beating well after each addition. Beat in almond and vanilla extracts. On medium-low speed, beat in flour mixture in three additions, alternating with coconut milk mixture, beginning and ending with the flour mixture.

• Pour batter evenly into prepared pans. Bake at 350° for 25 minutes, or until a toothpick inserted in the center comes out clean. Cool in pans 10 minutes, then turn onto a wire rack and cool completely.

• **Chocolate Ganache.** Heat cream in a small pot on medium-high heat just until it simmers. Immediately pour over chocolate in a medium bowl; let stand 3 minutes. Add vanilla and mix until smooth. Cover and cool to room temperature.

• **Filling.** Meanwhile, in the bowl of a stand mixer fitted with the whisk attachment, beat the butter and sugar on medium-low speed until blended, about 1 minute. Increase speed to medium-high and beat for another 3 minutes. Add vanilla and 3 tablespoons water and beat on medium-high speed for 30 seconds. Add coconut and almonds and beat for another 30 seconds. Set aside.

• To assemble: Place one cake on a stand (if slightly rounded, trim off a bit to make it flat). Spread half the filling on the cake. Repeat with second cake and remaining filling. Top with the third cake (do not trim). Ice cake evenly with chocolate ganache. Garnish with coconut and almonds.

PER SERVING 599 **CAL**; 32 g **FAT** (19 g **SAT**); 5 g **PRO**; 75 g **CARB**; 4 g **FIBER**; 174 mg **SODIUM**; 105 mg **CHOL**

CHILI 5 WAYS

Score big with slow-cooked versions of the fan favorite. Game on!

Smoky Brisket Chili

MAKES 8 servings **PREP** 15 minutes
SLOW COOK on HIGH for 6 hours or LOW for
8 hours

- 1 **cup low-sodium beef broth**
- 1 **cup dark beer (such as Guinness)**
- 1 **tablespoon cider vinegar**
- 2 **tablespoons cornstarch**
- 2 **tablespoons tomato paste**
- 2 **tablespoons molasses**
- 2 **tablespoons chili powder**
- 1 **tablespoon smoked paprika**
- ¾ **teaspoon salt**
- ½ **teaspoon pepper**
- 2 **pounds flat-cut beef brisket, fat trimmed, cut into 1½-inch chunks**
- 1 **sweet onion, diced**
- 3 **garlic cloves, chopped**
- 1 **can (14.5 ounces) fire-roasted diced tomatoes**
- 1 **can (15.5 ounces) red beans, drained and rinsed**
- 1 **can (15.5 ounces) kidney beans, drained and rinsed**
  Sour cream, sliced scallions and shredded cheese (optional)
  Cornbread (such as Jiffy, optional)

• In the base of a slow cooker, combine broth, beer and vinegar. Whisk in cornstarch until dissolved. Stir in tomato paste, molasses, chili powder, paprika, salt and pepper. Stir in beef, onion, garlic and tomatoes. Cover and cook on HIGH for 6 hours or LOW for 8 hours.

• Stir in beans to heat through. Garnish with sour cream, sliced scallions and cheese and serve with cornbread, if desired.

PER SERVING 308 **CAL**; 5 g **FAT** (2 g **SAT**);
32 g **PRO**; 30 g **CARB**; 8 g **FIBER**; 612 mg **SODIUM**;
49 mg **CHOL**

Fiery Green Chili

MAKES 8 servings **PREP** 15 minutes **SLOW COOK** on HIGH for 6 hours or LOW for 8 hours

- 1 **cup low-sodium beef broth**
- 1 **cup tomatillo salsa**
- 1 **large green pepper, seeded and diced**
- 1 **large yellow onion, diced**
- 3 **cloves garlic, chopped**
- 1 **teaspoon cumin**
- 1 **teaspoon ancho chile powder**
- ¾ **teaspoon salt**
- 1 **pound ground pork**
- 1 **pound ground beef**
- 1 **can (15.5 ounces) butter beans, drained and rinsed**
- ¼ **cup chopped fresh cilantro**
  Sliced scallions, lime wedges and sour cream (optional)

• Combine broth, salsa, green pepper, onion, garlic, cumin, chili powder and salt in the base of a slow cooker. Crumble in ground pork and beef; mix. Cover and cook on HIGH for 6 hours or LOW for 8 hours.

• Break up meat with a wooden spoon if necessary. Stir in beans and cilantro. Garnish with sliced scallions, lime and sour cream, if desired.

PER SERVING 306 **CAL**; 18 g **FAT** (7 g **SAT**);
24 g **PRO**; 13 g **CARB**; 3 g **FIBER**; 696 mg **SODIUM**;
78 mg **CHOL**

Lentil-Chickpea Chili

MAKES 8 servings PREP 15 minutes SLOW COOK on LOW for 8 hours

- **6 cups vegetable stock or broth**
- **2 tablespoons tomato paste**
- **1 tablespoon Dijon mustard**
- **2 teaspoons ground cumin**
- **½ teaspoon turmeric**
- **¼ teaspoon cayenne**
- **1 teaspoon salt**
- **1 bag (16 ounces) red lentils (such as Arrowhead Mills)**
- **1 can (14.5 ounces) diced tomatoes**
- **1 sweet onion, diced**
- **1 carrot, diced**
- **2 celery stalks, diced**
- **3 garlic cloves, diced**
- **2 bay leaves**
- **2 cans (15 ounces each) chickpeas, drained and rinsed**
- **¼ cup chopped fresh cilantro Flatbread (such as Stonefire naan, optional)**

• Whisk together stock, tomato paste, mustard, cumin, turmeric, cayenne and salt in the base of a slow cooker. Stir in lentils, diced tomatoes, onion, carrot, celery, garlic and bay leaves. Cover and cook on LOW for 8 hours.

• Stir in chickpeas and cilantro. Serve with flatbread, if desired.

PER SERVING 341 **CAL**; 3 g **FAT** (0 g **SAT**); 22 g **PRO**; 57 g **CARB**; 15 g **FIBER**; 778 mg **SODIUM**; 0 mg **CHOL**

Chipotle Chicken Chili

MAKES 8 servings **PREP** 15 minutes
SLOW COOK on HIGH for 6 hours or LOW
for 8 hours

2	medium yellow onions, halved and sliced
1	can (14.5 ounces) diced tomatoes
1	tablespoon tomato paste
3	garlic cloves, chopped
2	cups low-sodium chicken broth
1	chipotle in adobo, seeded and chopped, plus 1 tablespoon adobo sauce
1	teaspoon ground coriander
1	teaspoon salt
½	teaspoon pepper
2	pounds bone-in chicken thighs, skin removed
1	can (15.5 ounces) black beans, rinsed and drained
1	cup frozen corn kernels, thawed

• Combine onions, tomatoes, tomato paste, garlic, broth, chipotle and adobo, coriander, salt and pepper in the base of a slow cooker; wedge chicken thighs into the mixture, submerging at least half of the meat in the liquid. Cover and cook on HIGH for 6 hours or LOW for 8 hours.

• Remove chicken bones and shred meat back into slow cooker. Stir in beans and corn to heat through.

PER SERVING 229 **CAL**; 5 g **FAT** (1 g **SAT**); 27 g **PRO**; 17 g **CARB**; 5 g **FIBER**; 650 mg **SODIUM**; 94 mg **CHOL**

Cincinnati Chili

MAKES 8 servings **PREP** 15 minutes **SLOW COOK** on HIGH for 6 hours or LOW for 8 hours

2	cups low-sodium beef broth
1	can (8 ounces) tomato sauce
¼	cup tomato paste
2	tablespoons cider vinegar
2	tablespoons chili powder
2	teaspoons unsweetened cocoa powder
1	teaspoon ground cumin
1	teaspoon cinnamon
½	teaspoon ground cloves
¼	teaspoon ground allspice
1	teaspoon salt
½	teaspoon pepper
3	garlic cloves, chopped
1	large yellow onion, diced
2	pounds ground beef
1	pound spaghetti, cooked
	Finely shredded cheddar cheese and diced white onions (optional)

• Whisk together broth, tomato sauce, tomato paste, vinegar, chili powder, cocoa powder, cumin, cinnamon, cloves, allspice, salt and pepper in the base of a slow cooker. Add garlic and yellow onion, and crumble in beef; mix. Cover and cook on HIGH for 6 hours or LOW for 8 hours.

• Ladle chili over cooked spaghetti. Garnish with finely shredded cheddar cheese and diced white onions, if desired.

PER SERVING 325 **CAL**; 12 g **FAT** (5 g **SAT**); 28 g **PRO**; 24 g **CARB**; 3 g **FIBER**; 654 mg **SODIUM**; 74 mg **CHOL**

CORN & BLUEBERRY PANCAKES,
PAGE 81

MARCH

69

77

86

MEAL DEALS

Great-tasting, affordable dinners.

Roasted Salmon & Brussels Sprouts with Bacon Orzo

MAKES 4 servings **PREP** 10 minutes **ROAST** at 400° for 25 minutes **COOK** 21 minutes

BRUSSELS SPROUTS & SALMON

- **1 pound Brussels sprouts, trimmed and halved**
- **1 tablespoon olive oil**
- **¼ plus ⅛ teaspoon salt**
- **¼ teaspoon pepper**
- **4 salmon fillets (about 4 ounces each)**
- **1½ teaspoons Dijon mustard**

BACON ORZO

- **8 ounces orzo (about 1 cup dry)**
- **¼ pound thick-cut bacon, diced**
- **½ large yellow onion, diced**
- **2 tablespoons fresh lemon juice**
- **1 tablespoon Dijon mustard**

• **Brussels Sprouts & Salmon.** Heat oven to 400°. Toss Brussels sprouts with olive oil, ¼ teaspoon of the salt and ⅛ teaspoon of the pepper. Place on a baking sheet and roast at 400° for 20 to 25 minutes, flipping sprouts once.

• Place salmon skin-side down on a different baking sheet lined with nonstick foil. Season with remaining ⅛ teaspoon each salt and pepper. Spread mustard on top. Add to 400° oven during last 15 minutes of roasting Brussels sprouts.

• **Bacon Orzo.** Meanwhile, cook orzo in lightly salted boiling water for 8 minutes. Drain, reserving 1 cup of the cooking liquid.

• In a large sauté pan, cook bacon over medium heat for 8 minutes; remove with a slotted spoon. In same pan, add onion to bacon fat. Cook until softened, about 3 minutes. Stir in lemon juice, mustard and ½ cup of the reserved pasta water. Bring to a boil and simmer 1 to 2 minutes to thicken. Stir in orzo and bacon. Add more pasta water, if desired.

PER SERVING 512 **CAL**; 16 g **FAT** (3 g **SAT**); 37 g **PRO**; 56 g **CARB**; 7 g **FIBER**; 651 mg **SODIUM**; 73 mg **CHOL**

CHEAP TRICKS

Instead of relying on pricey olive oil, let the bacon's natural fat do some of the work for this recipe. Cooking the bacon low and slow releases the fat needed for sautéing onions, prevents the orzo from sticking together and adds an extra boost of smoky pork flavor to the dish.

A WORLD OF FLAVORS

Take your family on a culinary adventure without leaving the dinner table.

VIETNAMESE CHICKEN NOODLE
SOUP, PAGE 77

MIDDLE EASTERN STUFFED PEPPERS, PAGE 77

RIGATONI WITH CREAMY PEPPER SAUCE

Rigatoni with Creamy Pepper Sauce

MAKES 6 servings **PREP** 15 minutes
BROIL 10 minutes **COOK** 14 minutes

- **4** **sweet red and yellow peppers, halved, cored and seeded**
- **½** **cup reduced-sodium chicken broth**
- **3** **cloves garlic, chopped**
- **⅔** **cup heavy cream**
- **¾** **teaspoon salt**
- **¼** **teaspoon black pepper**
- **1** **pound rigatoni**
- **⅓** **pound small marinated bocconcini**
- **½** **cup basil leaves, thinly sliced**

• Heat broiler. Line a large broiler pan with foil and coat with nonstick cooking spray.

• Place peppers on prepared pan, cut side down. Broil for 9 to 10 minutes, about 4 inches from heat source. Place in a paper bag or covered bowl for 5 minutes. Peel skin off peppers and discard; thinly slice peppers.

• In a large nonstick skillet bring broth to a simmer; add garlic and simmer 2 minutes. Stir in cream, salt and pepper and simmer for an additional 2 minutes.

• Meanwhile, cook pasta following package directions, about 10 to 14 minutes for al dente. Drain and return to pot. Add cream mixture and sliced peppers; stir to combine.

• To serve, spoon into a large serving bowl and fold in bocconcini and basil.

PER SERVING 461 **CAL**; 17 g **FAT** (10 g **SAT**); 17 g **PRO**; 62 g **CARB**; 4 g **FIBER**; 491 mg **SODIUM**; 56 mg **CHOL**

Oven-Fried Tempura with Green Wasabi Sauce

MAKES 4 servings **PREP** 30 minutes **COOK** 3 minutes **BAKE** at 450° for 15 minutes

- **1** **teaspoon wasabi powder**
- **1** **cup reduced-fat sour cream**
- **1** **bunch scallions, trimmed and finely chopped**
- **½** **cup parsley, chopped**
- **½** **plus ⅛ teaspoon salt**
- **6** **ounces carrots, peeled and cut into 3 x ½-inch sticks**
- **3** **egg whites, lightly beaten**
- **1½** **cups panko**
- **1½** **pounds large shrimp, shelled and deveined**
- **6** **ounces zucchini, cut into 3 x ½-inch sticks**
  Reduced-sodium teriyaki sauce for dipping (optional)

• Heat oven to 450°. Place a large wire rack on a large baking sheet and coat with nonstick cooking spray.

• In a small bowl, mix wasabi powder with 1 tablespoon water. Stir in sour cream, scallions, parsley and ¼ teaspoon of the salt; refrigerate.

• Place the carrots in a small saucepan of boiling water and cook 3 minutes until crisp tender. Drain and pat carrots dry.

• Place egg whites in a shallow dish and add remaining ¼ teaspoon of the salt. Spread the panko in a second dish.

• Dip shrimp in egg, coat with panko and place on prepared pan. Repeat with carrots and zucchini.

• Bake shrimp and vegetables at 450° for 12 to 15 minutes or until shrimp and vegetables are cooked through. Sprinkle vegetables with remaining ⅛ teaspoon salt.

• Serve with wasabi sauce and, if desired, teriyaki sauce.

PER SERVING 498 **CAL**; 11 g **FAT** (5 g **SAT**); 47 g **PRO**; 51 g **CARB**; 2 g **FIBER**; 786 mg **SODIUM**; 290 mg **CHOL**

Slow Cooker Lamb & Cilantro Curry

MAKES 6 servings **PREP** 25 minutes
SLOW COOK on LOW for 8 hours

- **2** bunches cilantro, leaves picked off stems
- **3** tablespoons lemon juice
- **2** tablespoons chopped ginger
- **4** cloves garlic, chopped
- **2** jalapeño peppers, seeded and chopped
- **1¼** teaspoons salt
- **1** teaspoon curry powder
- **⅛** teaspoon cayenne pepper
- **1¼** pounds boneless lamb shoulder, cut into 1-inch cubes
- **1** large onion, chopped
- **1** can (15½ ounces) chickpeas, drained and rinsed
- **1** cup light coconut milk
- **3** cups cooked basmati rice

• Place cilantro leaves, lemon juice, ginger, garlic, jalapeños, salt, curry powder, cayenne and ½ cup water into a blender. Blend until smooth.

• Coat bowl of a slow cooker with nonstick cooking spray. Add lamb, onion and cilantro mixture; stir to combine. Cover and cook on LOW for 7½ hours. Stir in chickpeas and coconut milk; cook 30 minutes more.

• Serve curry over cooked basmati rice.

PER SERVING 500 CAL; 18 g FAT (8 g SAT); 26 g PRO; 57 g CARB; 4 g FIBER; 661 mg SODIUM; 68 mg CHOL

Lomo Saltado

MAKES 4 servings **PREP** 25 minutes **STIR-FRY** 10 minutes **BAKE** at 400° for 25 minutes

- **1** pound sweet potatoes, peeled and cut into 2 x ½-inch pieces
- **2** tablespoons canola oil
- **¼** teaspoon salt
- **¼** teaspoon paprika
- **⅛** teaspoon black pepper
- **1** pound flank steak, thinly sliced against the grain
- **1** large red onion, thinly sliced
- **2** sweet red peppers, cored, seeded and cut into 1-inch pieces
- **2** cubano or Italian frying peppers, cored, seeded and cut into 1-inch pieces
- **1** large jalapeño pepper, cored, seeded and chopped
- **3** cloves garlic, chopped
- **½** teaspoon cumin
- **3** tablespoons reduced-sodium soy sauce
- **2** tablespoons red wine vinegar
- **2** plum tomatoes, seeded and chopped
- **½** cup roughly chopped cilantro
- **1½** cups cooked brown rice

• Heat oven to 400°. Coat rimmed baking sheet with nonstick cooking spray. Place sweet potatoes on baking sheet and toss with 1 tablespoon of the canola oil and season with salt, paprika and pepper. Bake at 400° for 20 to 25 minutes until tender, turning once.

• Meanwhile, heat remaining 1 tablespoon oil in a large nonstick skillet over medium-high heat. Add flank steak and stir-fry for 4 minutes; remove to a plate. Add onion, peppers, garlic and cumin; stir-fry for 6 minutes. Stir in soy sauce, vinegar and tomatoes; bring to a simmer.

• Stir beef with any accumulated juices, sweet potatoes and cilantro into the skillet. Heat gently and serve over cooked brown rice.

PER SERVING 497 CAL; 18 g FAT (5 g SAT); 38 g PRO; 47 g CARB; 8 g FIBER; 704 mg SODIUM; 62 mg CHOL

Turkey Schnitzel with Creamy Dill Sauce

MAKES 4 servings   **PREP** 20 minutes   **COOK** 8 minutes

- ¼   cup all-purpose flour
- 2   eggs, lightly beaten
- ¾   cup cracker meal or unseasoned bread crumbs
- 1   teaspoon paprika
- ¾   teaspoon salt
- ¼   teaspoon black pepper
- 1   pound thinly sliced turkey cutlets
- 3   tablespoons vegetable oil
- ½   cup reduced-sodium chicken broth
- ½   cup reduced-fat sour cream
- 1   tablespoon chopped fresh dill
- 1   pound green beans, steamed
   Lemon wedges
   Cooked noodles (optional)

• Place flour in a shallow dish and eggs in a second dish. In a third dish, whisk together cracker meal, paprika, ¼ teaspoon of the salt and the pepper.

• Season turkey with ¼ teaspoon of the salt and coat with flour, shaking off excess. Dip in egg and coat with cracker meal mixture.

• Heat oil in a large nonstick skillet over medium-high heat. Add turkey and cook 3 minutes per side, in batches if necessary. Remove to a plate and keep warm.

• Add chicken broth to skillet and bring to a simmer, scraping up any browned bits from bottom of pan. Reduce heat to low and stir in sour cream, dill and remaining ¼ teaspoon salt. Stir until smooth and slightly thickened, about 2 minutes.

• To serve, spoon some of the sauce over the turkey and serve with lemon wedges, green beans and cooked noodles, if desired.

PER SERVING 429 **CAL**; 18 g **FAT** (4 g **SAT**); 37 g **PRO**; 29 g **CARB**; 4 g **FIBER**; 653 mg **SODIUM**; 166 mg **CHOL**

Jerk Pork Tenderloin

MAKES 4 servings   **PREP** 15 minutes   **MARINATE** 6 to 8 hours   **COOK** 14 minutes   **GRILL** 5 minutes

½	teaspoon ground allspice
½	teaspoon dried thyme
½	teaspoon salt
½	teaspoon black pepper
3	tablespoons lime juice
2	tablespoons vegetable oil
4	cloves garlic, chopped
½	teaspoon hot sauce
1	pork tenderloin (about 1¼ pounds)
8	thin slices prepared polenta (such as Zerto) from an 18-ounce package (about 8 ounces)
1	can (14½ ounces) stewed tomatoes
1	bag (6 ounces) baby spinach blend, steamed (optional)

• In a small bowl, combine allspice, thyme, salt and pepper. Set aside ½ teaspoon. Stir into the remaining spices the lime juice, 1 tablespoon of the oil, the garlic and hot sauce. Place pork in a resealable plastic bag and spoon in the spice–lime juice mixture. Shake to coat pork with mixture. Refrigerate for 6 to 8 hours.

• Heat remaining 1 tablespoon oil in a large nonstick skillet over medium-high heat; add pork and cook 12 to 14 minutes, until internal temperature reaches 140°, turning so all sides brown. Remove to a plate.

• Heat a lightly greased stovetop grill pan and grill the polenta slices about 5 minutes, turning once.

• Heat stewed tomatoes and stir in reserved ½ teaspoon seasoning mix.

• Slice pork and serve over a bed of spinach, if desired, with the grilled polenta and stewed tomatoes.

PER SERVING 269 **CAL**; 11 g **FAT** (2 g **SAT**); 26 g **PRO**; 17 g **CARB**; 2 g **FIBER**; 782 mg **SODIUM**; 74 mg **CHOL**

Vietnamese Chicken Noodle Soup

MAKES 4 servings **PREP** 15 minutes
COOK 6 minutes

- **2** **cans (14½ ounces each) reduced-sodium chicken broth**
- **1½** **pounds boneless, skinless chicken thighs, cut into bite-size pieces**
- **1** **cup shredded carrots**
- **1** **cup snow peas, thinly sliced**
- **2** **tablespoons chopped fresh ginger**
- **2** **scallions, thinly sliced**
- **1** **tablespoon reduced-sodium soy sauce**
- **1** **tablespoon lime juice**
- **2** **teaspoons Asian hot sauce (such as Sriracha)**
- **6** **ounces rice noodles**
- **¼** **cup mint leaves**
- **¼** **cup cilantro leaves**

● In a large pot, bring chicken broth and 1½ cups water to a boil. Add chicken and simmer 3 minutes. Add carrots, snow peas and ginger; simmer 3 minutes.

● Stir in scallions, soy sauce, lime juice and hot sauce.

● Meanwhile, boil rice noodles for 6 minutes. Drain.

● Divide cooked noodles among four bowls. Spoon an equal amount of soup into each bowl of noodles.

● Scatter mint and cilantro over each dish and serve immediately.

PER SERVING 390 **CAL**; 10 g **FAT** (2 g **SAT**); 38 g **PRO**; 37 g **CARB**; 3 g **FIBER**; 705 mg **SODIUM**; 166 mg **CHOL**

Middle Eastern Stuffed Peppers

MAKES 6 servings **PREP** 20 minutes **MICROWAVE** 10 minutes

- **6** **medium-size sweet red peppers**
- **1** **cup tricolor pearl couscous (such as Bob's Red Mill) cooked following package directions**
- **1** **can (15 ounces) chickpeas, drained and rinsed**
- **1** **small cucumber, peeled, seeded and chopped**
- **1** **cup crumbled feta cheese**
- **2** **large scallions, trimmed and chopped**
- **¼** **cup parsley, chopped**
- **¼** **cup lemon juice**
- **3** **tablespoons olive oil**
- **¾** **teaspoon salt**
- **¼** **teaspoon black pepper**
  Leafy lettuce (optional)

● Trim about ½ inch off tops of peppers; remove seeds and core. Place cut side down in a microwave-safe glass baking dish. Pour in ½ cup water and cover with microwave-safe plastic wrap, venting at one corner. Microwave on high for 8 to 10 minutes until tender. Remove peppers from dish and set aside.

● In a large bowl, combine cooked couscous, chickpeas, cucumber, feta, scallions and parsley.

● In a small bowl, whisk together lemon juice, olive oil, salt and pepper. Stir into couscous mixture.

● Stuff peppers with an equal amount of couscous mixture, about a scant cup in each. Serve at room temperature or chilled, on a bed of leafy lettuce, if desired.

PER SERVING 341 **CAL**; 7 g **FAT** (4 g **SAT**); 14 g **PRO**; 57 g **CARB**; 8 g **FIBER**; 792 mg **SODIUM**; 22 mg **CHOL**

POWER BREAKFASTS

10 great-tasting, good-for-you morning meals.

HEARTY WAFFLES, PAGE 85

EGGS BENEDICT WITH ROASTED
PEPPERS, PAGE 86

HOMEMADE GRANOLA

You know what they say: Breakfast is the most important meal of the day. Fuel up with wholesome, healthy food.

Homemade Granola

MAKES 5 cups (10 servings) **PREP** 15 minutes
COOK 3 minutes **BAKE** at 325° for 30 minutes

- **2   cups rolled oats**
- **¾   cup raisins**
- **½   cup sliced almonds**
- **½   cup hulled pumpkin seeds (pepitas)**
- **½   cup agave syrup**
- **2   tablespoons unsalted butter**
- **¼   teaspoon salt**
- **¼   teaspoon ground cinnamon**
- **¼   teaspoon ground allspice**

• Heat oven to 325°. Combine oats, raisins, almonds and pumpkin seeds in a large bowl.

• Combine agave syrup, butter, salt, cinnamon and allspice in a small saucepan. Heat over low heat until butter is melted, about 3 minutes. Whisk to blend, then pour over oat mixture in bowl. Stir to evenly coat pieces.

• Spread mixture onto one large or two smaller rimmed baking sheets. Bake at 325° for 15 minutes. Stir and rotate pans (if using more than one). Bake an additional 15 minutes until mixture is golden. Transfer from pan to bowl or canister. Serve with fruit and milk or over yogurt.

PER ½ CUP SERVING 256 **CAL**; 11 g **FAT** (3 g **SAT**); 8 g **PRO**; 36 g **CARB**; 3 g **FIBER**; 62 mg **SODIUM**; 6 mg **CHOL**

Corn & Blueberry Pancakes

MAKES 12 pancakes (4 servings) **PREP** 15 minutes **COOK** 5 minutes per batch **KEEP WARM** at 200°

- **¾   cup all-purpose flour**
- **¾   cup yellow cornmeal**
- **¼   cup sugar**
- **¾   teaspoon baking soda**
- **¼   teaspoon salt**
- **1½   cups buttermilk**
- **1   large egg**
- **2   tablespoons vegetable oil**
- **1   cup fresh or frozen blueberries**
    Butter and maple syrup, for serving (optional)

• Heat a griddle or two large nonstick skillets over medium-low heat. Heat oven to 200°.

• In a bowl, whisk flour, cornmeal, sugar, baking soda and salt until blended. Make a well in the center.

Whisk buttermilk, egg and oil in a bowl; add to flour mixture. Gently whisk just until moistened. Fold in blueberries.

• Using a ladle, drop batter in scant ⅓-cup rounds onto hot griddle. Let cook 2 to 3 minutes until edge is firm and bubbles form. Carefully flip over and cook an additional 2 minutes. Keep pancakes warm on a cookie sheet in 200° oven.

• Repeat with remaining batter. Serve with butter and maple syrup, if desired.

PER SERVING 381 **CAL**; 9 g **FAT** (1 g **SAT**); 9 g **PRO**; 64 g **CARB**; 2 g **FIBER**; 496 mg **SODIUM**; 57 mg **CHOL**

Breakfast Burritos

MAKES 6 servings **PREP** 20 minutes **COOK** 8 minutes **MICROWAVE** 1 minute

1	**can (15 ounces) black beans, drained and rinsed**
⅓	**cup jarred salsa**
1½	**cups baby spinach, roughly chopped**
3	**large eggs plus 3 egg whites (see Note)**
2	**scallions, trimmed and sliced**
¼	**cup cilantro, chopped**
¼	**teaspoon chili powder**
¼	**teaspoon salt**
6	**fajita-size (or slightly larger) whole-wheat tortillas**
¾	**cup shredded taco cheese blend**

• Combine beans and salsa in a small saucepan and cook, stirring occasionally, over medium-low heat until warm.

• Meanwhile, coat a large nonstick skillet with nonstick cooking spray; set over medium heat. Add spinach and cook until wilted, 3 minutes. Whisk eggs, egg whites, scallions, cilantro, chili powder and salt in a bowl.

• Once spinach is wilted, add egg mixture to skillet. Cook 3 minutes without stirring. Scramble and continue to cook and stir for 2 minutes until just set.

• Cover tortillas with a damp paper towel and microwave 1 minute. Spread onto a cutting board. Sprinkle equal amount of cheese in center of each tortilla. Divide bean-salsa mixture among tortillas and top with egg mixture. Fold short ends over filling and then continue to roll, burrito-style. Serve immediately.

Note To lower cholesterol and fat levels, use 1¼ cups egg substitute in place of the eggs and egg whites.

PER BURRITO 305 **CAL**; 11 g **FAT** (4 g **SAT**); 17 g **PRO**; 36 g **CARB**; 7 g **FIBER**; 761 mg **SODIUM**; 154 mg **CHOL**

Apple Cider Doughnuts

MAKES 12 doughnuts **PREP** 15 minutes
BAKE at 325° for 15 minutes

DOUGHNUTS

3	**cups all-purpose flour**
1	**teaspoon baking soda**
¼	**teaspoon salt**
¾	**cup apple cider, plus more for brushing**
½	**cup reduced-fat sour cream**
⅔	**cup packed dark-brown sugar**
2	**eggs**
8	**teaspoons unsalted butter, melted**
1	**tablespoon fresh ginger, peeled and grated**
1	**teaspoon vanilla extract**

CINNAMON SUGAR

½	**cup granulated sugar**
1	**teaspoon ground cinnamon**

• **Doughnuts.** Heat oven to 325°. Coat two 6-indentation doughnut pans with nonstick cooking spray.

• In a large bowl, whisk flour, baking soda and salt. In a small bowl, whisk ¾ cup of the apple cider, the sour cream, brown sugar, eggs, butter, ginger and vanilla extract until smooth. Add milk mixture to flour mixture; whisk until smooth.

• Spoon batter into a large resealable plastic bag. Cut off a corner and squeeze batter into prepared indents, about ⅔ full. Smooth tops. Bake at 325° for 13 to 15 minutes, until doughnuts spring back when lightly pressed. Cool in pan on rack 3 minutes.

• **Cinnamon Sugar.** Stir granulated sugar and cinnamon together in a small bowl. Carefully remove doughnuts from pans and brush tops lightly with additional apple cider. Quickly toss in cinnamon sugar to coat.

PER DOUGHNUT 231 **CAL**; 5 g **FAT** (3 g **SAT**); 5 g **PRO**; 42 g **CARB**; 1 g **FIBER**; 178 mg **SODIUM**; 47 mg **CHOL**

APPLE CIDER DOUGHNUTS

Wake to the aroma of Irish oatmeal made from steel-cut oats bubbling in the slow cooker. A topping of sautéed apples gives it a special touch.

Overnight Oatmeal

MAKES 6 servings **PREP** 15 minutes
SLOW COOK on LOW for 10 hours
COOK 5 minutes

OATMEAL

3	cups 1% milk
1½	cups steel cut oats
½	cup packed dark-brown sugar
¾	teaspoon salt

TOPPING

2	apples (such as Gala or Granny Smith), cored and diced
2	tablespoons packed dark-brown sugar
3	tablespoons sweetened dried cranberries or raisins
3	tablespoons chopped walnuts

• **Oatmeal.** Coat a slow cooker with nonstick cooking spray. Combine milk, 3 cups water, the oats, ¼ cup of the brown sugar and the salt in slow cooker. Cover and cook overnight on LOW for 9½ to 10 hours.

• Uncover and stir in remaining ¼ cup brown sugar. Set aside. **Topping.** Coat a large nonstick skillet with nonstick cooking spray and place over medium heat. Add apples and cook 4 minutes, stirring occasionally. Add brown sugar, 1 tablespoon water and dried cranberries. Cook 1 minute. Remove from heat and stir in nuts.

• Stir oatmeal in slow cooker until smooth. Spoon about 1 cup into a bowl and add a few tablespoons of the topping. Serve warm.

PER SERVING 335 **CAL**; 6 g **FAT** (2 g **SAT**); 11 g **PRO**; 65 g **CARB**; 5 g **FIBER**; 644 mg **SODIUM**; 6 mg **CHOL**

Hearty Waffles

MAKES 12 4-inch waffles (6 servings) **PREP** 15 minutes **COOK** 4 minutes per batch
KEEP WARM at 200°

TOPPING

1	pint strawberries, hulled and sliced
1	tablespoon granulated sugar
1	tablespoon confectioners' sugar

WAFFLES

1½	cups all-purpose flour
1¼	cups white whole-wheat flour
½	cup packed brown sugar
¼	cup wheat germ
2	teaspoons baking powder
½	teaspoon pumpkin pie spice
¾	teaspoon baking soda
½	teaspoon salt
1¾	cups low-fat buttermilk
2	eggs, separated
2	tablespoons canola oil
1	teaspoon vanilla extract

• Heat oven to 200°. Heat a Belgian waffle maker as per manufacturer's directions. Lightly coat with nonstick cooking spray.

• **Topping.** Combine berries and granulated sugar in a bowl. Set aside.

• **Waffles.** In a large bowl, combine flours, brown sugar, wheat germ, baking powder, pumpkin pie spice, baking soda and salt.

• In a small bowl or large measuring cup, blend buttermilk, ¾ cup water, egg yolks, oil and vanilla. Whip egg whites to stiff peaks.

• Mix buttermilk mixture into flour mixture. Fold in egg whites. Pour ½ cup batter onto each section of prepared waffle maker. Cook as per manufacturer's instructions, about 4 minutes per batch. Transfer waffles directly to oven rack in 200° oven. Repeat. Sprinkle waffles with confectioners' sugar and serve with strawberries.

PER SERVING 377 **CAL**; 8 g **FAT** (2 g **SAT**); 13 g **PRO**; 65 g **CARB**; 6 g **FIBER**; 594 mg **SODIUM**; 75 mg **CHOL**

Eggs Benedict with Roasted Peppers

MAKES 4 servings PREP 10 minutes COOK 12 minutes MICROWAVE 2 minutes BROIL 3 minutes

- **2** tablespoons white vinegar
- **1** packet (0.9 ounce) Knorr's hollandaise sauce mix
- **1** cup skim milk
- **2** tablespoons unsalted butter
- **8** slices turkey bacon
- **8** large eggs
- **4** 100-calorie English muffins, split
- **1** jar (12 ounces) roasted red peppers, drained
  Cracked black pepper

• Heat oven to broil. Pour water into a shallow sauté pan to measure 1 inch deep. Add vinegar and bring to a simmer.

• In small saucepan, combine hollandaise mix, milk and butter. Cook, whisking over medium heat until thickened, 3 to 4 minutes. Remove from heat and cover.

• Line a microwave-safe plate with paper towels. Add 4 slices of the turkey bacon and cover with a second layer of towels. Repeat layering. Microwave 2 minutes. Keep warm.

• Meanwhile, crack an egg into a small bowl; slip egg into simmering water. Repeat with 3 more eggs. Cook 4 minutes, or until desired doneness. Remove with a slotted spoon to a paper towel–lined plate. Repeat with the 4 remaining eggs.

• Toast muffins under broiler for 3 minutes and then put both halves on a plate. Top muffin half with 1 slice of bacon, halved, a piece of roasted pepper, 1 egg and a spoonful of hollandaise sauce (refrigerate remaining sauce). Season with black pepper and serve.

PER SERVING 341 CAL; 16 g FAT (5 g SAT); 21 g PRO; 32 g CARB; 6 g FIBER; 827 mg SODIUM; 446 mg CHOL

Breakfast Strata

MAKES 10 servings PREP 30 minutes
COOK 11 minutes REFRIGERATE overnight
BAKE at 350° for 1 hour BROIL 3 minutes

- **3** cups small broccoli florets (about 6 ounces)
- **3** sweet or hot Italian turkey sausage links (about 10 ounces), casings removed
- **2** plum tomatoes, seeded and chopped
- **3** scallions, trimmed and sliced
- **1** loaf Italian bread (about 14 ounces), cut into 1-inch cubes
- **8** large eggs
- **4** egg whites
- **1¼** cups skim milk
- **¼** teaspoon salt
- **1** package (10 ounces) 2% white cheddar cheese, shredded

• Bring a large pot of lightly salted water to boiling. Add broccoli and cook 3 minutes. Drain and set aside.

• Coat a large nonstick skillet with nonstick cooking spray. Heat over medium-high heat and crumble in sausage. Cook 5 minutes, breaking apart with a spoon, until cooked through. Add tomatoes and scallions; cook 3 more minutes. Remove from heat.

• Place bread cubes in a large bowl. In a medium-size bowl, whisk eggs, egg whites, milk and salt. Pour sausage mixture and broccoli florets over bread. Stir to combine. Add egg mixture and 1½ cups of the cheese and stir to blend evenly. Coat a large rectangular or oval dish with nonstick spray. Transfer mixture to prepared dish, cover with plastic and refrigerate overnight.

• Heat oven to 350°. Uncover dish and top with remaining 1 cup cheese. Cover with nonstick foil and bake at 350° for 45 minutes. Uncover and cook 15 minutes more. Increase oven temp to broil and crisp under broiler for 3 minutes. Let rest 5 minutes before serving.

PER SERVING 344 CAL; 14 g FAT (6 g SAT); 25 g PRO; 27 g CARB; 3 g FIBER; 823 mg SODIUM; 207 mg CHOL

BREAKFAST STRATA

SMOKED SALMON
BREAKFAST PIZZA

Smoked Salmon Breakfast Pizza

MAKES 6 servings PREP 15 minutes
BAKE at 450° for 10 minutes

- 1 **package (14 ounces) prepared pizza crust (such as Boboli)**
- ½ **cup ⅓-less-fat chive and onion cream cheese**
- 1 **plum tomato, cored and thinly sliced**
- 4 **ounces smoked salmon, torn into small pieces**
- ½ **small red onion, peeled and sliced (¼ cup)**
- 1 **tablespoon capers**
  Freshly ground black pepper

• Heat oven to 450°. Place pizza crust onto middle rack. Bake at 450° for 8 to 10 minutes. Transfer to a large cutting board.

• Spread crust with cream cheese within ½ inch of edge. Place tomato slices over cream cheese. Spread salmon pieces over tomatoes. Scatter red onion slices and capers evenly over salmon. Sprinkle with freshly ground black pepper and cut into 6 slices.

PER SERVING 300 CAL; 9 g FAT (3 g SAT); 20 g PRO; 34 g CARB; 2 g FIBER; 710 mg SODIUM; 37 mg CHOL

Banana Berry Smoothie

MAKES 6 servings PREP 10 minutes

- 2 **ripe bananas, peeled**
- 2 **cups orange juice**
- 1 **bag (12 ounces) frozen mixed berries**
- 1 **cup 0% Fat Greek yogurt**
- ⅓ **cup wheat germ**
- ¼ **cup honey**

• Combine bananas, 1 cup of the orange juice, the berries, yogurt, wheat germ and honey in a blender.

• Cover and blend for about 1 minute, until all ingredients are mixed. While blending, pour in remaining 1 cup orange juice. Blend until smooth. Pour into glasses and serve.

PER SERVING 194 CAL; 1 g FAT (0 g SAT); 7 g PRO; 42 g CARB; 4 g FIBER; 19 mg SODIUM; 0 mg CHOL

BANANA BERRY SMOOTHIE

CREOLE SAUSAGE
& SHRIMP, PAGE 98

APRIL

93

104

110

MEAL DEALS

Great-tasting, affordable dinners.

Chicken Paprikash with Spaetzle

MAKES 6 servings PREP 20 minutes COOK 24 minutes BAKE at 325° for 45 minutes

1	whole chicken (about 4 pounds), cut into 12 pieces (2 drumsticks, 2 thighs, 2 wings, breasts in thirds), skin removed
1¼	teaspoons salt
2	tablespoons vegetable oil
1	medium sweet onion, diced
1	sweet red pepper, diced
3	tablespoons all-purpose flour
2	tablespoons sweet paprika
1	tablespoon smoked paprika
¼	teaspoon cayenne pepper
2	cups low-sodium chicken broth
2	medium tomatoes, seeded and diced
1	cup sour cream
1	box (10 ounces) spaetzle (such as Maggi) or egg noodles, cooked Fresh chopped parsley, if desired

• Heat oven to 325°. Season chicken pieces with ¼ teaspoon of the salt. Heat oil in a Dutch oven over medium-high heat. Brown chicken in two batches, 3 to 4 minutes per side (12 to 16 minutes total). Remove to a plate, keeping as much oil in the pan as possible.

• Reduce heat to medium. Add onion and red pepper; cook 3 minutes to soften slightly. Mix in flour, sweet and smoked paprika, and cayenne pepper. Cook 2 minutes, stirring constantly. Add broth, tomatoes and remaining 1 teaspoon salt. Bring to a boil and simmer 3 minutes to thicken. Add browned chicken back to pot, ladling a bit of sauce on top. Cover and bake at 325° for 45 minutes or until chicken is very tender.

• Remove chicken; cover to keep warm. Add sour cream to a bowl; whisk in a cup of the hot sauce to temper. Whisk sour cream mixture back into pot. Serve two pieces of chicken over cooked spaetzle with several spoonfuls of sauce. Garnish with parsley, if desired.

PER SERVING 482 CAL; 17 g FAT (6 g SAT.); 31 g PRO; 48 g CARB; 5 g FIBER; 598 mg SODIUM; 128 mg CHOL

CHEAP TRICKS

Purchasing a whole, precut chicken instead of individual pieces is much more economical and can save at least $2 per pound. Don't remove the bones before cooking—they enhance poultry's flavor and help it stay tender. If a complete cut-up fryer isn't available in the grocery's meat section, just ask the butcher to prepare one for you. Use extra chicken pieces to make homemade stock for even more savings.

SIMMER DOWN

Low-cal slow cooker suppers—dig in!

INDIAN-SPICED
TURKEY BREAST,
PAGE 97

Pulled Buffalo Chicken Sliders

MAKES 16 sliders (8 servings)
PREP 10 minutes **SLOW COOK** on HIGH for
6 hours or LOW for 8 hours

4	boneless, skinless chicken breasts, about 1½ pounds
¼	cup hot wing sauce (such as Frank's), plus more for serving (optional)
16	dinner-size potato rolls, 1¼ ounces each
1	cup reduced-fat blue cheese dressing
	Celery and carrot sticks (optional)

• Coat slow cooker bowl with nonstick cooking spray. Place chicken breasts in a single layer in bottom; combine hot sauce with ⅔ cup water; pour over chicken.

• Cover and cook on HIGH for 6 hours or LOW for 8 hours. Remove chicken to a plate and shred with two forks. Return to slow cooker and stir to coat with sauce.

• To serve, place shredded chicken on bottom halves of rolls and top each with 1 tablespoon of dressing. If desired, serve with celery sticks, carrot sticks and additional hot sauce.

PER SERVING 294 **CAL**; 7 g **FAT** (1 g **SAT**); 23 g **PRO**; 34 g **CARB**; 2 g **FIBER**; 792 mg **SODIUM**; 49 mg **CHOL**

Chinese Hacked Pork

MAKES 6 servings **PREP** 10 minutes **MARINATE** overnight **SLOW COOK** on HIGH for 4 hours or LOW for 6 hours **COOK** 1 minute

- ¼ **cup reduced-sodium soy sauce**
- ¼ **cup honey**
- 2 **tablespoons hoisin sauce**
- 4 **cloves garlic, chopped**
- 2 **tablespoons chopped ginger**
- 1 **teaspoon Chinese five-spice powder**
- 2 **pounds boneless center-cut pork roast**
- 1 **tablespoon cornstarch**
- ¾ **cup reduced-sodium chicken broth**
- 12 **ounces wide lo mein noodles, cooked following package directions**
- 2 **scallions, thinly sliced**
  Steamed snow peas (optional)

• In a small bowl, whisk together soy sauce, honey, hoisin, garlic, ginger and five-spice powder. Place in a resealable plastic bag and add pork; shake to coat. Refrigerate overnight.

• Coat slow cooker bowl with nonstick cooking spray. Place pork in bowl and pour marinade over top. Cover and cook on HIGH for 4 hours or LOW for 6 hours.

• Remove pork to a large baking dish and keep warm. Pour liquid from slow cooker into a saucepan. In a small bowl, stir cornstarch into broth. Bring liquid in saucepan to a boil and whisk in the broth mixture. Cook for 1 minute.

• Shred pork into large pieces with two forks; stir in sauce. Spoon over noodles; garnish with scallions and serve with steamed snow peas, if desired.

PER SERVING 485 **CAL**; 8 g **FAT** (3 g **SAT**); 39 g **PRO**; 65 g **CARB**; 1 g **FIBER**; 741 mg **SODIUM**; 95 mg **CHOL**

A squeeze of lemon and a dash of hot sauce is an easy way to perk up soups and stews.

Indian-Spiced Turkey Breast

MAKES 6 servings **PREP** 10 minutes
SLOW COOK on HIGH for 4 hours or LOW
for 6 hours

1	boneless, skinless turkey breast half, about 2½ pounds
1	cup reduced-sodium chicken broth
1½	teaspoons curry powder
¼	teaspoon cayenne pepper
½	teaspoon salt
1	large onion, chopped
2	tablespoons chopped ginger
¼	cup cilantro leaves
1	can (15 ounces) chickpeas, drained and rinsed
½	cup reduced-fat (2%) plain yogurt
2	tablespoons chopped cilantro
3	cups cooked brown basmati rice

• Coat slow cooker bowl with nonstick cooking spray. Place turkey in bottom and pour broth over top. Mix together curry powder, cayenne pepper and salt; sprinkle over turkey. Scatter onion, ginger and cilantro leaves over turkey.

• Cover and cook on HIGH for 4 hours or LOW for 6 hours. Add chickpeas during last 30 minutes of cooking.

• Remove turkey to a cutting board and cover. Gradually whisk yogurt into slow cooker bowl; stir in chopped cilantro. Allow sauce to heat through.

• Slice turkey and serve with cooked rice and the yogurt and chickpea sauce.

PER SERVING 397 **CAL**; 3 g **FAT** (1 g **SAT**);
52 g **PRO**; 38 g **CARB**; 5 g **FIBER**; 578 mg
SODIUM; 125 mg **CHOL**

Beef & Hominy Stew

MAKES 6 servings **PREP** 15 minutes **SLOW COOK** on HIGH for 6 hours or LOW for 8 hours

1	large onion, chopped
1¾	pounds boneless beef chuck, cut into 1½-inch pieces
¼	teaspoon salt
1	green pepper, cored, seeded and chopped
3	carrots, peeled and cut into 1-inch pieces
3	ribs celery, cut into 1-inch pieces
3	cloves garlic, chopped
1	can (14½ ounces) petite diced tomatoes with chiles
1	cup reduced-sodium beef broth
2	tablespoons cornstarch
1	can (15 ounces) hominy, drained and rinsed
	Corn tortillas and salad (optional)

• Coat slow cooker bowl with nonstick cooking spray. Place onion in bottom and add beef; season with salt. Add green pepper, carrots, celery and garlic. Pour tomatoes and ¾ cup of the broth over the top.

• Cover and cook on HIGH for 6 hours or LOW for 8 hours.

• Mix cornstarch with remaining ¼ cup of broth until smooth. Stir into slow cooker during last 15 minutes of cooking; add hominy.

• Serve with corn tortillas and salad, if desired.

PER SERVING 274 **CAL**; 8 g **FAT** (2 g **SAT**);
28 g **PRO**; 24 g **CARB**; 5 g **FIBER**; 799 mg
SODIUM; 75 mg **CHOL**

Creole Sausage & Shrimp

MAKES 6 servings **PREP** 15 minutes
SLOW COOK on HIGH for 6 hours or LOW for
8 hours, plus 7 minutes

1	**large onion, chopped**
1	**green pepper, cored, seeded and chopped**
2	**ribs celery, sliced**
2	**large carrots, peeled and diced**
4	**cloves garlic, chopped**
1	**can (14½ ounces) no-salt-added diced tomatoes**
¾	**cup reduced-sodium chicken broth**
2	**teaspoons Creole seasoning**
3	**jalapeño-flavor fully cooked chicken sausages from a 12-ounce package (such as Aidells), sliced into ½-inch-thick coins**
1	**package (10 ounces) frozen corn, thawed**
1	**tablespoon tomato paste**
1	**pound raw, cleaned and deveined large shrimp**
3	**cups cooked brown rice**

• Coat slow cooker bowl with nonstick cooking spray. Place onion, green pepper, celery, carrots, garlic, tomatoes, broth and Creole seasoning in bowl; stir to combine. Mix in sausage and corn.

• Cover and cook on HIGH for 6 hours or LOW for 8 hours. Stir in tomato paste and shrimp; cook until shrimp is just cooked through, about 5 to 7 minutes.

• Serve over cooked brown rice.

PER SERVING 345 **CAL**; 7 g **FAT** (2 g **SAT**);
28 g **PRO**; 42 g **CARB**; 5 g **FIBER**; 800 mg
SODIUM; 173 mg **CHOL**

White Bean & Ham Soup

MAKES 6 servings **PREP** 15 minutes **SOAK** overnight **SLOW COOK** on HIGH 6 hours

1	**pound dry cannellini beans**
1	**large onion, chopped**
2	**carrots, peeled and sliced**
3	**cloves garlic, chopped**
1	**can (14½ ounces) stewed tomatoes**
1½	**teaspoons dried Italian seasoning**
8	**ounces low-sodium ham, diced**
½	**teaspoon salt**
½	**teaspoon black pepper**
	Crusty bread (optional)
	Fresh parsley (optional)

• Place beans in a large pot and cover with water. Bring to boiling, cover and turn off heat. Allow to soak overnight.

• Coat slow cooker bowl with nonstick cooking spray. Drain beans and add to bowl. Add 4 cups water, onion, carrots, garlic, tomatoes, Italian seasoning and ham. Stir to combine, breaking up tomatoes with a wooden spoon.

• Cover and cook on HIGH for 6 hours.

• Season with salt and pepper; mash beans slightly to thicken soup. Serve with crusty bread and garnish with parsley, if desired.

PER SERVING 349 **CAL**; 5 g **FAT** (2 g **SAT**);
21 g **PRO**; 57 g **CARB**; 21 g **FIBER**; 795 mg
SODIUM; 21 mg **CHOL**

CREOLE SAUSAGE
& SHRIMP

BUDGET GOURMET

10 of our favorite family meals for less than $10.

Chicken Meatballs with Peanut Sauce

MAKES 4 servings **PREP** 20 minutes **COOK** 20 minutes

- **1**   **pound ground chicken**
- **½**   **cup plain bread crumbs**
- **½**   **cup finely diced onion**
- **½**   **cup finely diced sweet red pepper**
- **⅓**   **cup cilantro, chopped, plus more for garnish**
- **1**   **egg**
- **½**   **teaspoon salt**
- **¼**   **teaspoon cayenne pepper**
- **1½**   **teaspoons grated ginger**
- **2**   **tablespoons vegetable oil**
- **1**   **cup light coconut milk**
- **⅓**   **cup reduced-fat chunky peanut butter**
- **½**   **cup low-sodium chicken broth**
- **2**   **tablespoons low-sodium soy sauce**
- **3**   **cups cooked basmati rice**

● In a large bowl, combine chicken, bread crumbs, onion, red pepper, cilantro, egg, salt, cayenne and 1 teaspoon of the ginger. Mix well and form into 20 meatballs. Add 1 tablespoon of the oil to a large, lidded sauté pan over medium heat. Add half the meatballs and brown on all sides, 5 to 6 minutes total; remove to a plate. Repeat with remaining 1 tablespoon oil and remaining meatballs; set aside.

● In same pan, combine coconut milk, peanut butter, chicken broth, soy sauce and remaining ½ teaspoon ginger. Stir constantly over medium heat to melt peanut butter. Bring to a simmer and cook 2 to 3 minutes, until slightly thickened. Add meatballs to sauce, cover pan and cook 5 minutes, or until meatballs are cooked through.

● Serve meatballs and peanut sauce over rice. Garnish with cilantro, if desired.

PER SERVING 695 **CAL**; 35 g **FAT** (10 g **SAT**); 33 g **PRO**; 65 g **CARB**; 3 g **FIBER**; 917 mg **SODIUM**; 190 mg **CHOL**

**ASPARAGUS & RICOTTA PIZZA,
PAGE 107**

Salmon Cakes with Old Bay Aïoli

MAKES 4 servings **PREP** 20 minutes **COOK** 17 minutes

SALMON CAKES

- 3   tablespoons vegetable oil
- ½   sweet onion, diced small
- 1   medium carrot, finely diced
- 1   rib celery, finely diced
- 2   cans (7.5 ounces each) canned pink salmon
- 1   cup plain bread crumbs
- 1¼   teaspoons Old Bay seasoning
- 1   teaspoon Dijon mustard
- ¼   teaspoon cayenne pepper
- ¼   cup light mayonnaise
- ¼   cup parsley, chopped
- 1   tablespoon lemon juice
- 1   head escarole, chopped
-   Bottled dressing (optional)

OLD BAY AÏOLI

- ¼   cup light mayonnaise
- 1   teaspoon Dijon mustard
- ½   teaspoon grated garlic
- ¼   teaspoon Old Bay seasoning

• **Salmon Cakes.** In a large nonstick skillet, heat 1 tablespoon of the oil over medium heat. Add onion, carrot and celery; cook 5 minutes until slightly softened. Remove to a large bowl.

• Drain salmon; remove bones, if desired. Add to bowl with cooked vegetables along with bread crumbs, Old Bay, mustard, cayenne, mayonnaise, parsley and lemon juice. Combine well and form into 12 cakes, about ⅓ cup each.

• In same skillet, add another 1 tablespoon of the oil over medium heat. When oil is hot, add half the cakes to the pan and cook 2 to 3 minutes per side or until browned. Repeat with remaining 1 tablespoon oil and remaining cakes.

• **Old Bay Aïoli.** In a small bowl, combine mayonnaise, mustard, garlic and Old Bay. Mix and serve alongside cakes and escarole. Drizzle escarole with dressing, if desired.

PER SERVING (Salmon Cakes) 432 **CAL**; 22 g **FAT** (4 g **SAT**); 31 g **PRO**; 29 g **CARB**; 6 g **FIBER**; 1,032 mg **SODIUM**; 92 mg **CHOL**

PER SERVING (Old Bay Aïoli) 52 **CAL**; 5 g **FAT** (1 g **SAT**); 0 g **PRO**; 2 g **CARB**; 0 g **FIBER**; 191 mg **SODIUM**; 5 mg **CHOL**

Caramelized Onion Quiche

MAKES 6 servings PREP 15 minutes
COOK 40 minutes BAKE at 375° for 45 minutes
COOL 10 minutes

1	refrigerated piecrust
¼	cup olive oil
5	cups thinly sliced onions
5	eggs
1	cup 2% milk
1	tablespoon Dijon mustard
½	teaspoon salt
¼	teaspoon nutmeg
4	ounces Swiss or Gruyère cheese, shredded (1 cup)
	Arugula (optional)

• Heat oven to 375°. Fit crust into a 9-inch pie plate, cover loosely with plastic wrap and refrigerate.

• Heat oil in a large sauté pan over medium heat. Add onions and cook until browned and soft, stirring once in a while, about 35 to 40 minutes. (If onions begin to burn, reduce heat to medium-low.) Set aside to cool a bit.

• In a bowl, whisk together eggs, milk, mustard, salt and nutmeg. Remove pie plate from refrigerator. Sprinkle cheese evenly on bottom of crust. Scatter onions on top. Pour egg mixture over cheese and onions. Bake quiche at 375° for 45 minutes, or until eggs are set and crust is browned. Cool 10 minutes on a wire rack. Serve with arugula, if desired.

PER SERVING 444 CAL; 28 g FAT (10 g SAT); 14 g PRO; 34 g CARB; 2 g FIBER; 506 mg SODIUM; 201 mg CHOL

Roasted Beet, Apple & White Bean Salad

MAKES 4 servings PREP 25 minutes BAKE at 425° for 35 minutes

3	beets (about 1 pound with leaves trimmed), halved
⅓	cup plus 2 tablespoons olive oil
⅛	teaspoon plus ¼ teaspoon salt
¼	teaspoon pepper
3	tablespoons balsamic vinegar
2	teaspoons Dijon mustard
1	shallot, finely diced
1	bunch kale (about 1 pound), tough stems removed and sliced in ¼-inch strips
1	can (15 ounces) cannellini beans, drained and rinsed
1	Granny Smith apple, thinly sliced
½	cup diced ricotta salata or crumbled feta cheese

• Heat oven to 425°. Toss beets in 2 tablespoons of the olive oil and ⅛ teaspoon each of the salt and pepper. Seal beets inside a large piece of aluminum foil. Place foil-wrapped beets on a baking sheet and bake at 425° for 35 minutes or until knife-tender. Allow to cool a bit, then remove skins with a paper towel or gloves. Cut into ½-inch pieces.

• Meanwhile, make the dressing. In a medium bowl, combine vinegar, mustard, shallot, remaining ¼ teaspoon salt and remaining ⅛ teaspoon pepper. Slowly whisk in remaining ⅓ cup olive oil.

• Toss kale with half the dressing. Arrange on a platter with beets, beans and apple. Scatter cheese on top and drizzle with remaining dressing.

PER SERVING 484 CAL; 30 g FAT (6 g SAT); 13 g PRO; 45 g CARB; 9 g FIBER; 727 mg SODIUM; 17 mg CHOL

Chicken Tostadas with Pickled Red Onion

MAKES 4 servings **PREP** 15 minutes **COOK** 46 minutes **BAKE** at 400° for 10 minutes

PICKLED RED ONION

- **1** red onion, thinly sliced
- **½** cup distilled white vinegar
- **1** teaspoon granulated sugar
  Pinch of salt

CHICKEN TOSTADAS

- **1** tablespoon chili powder
- **2** teaspoons ground cumin
- **1** teaspoon ground coriander
- **¼** teaspoon cayenne pepper
- **½** teaspoon salt
- **1½** pounds bone-in chicken thighs, skin removed
- **2** tablespoons vegetable oil, plus more for brushing tortillas
- **1** cup diced yellow onion
- **3** cloves garlic, chopped
- **1** can (14.5 ounces) diced tomatoes
- **½** cup low-sodium chicken broth
- **8** corn tortillas
  Shredded pepper Jack cheese (optional)
  Fresh cilantro (optional)

• **Pickled Red Onion.** Combine onion, vinegar, sugar, salt and 1 cup water in a small saucepan. Bring to a boil; simmer 1 minute. Pour into a heat-proof bowl, cover and chill until using.

• **Chicken Tostadas.** Heat oven to 400°. Combine chili powder, cumin, coriander, cayenne and salt in a small bowl. Rub spice mixture on chicken thighs. Heat the 2 tablespoons of oil in a large, lidded sauté pan on medium-high heat. Sear chicken 2 to 3 minutes per side; remove to a plate. Reduce heat to medium and add onion; sauté 3 minutes. Add garlic and sauté 1 more minute.

• Pour tomatoes and broth into pan, scraping brown bits from bottom. Bring to a simmer, then return chicken to pan and reduce heat to low. Cover and simmer for 35 minutes.

• Meanwhile, lightly brush both sides of tortillas with vegetable oil and place them in a single layer on two baking sheets. Bake at 400° for 5 minutes, flip and bake another 3 to 5 minutes, until browned and crispy. Remove from oven, cover with aluminum foil and set aside. Remove chicken, shred and return to pan; discard bones.

• To assemble: Place 1 tortilla on plate. Transfer a bit of chicken mixture to tortilla using a slotted spoon. Place another tortilla on top. Garnish with Pickled Red Onion and, if desired, cheese and cilantro.

PER SERVING 446 **CAL**; 16 g **FAT** (3 g **SAT**); 39 g **PRO**; 37 g **CARB**; 7 g **FIBER**; 734 mg **SODIUM**; 141 mg **CHOL**

Falafel with Spicy Yogurt Sauce

MAKES 4 servings (12 falafel) **PREP** 20 minutes
COOK 16 minutes

SPICY YOGURT SAUCE

1	container (6 ounces) plain low-fat yogurt
1	clove garlic, grated
1	teaspoon fresh lemon juice
¼	teaspoon cayenne pepper
⅛	teaspoon salt

FALAFEL

2	cans (15.5 ounces each) chickpeas, drained and rinsed
1	cup packed fresh parsley
½	cup packed fresh cilantro
2	cloves garlic, halved
2	scallions, roughly chopped
¼	cup all-purpose flour
1	teaspoon ground cumin
1	teaspoon ground coriander
¾	teaspoon salt
¼	teaspoon pepper
2	tablespoons vegetable oil
2	pitas, halved
1	tomato, sliced
½	cucumber, sliced

• **Spicy Yogurt Sauce.** Combine yogurt, garlic, lemon juice, cayenne and salt in a small bowl. Cover and refrigerate until using.

• **Falafel.** Combine chickpeas, parsley, cilantro, garlic, scallions, flour, cumin, coriander, salt and pepper in a food processor. Run until well combined. Transfer mixture to a bowl. Form into 12 falafel balls.

• Heat oven to 200°. Heat 1 tablespoon of the oil in a large nonstick sauté pan over medium to medium-high heat. Add 6 falafel to pan and brown 2 minutes per side, about 8 minutes total. Transfer to 200° oven to keep warm. Repeat with second batch.

• Serve falafel in a pita half with tomato, cucumber and Spicy Yogurt Sauce.

PER SERVING 416 **CAL**; 11 g **FAT** (2 g **SAT**); 17 g **PRO**; 62 g **CARB**; 11 g **FIBER**; 967 mg **SODIUM**; 4 mg **CHOL**

Pork Dumplings

MAKES 6 servings (48 dumplings)
PREP 45 minutes **COOK** 18 minutes

2	small beef bouillon cubes plus 4 cups water or 4 cups low-sodium beef broth
2	whole cloves
5	peppercorns
1	teaspoon fennel seeds
2	1-inch pieces of ginger, peeled
2	tablespoons low-sodium soy sauce
½	teaspoon salt
10	large napa cabbage leaves, coarsely chopped (6 cups)
1	pound ground pork
4	scallions, sliced
1	teaspoon sesame oil
2	cloves garlic, grated
1	package (12 ounces) wonton wrappers

• In a lidded saucepan, combine broth, cloves, peppercorns, fennel seeds, 1 piece of the ginger, 1 tablespoon of the soy sauce and ¼ teaspoon of the salt. Bring to a boil, remove from heat and cover.

• Meanwhile, bring a large pot of lightly salted water to boiling. Add cabbage leaves and boil for 2 minutes. Remove with tongs to a colander and press out water. Chop into small pieces and place in a large bowl. Reserve pot of water for later use.

• Grate remaining piece of ginger. Add to bowl with cooked cabbage, along with the pork, 2 of the scallions, sesame oil, garlic, remaining 1 tablespoon soy sauce and remaining ¼ teaspoon salt. Mix well.

• Fill a small bowl with water. Place 1 wonton wrapper on a dry surface. Add 1 tablespoon of the pork mixture to center of wrapper and brush edges with water. Fold wrapper to form a triangle and press sides together firmly to seal. Set aside. Repeat with remaining wonton wrappers and pork filling.

• Bring pot of water back to a boil. Add 12 of the dumplings and cook 3 to 4 minutes; dumplings will float to surface. Remove with a slotted spoon to six bowls and cover with plastic wrap. Repeat three more times until all dumplings are cooked. Reheat broth and pour evenly into bowls. Garnish with remaining 2 scallions.

Note Dumplings can be made ahead of time: Freeze uncooked dumplings on a baking sheet in single layers, separated by wax or parchment paper, then transfer to a resealable plastic bag for up to 3 months.

PER SERVING 400 **CAL**; 18 g **FAT** (6 g **SAT**); 22 g **PRO**; 36 g **CARB**; 2 g **FIBER**; 1,071 mg **SODIUM**; 60 mg **CHOL**

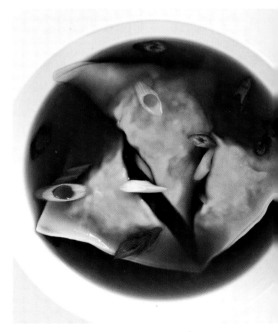

and 1 cup of the reserved pasta water. Mix constantly for 2 minutes, making sure not to scramble the eggs. Stir in salt and pepper, cover and set aside.

• Heat 1 teaspoon of the oil in a medium nonstick skillet. Add 2 of the eggs and fry sunny-side up for 3 to 4 minutes over medium heat; set aside. Repeat with remaining 1 teaspoon oil and 2 eggs. Divide pasta evenly among four bowls (if pasta seems a bit dry, stir in remaining ½ cup reserved pasta water just before serving). Place 1 egg on each serving and garnish with parsley.

PER SERVING 572 CAL; 33 g FAT (12 g SAT); 28 g PRO; 38 g CARB; 2 g FIBER; 1,017 mg SODIUM; 360 mg CHOL

Spaghetti Carbonara

MAKES 4 servings PREP 10 minutes
COOK 19 minutes

1	pound spaghetti
⅓	pound bacon (about 5 slices), diced
6	eggs
1	cup grated Parmesan cheese
4	cloves garlic, sliced
½	teaspoon salt
1½	teaspoons freshly cracked black pepper
2	teaspoons olive oil
¼	cup fresh parsley, chopped

• Bring a pot of lightly salted water to boiling. Add spaghetti and cook 10 minutes or as per package directions. Reserve 1½ cups hot pasta water.

• Meanwhile, add bacon to a large, lidded sauté pan. Cook over medium heat for 6 minutes or until slightly crispy. While bacon is cooking, whisk together 2 of the eggs and the cheese in bowl. Add garlic to pan and cook 1 to 2 minutes.

• When pasta has finished cooking, drain and immediately add to pan with cooked bacon and garlic. Toss for 1 minute to coat noodles. Remove pan from heat and stir in egg-cheese mixture

Sausage & Mushroom Risotto

MAKES 4 servings PREP 15 minutes
COOK 44 minutes

2	cans (14.5 ounces each) low-sodium chicken broth
½	pound bulk pork sausage
2	tablespoons olive oil
1	cup diced sweet onion
10	ounces button mushrooms, sliced
2	cloves garlic, chopped
1	cup arborio rice
¼	teaspoon salt
¼	teaspoon pepper
½	cup grated Parmesan cheese
¼	cup chopped fresh parsley

• Warm broth in a small, lidded pot over low heat.

• Crumble sausage into a large, nonstick sauté pan over medium heat. Brown 5 to 7 minutes, breaking apart meat with a wooden spoon. Transfer sausage to a medium bowl with a slotted spoon.

• Pour oil into the same pan. Add onion and sauté 3 minutes. Stir in mushrooms; sauté 5 to 7 minutes until they are browned and soft. Add garlic and cook 1 more minute. Transfer mixture to bowl with sausage.

With fresh, wholesome ingredients and fabulous flavor, you'd never guess these delicious dinners go easy on the pocketbook.

• Reduce heat to medium-low. Add rice; toast 1 minute. Add ⅓ cup of the warm broth. Scrape brown bits from bottom of pan. Bring to a very low simmer. When liquid is almost absorbed, add another ⅓ cup of broth. Continue adding broth ⅓ cup at a time, stirring frequently, until it is gone and rice is tender, about 20 to 25 minutes.

• Stir in cooked sausage-vegetable mixture, salt, pepper, cheese and parsley. Serve immediately.

PER SERVING 524 CAL; 28 g FAT (9 g SAT); 20 g PRO; 51 g CARB; 3 g FIBER; 795 mg SODIUM; 52 mg CHOL

Asparagus & Ricotta Pizza

MAKES 4 servings   **PREP** 20 minutes   **RISE** 45 minutes   **BAKE** at 500° for 12 minutes

DOUGH (ENOUGH FOR 2 LARGE PIZZAS)

1	package (¼ ounce) active dry yeast
	Pinch of sugar
3¾	cups all-purpose flour, plus more if needed
2	teaspoons sea salt
1	tablespoon olive oil

ASPARAGUS & RICOTTA TOPPING

½	pound asparagus (about 15 to 20 thin spears)
1	tablespoon olive oil, plus more for drizzling (optional)
¼	teaspoon plus ⅛ teaspoon salt
¼	teaspoon pepper
½	cup part-skim ricotta cheese
1	clove garlic, grated
	Cornmeal or semolina flour, for pizza stone
	Zest of ½ a lemon

• Heat oven with pizza stone inside to 500° at least 1 hour prior to baking.

• **Dough.** In a small bowl, stir together 1½ cups warm water (between 100° and 110°), yeast and sugar. Set aside for 10 minutes.

• Combine flour and salt in a large bowl. Make a well in the center and pour yeast mixture and oil into it. Slowly stir yeast mixture into flour (from the inside out). Finish bringing together dough by hand in bowl until most of flour is absorbed (if it feels too sticky, add more flour). Place dough on a clean surface and knead until it slowly springs back when pressed, about 2 to 3 minutes. Divide dough in half. Lightly coat two bowls with olive oil and place one piece of dough into each. Cover and set aside in a warm place to rise for 45 minutes.

• Meanwhile, make **Topping.** Break tough ends off asparagus and cut each stalk into thirds. Place asparagus in a bowl and toss in oil, ¼ teaspoon of the salt and ⅛ teaspoon of the pepper. In another bowl, mix together ricotta,

garlic and remaining ⅛ teaspoon each of the salt and pepper.

• Punch down dough in both bowls. Wrap one ball tightly in plastic wrap, place in a resealable bag and freeze for later use. Form other ball into 12- to 14-inch circle. Sprinkle cornmeal on pizza peel and place dough on top. Scatter asparagus over dough. Dollop ricotta mixture on top. Transfer from peel to stone, and bake at 500° for 12 minutes or until crust is browned and cooked through. (If you don't have a peel, use the back of a pizza pan to transfer to the stone. No stone? Bake pizza on pan at 500° for 14 minutes or until browned.) Zest lemon on top of pizza and drizzle with more olive oil, if desired.

PER SERVING 303 **CAL**; 8 g **FAT** (2 g **SAT**.); 11 g **PRO**; 47 g **CARB**; 3 g **FIBER**; 740 mg **SODIUM**; 10 mg **CHOL**

SWEET SUCCESS

With these bake-sale treats, raising money for your favorite cause is a piece of cake.

MINI BROWNIE BARS,
PAGE 112

COOKIEPOPS,
PAGE 112

Cookies 'n' Cream Cake Pops

MAKES 48 pops **PREP** 15 minutes **BAKE** at 350° for 35 minutes **DECORATE** 2 hours

FILLING

- **1 box (18.25 ounces) white cake mix**
- **3 large egg whites**
- **2 tablespoons vegetable oil**
- **1 cup chopped Oreo cookies (8 cookies)**
- **1 cup canned vanilla frosting**

COATING

- **3 bags (14 ounces each) pink, yellow and white candy melts (such as Wilton)**
- **48 lollipop sticks**
- **½ cup white nonpareils**
- **2 crushed Oreo cookies**

• **Filling.** Heat oven to 350°. Coat a 13 x 9 x 2-inch baking pan with nonstick cooking spray. In a large bowl, combine cake mix, 1⅓ cups water, the egg whites and oil. Prepare as per package directions. Fold in chopped cookies and pour into prepared pan. Bake at 350° for 32 to 35 minutes. Cool completely in pan on a wire rack.

• Finely crumble cake into a large bowl. Stir in frosting and press together with the back of a spoon. Shape mixture into 1¼-inch balls and place on a baking sheet. Refrigerate 2 hours or freeze for 20 minutes.

• **Coating.** Once cake balls are chilled, melt candy as per package directions. Remove a few balls from the refrigerator or freezer. Dip a lollipop stick about ½ inch into the melted candy. Press a cake ball onto the stick, being careful not to press stick too far. Dip ball into desired coating and gently tap so excess coating drips back into bowl. Garnish with contrasting-color drizzle, nonpareils, crushed cookies or a combination of ingredients. Transfer decorated pops to a wax paper-lined sheet. Repeat, reheating candy melts as needed. Refrigerate for 30 minutes, then store at room temp up to 2 weeks.

PER POP 111 **CAL**; 6 g **FAT** (4 g **SAT**); 1 g **PRO**; 13 g **CARB**; 0 g **FIBER**; 46 mg **SODIUM**; 0 mg **CHOL**

Chocolate-Strawberry Mini Cupcakes

MAKES 24 minis **PREP** 10 minutes
BAKE at 350° for 17 minutes

CUPCAKES

¾	cup all-purpose flour
¼	cup unsweetened cocoa powder
1	teaspoon baking powder
⅛	teaspoon salt
6	tablespoons (¾ stick) unsalted butter, softened
½	cup granulated sugar
1	large egg
⅓	cup whole milk
½	teaspoon vanilla extract

FROSTING

1¼	cups confectioners' sugar
¼	cup strawberry-flavor cream cheese spread
2	tablespoons unsalted butter, softened
2	tablespoons strawberry preserves
	Red food coloring

• Heat oven to 350°. Line indents of two 12-cup mini cupcake pans with paper or foil liners.

• **Cupcakes.** In a medium-size bowl, whisk together flour, cocoa powder, baking powder and salt. In a second medium-size bowl, combine butter and sugar. Beat with an electric mixer on medium-high for 1 minute. Add egg and beat until combined. On low speed, beat in half the flour mixture, then all the milk, followed by remaining flour mixture. Beat in vanilla extract.

• Spoon evenly into prepared liners. Bake at 350° for 17 minutes. Cool in pans on wire racks.

• **Frosting.** In a medium-size bowl, combine confectioners' sugar, cream cheese, butter, preserves and enough food coloring to tint desired shade of pink. Beat until smooth. Spread onto mini cupcakes.

PER CUPCAKE 108 **CAL**; 5 g **FAT** (3 g **SAT**); 1 g **PRO**; 16 g **CARB**; 0 g **FIBER**; 42 mg **SODIUM**; 21 mg **CHOL**

Key Lime Mini Cupcakes

MAKES 24 minis **PREP** 10 minutes **BAKE** at 350° for 17 minutes

CUPCAKES

1	cup all-purpose flour
1	teaspoon baking powder
⅛	teaspoon salt
6	tablespoons (¾ stick) unsalted butter, softened
½	cup plus 2 tablespoons granulated sugar
1	large egg
¼	cup Key lime or traditional lime juice

FROSTING

1½	cups confectioners' sugar
6	tablespoons unsalted butter, softened
1	tablespoon Key lime juice

• Heat oven to 350°. Line indents of two 12-cup mini cupcake pans with paper or foil liners.

• **Cupcakes.** In a medium bowl, combine flour, baking powder and salt. In a second medium-size bowl, combine butter and sugar. Beat with an electric mixer on medium-high for 1 minute. Add egg and beat until combined. On low, beat in half the flour mixture, then the Key lime juice, followed by remaining flour mixture.

• Spoon evenly into prepared liners. Bake at 350° for 17 minutes. Cool in pans on wire racks.

• **Frosting.** In a small bowl, combine confectioners' sugar, butter and Key lime juice. Beat until smooth. Spread frosting onto cooled cupcakes.

PER CUPCAKE 122 **CAL**; 6 g **FAT** (4 g **SAT**); 1 g **PRO**; 17 g **CARB**; 0 g **FIBER**; 33 mg **SODIUM**; 24 mg **CHOL**

CookiePops

MAKES 2½ dozen **PREP** 15 minutes
BAKE at 350° for 14 minutes

COOKIES

1	**cup all-purpose flour**
½	**teaspoon baking soda**
¼	**teaspoon salt**
½	**cup (1 stick) unsalted butter, softened**
⅓	**cup packed light-brown sugar**
1	**large egg**
1	**teaspoon vanilla extract**
¾	**cup mini semisweet chocolate chips**

FILLING

2	**cups confectioners' sugar**
¾	**cup (1½ sticks) unsalted butter, softened**
1	**tablespoon milk**
30	**lollipop sticks**

• Heat oven to 350°. **Cookies.** Whisk
together flour, baking soda and salt in a
medium bowl. With an electric mixer,
beat together butter and brown sugar
on medium-high speed for 1 minute.
Add egg and beat until smooth. On low,
beat in vanilla and flour mixture just
until blended. Stir in mini chips.

• Drop batter by the teaspoonful onto
two large baking sheets (you should
have 5 dozen cookies). Bake at 350° for
14 minutes or until slightly browned.
Cool 1 minute on pans, then transfer
directly to a rack to cool completely.

• **Filling.** On medium speed, beat
together confectioners' sugar, butter
and milk until smooth, thick frosting is
created. Spread about 2 teaspoons of
filling onto flat side of one cookie. Press
a lollipop stick into frosting, then
sandwich with a second cookie (flat side
down). Refrigerate until firm.

PER COOKIE POP 153 **CAL**; 9 g **FAT** (6 g **SAT**);
1 g **PRO**; 17 g **CARB**; 0 g **FIBER**; 45 mg **SODIUM**;
27 mg **CHOL**

Mini Brownie Bars

MAKES 24 brownies **PREP** 15 minutes **MICROWAVE** 1 minute **BAKE** at 350° for 12 minutes

BROWNIES

¼	**cup (½ stick) unsalted butter, softened**
4	**ounces semisweet chocolate, chopped**
⅔	**cup all-purpose flour**
½	**cup sugar**
½	**teaspoon salt**
2	**large eggs**
1	**teaspoon vanilla extract**

TOPPINGS

⅔	**cup canned vanilla frosting**
	Toasted shredded coconut, chopped Andes mints, chopped pretzels, chopped pecans, warmed bottled hot fudge and caramel

• Heat oven to 350°. Coat one 24-square
silicone mini brownie pan or two
12-cup mini muffin pans with nonstick
cooking spray.

• **Brownies.** Microwave butter and
chocolate together for 1 minute. Stir
until smooth. Mix in flour, sugar and
salt. Whisk in eggs and vanilla until
smooth. Transfer batter to a plastic bag.
Snip off a corner and squeeze batter
into indentations. Bake at 350° for
12 minutes. Cool in pan(s) on wire rack.

• Once cooled, remove brownies to a
platter. Transfer frosting to a plastic bag
and snip off a corner. Pipe onto brownies,
then top with toasted coconut, chopped
mints, chopped pretzels or chopped
pecans. Drizzle hot fudge over the
mints and pretzels and caramel over
the pecans.

PER BROWNIE 99 **CAL**; 5 g **FAT** (3 g **SAT**);
1 g **PRO**; 13 g **CARB**; 1 g **FIBER**; 73 mg **SODIUM**;
23 mg **CHOL**

Dulce de Leche Bars

MAKES 24 servings **PREP** 10 minutes **COOK** 5 minutes

- ¼ **cup (½ stick) unsalted butter, cut up**
- 1 **bag (10 ounces) marshmallows**
- 6 **cups Dulce de Leche (or original) Cheerios**
- 1 **cup golden raisins**
- 1 **bag (11 ounces) butterscotch morsels**

• Coat a 15 x 10 x 1-inch or 13 x 9 x 2-inch pan with nonstick cooking spray. Melt butter in a large pot over medium-low heat. Add marshmallows and cook until melted and smooth, about 5 minutes.

• Remove pot from heat and stir in Cheerios and raisins. Let stand 2 minutes (mixture will stick to pot if you wait too long).

• Fold in butterscotch morsels until well distributed. With greased hands, gently press mixture into prepared dish.

• Let stand at room temperature until cool. Cut into 24 bars.

PER BAR 174 **CAL**; 6 g **FAT** (4 g **SAT**); 1 g **PRO**; 29 g **CARB**; 1 g **FIBER**; 61 mg **SODIUM**; 5 mg **CHOL**

RADICCHIO &
SHAVED FENNEL,
PAGE 122

SKILLET VEGGIE MEATBALLS
& CAVATAPPI, PAGE 122

MAY

121

137

140

MEAL DEALS

Great-tasting, affordable dinners.

Mussels & Fries

MAKES 4 servings   PREP 20 minutes   COOK 13 minutes   BAKE at 450° for 32 minutes

- **4   pounds fresh mussels**
- **2   pounds baking potatoes**
- **2   tablespoons olive oil**
- **¾   teaspoon salt**
- **¼   teaspoon pepper**
- **2   tablespoons unsalted butter**
- **3   shallots, finely diced (about ½ cup)**
- **6   cloves garlic, sliced**
- **2   cups dry white wine**
- **½   cup chopped fresh parsley, plus more for garnishing fries (optional)**

• Heat oven to 450°. Place mussels in a large bowl of lightly salted cold water. Set aside.

• Peel potatoes and slice into 3 x ½-inch sticks. Toss with olive oil, ¼ teaspoon of the salt and the pepper. Scatter in a single layer on a baking sheet and bake at 450° for 17 minutes; flip potatoes and bake 15 more minutes or until they are browned. Remove from oven; toss with another ¼ teaspoon of the salt while hot.

• Meanwhile, debeard mussels by pulling off the seaweed-like string between the shells. Discard any open mussels. (If open, tap on the counter; if shell closes, you can keep it.) Place mussels in a new bowl.

• Melt butter in a large, lidded pot over medium heat. Stir in shallots and sauté 3 minutes. Stir in garlic and sauté another 1 to 2 minutes. Add wine and remaining ¼ teaspoon salt; bring to a simmer. Add mussels, cover and cook 6 to 8 minutes, or until shells have opened and mussels are cooked through. Stir in parsley. Discard any mussels that did not open.

• Garnish fries with additional parsley, if desired, and serve alongside mussels and cooking liquid.

PER SERVING 520 CAL; 17 g FAT (5 g SAT); 29 g PRO; 54 g CARB; 4 g FIBER; 813 mg SODIUM; 71 mg CHOL

CHEAP TRICKS

Although mussels are generally inexpensive and widely available nowadays, it's most economical to purchase them during spring and winter months. Most of the mussels in the U.S. are cultivated, which means they're highly sustainable and relatively clean. Look for 2-pound mesh bags in your supermarket's seafood section. Buy them no more than a day before using and store them loosely wrapped in the fridge.

GARDEN VARIETY

Easy, delicious vegetarian meals that are anything but boring.

Bow Ties with Chickpeas & Tomato Sauce

MAKES 6 servings **PREP** 10 minutes **COOK** 12 minutes

- **1** **pound tricolor bow tie (farfalle) pasta**
- **2** **tablespoons olive oil**
- **4** **cloves garlic, sliced**
- **1** **can (28 ounces) crushed tomatoes**
- **1** **can (15 ounces) chickpeas, drained and rinsed**
- **¾** **teaspoon salt**
- **¼** **teaspoon red pepper flakes**
- **½** **cup raisins**
- **⅛** **teaspoon cinnamon**
- **2** **tablespoons chopped parsley**

• Bring a large pot of lightly salted water to boiling. Cook pasta 12 minutes or as per package directions. Drain, reserving 1 cup of the pasta cooking water.

• Meanwhile, heat olive oil in a large nonstick skillet over medium-high heat. Add garlic and cook 2 minutes or until browned. Stir in tomatoes, chickpeas, salt and red pepper flakes. Simmer 10 minutes. Add raisins and cinnamon.

• Toss pasta with sauce, adding pasta water to thin sauce, if necessary. Garnish with parsley.

PER SERVING 481 **CAL**; 8 g **FAT** (1 g **SAT**); 17 g **PRO**; 88 g **CARB**; 9 g **FIBER**; 697 mg **SODIUM**; 0 mg **CHOL**

TACO PIZZA, PAGE 122

Toothsome tofu and meaty mushrooms take the place of meat in these satisfying dinners. Not even dedicated carnivores will miss it.

Grilled Tofu Salad

MAKES 4 servings PREP 15 minutes
COOK 6 minutes

- **3 tablespoons white balsamic vinegar**
- **2 tablespoons extra virgin olive oil**
- **2 teaspoons Dijon mustard**
- **¼ teaspoon salt**
- **⅛ teaspoon black pepper**
- **12 ounces smoked or baked tofu (such as Soy Boy)**
- **12 cups mixed salad greens**
- **2 hard-cooked eggs, chopped**
- **¼ cup crumbled blue cheese**
- **8 plum tomatoes, each cut into 4 wedges**

• In a small bowl, whisk together vinegar, olive oil, mustard, salt and pepper. Set aside.

• Heat a nonstick grill pan or skillet over medium-high heat. Coat with nonstick cooking spray; add tofu and grill 3 minutes per side. Remove to a plate and cut into bite-size pieces.

• Toss salad greens with 3 tablespoons of the dressing and distribute evenly over four dinner plates. Arrange tofu, eggs, blue cheese and tomatoes on top. Serve remaining dressing on the side.

PER SERVING 279 **CAL**; 17 g **FAT** (4 g **SAT**); 17 g **PRO**; 16 g **CARB**; 6 g **FIBER**; 406 mg **SODIUM**; 116 mg **CHOL**

Mixed Mushroom Pie

MAKES 6 servings PREP 20 minutes COOK 7 minutes BAKE at 375° for 50 minutes

- **1 ready-to-roll piecrust**
- **1 teaspoon coarsely ground black pepper**
- **1 pound sliced mixed mushrooms**
- **4 eggs**
- **1¼ cups fat-free milk**
- **1 tablespoon coarse-grain Dijon mustard**
- **1 teaspoon garlic salt**
- **1 teaspoon onion powder**
- **½ teaspoon dried thyme**
- **⅛ teaspoon ground nutmeg**
- **⅛ teaspoon cayenne pepper**
- **1 cup shredded reduced-fat Swiss cheese**

• Heat oven to 375°.

• On a lightly floured surface, unroll piecrust. Sprinkle pepper over crust and gently roll into piecrust. Fit into 9-inch pie plate and crimp edges. Refrigerate.

• Heat a large nonstick skillet over medium-high heat. Add mushrooms and cook 5 to 7 minutes, stirring occasionally, until lightly browned. Set aside.

• Whisk together eggs, milk, mustard, garlic salt, onion powder, dried thyme, nutmeg and cayenne. Stir in ½ cup of the cheese.

• Sprinkle remaining ½ cup cheese over bottom of piecrust and spoon mushrooms over cheese. Pour egg mixture evenly over mushrooms.

• Bake at 375° for 50 minutes or until egg mixture is set and knife inserted in center comes out clean.

• Cool to room temperature before slicing. Serve with Broccoli and Cauliflower Toss, if desired.

PER SERVING 307 **CAL**; 17 g **FAT** (8 g **SAT**); 15 g **PRO**; 24 g **CARB**; 1 g **FIBER**; 450 mg **SODIUM**; 162 mg **CHOL**

Broccoli and Cauliflower Toss

Steam 1 pound broccoli and cauliflower mix (such as Mann's). Dress with 2 tablespoons olive oil, 1 tablespoon lemon juice, ¼ teaspoon red pepper flakes and a pinch of garlic salt.

Skillet Veggie Meatballs & Cavatappi

MAKES 6 servings **PREP** 20 minutes
COOK 13 minutes

- ¾ **pound soy breakfast sausage patties, chopped**
- ½ **cup bread crumbs**
- ½ **cup fat-free milk**
- ¾ **teaspoon dried Italian seasoning**
- ½ **small onion, chopped**
- 2 **cloves garlic, chopped**
- 1 **can (14.5 ounces) fire-roasted diced tomatoes**
- 1 **can (8 ounces) no-salt-added tomato sauce**
- 1 **pound cavatappi**
  Grated Asiago cheese (optional)

• In a large bowl, combine sausage, bread crumbs, milk and Italian seasoning. Form into 36 meatballs.

• Heat a large nonstick skillet over medium heat and coat with nonstick cooking spray. Add onion and garlic; cook 3 minutes. Stir in diced tomatoes and tomato sauce; bring to a simmer.

• Add meatballs to sauce. Cook, covered, on medium-low for 5 minutes. Turn meatballs and cook an additional 5 minutes. Meanwhile, cook cavatappi as per package directions, about 8 minutes. Drain, reserving 1 cup of the pasta cooking water.

• Spoon meatballs and sauce plus reserved pasta water over pasta. Sprinkle with cheese, if desired. Serve with Radicchio and Shaved Fennel, if desired.

PER SERVING 472 **CAL**; 6 g **FAT** (1 g **SAT**); 25 g **PRO**; 77 g **CARB**; 5 g **FIBER**; 623 mg **SODIUM**; 0 mg **CHOL**

Radicchio & Shaved Fennel

Combine 2 tablespoons olive oil, 1 tablespoon balsamic vinegar, ½ teaspoon mustard and a pinch of salt and pepper. Toss with 1 head sliced radicchio and 1 bulb thinly sliced fennel. Top with shaved Parmesan.

Taco Pizza

MAKES 6 servings **PREP** 15 minutes **BAKE** at 475° for 17 minutes

- 1 **pound frozen pizza dough, thawed**
- 1 **can (15 ounces) refried beans, stirred to loosen**
- ¾ **cup medium-hot jarred salsa**
- 1 **can (15 ounces) black beans, drained and rinsed**
- ¾ **cup shredded pepper Jack cheese**
- 2 **tablespoons chopped cilantro**
- 2 **cups shredded iceberg lettuce**
- 2 **cups grape tomatoes, quartered**

• Heat oven to 475°. Coat a 14-inch pizza pan with nonstick cooking spray.

• On a lightly floured surface, roll out dough into a 14-inch circle. Gently roll up on a lightly floured rolling pin and unroll onto prepared pizza pan.

• Spread refried beans over dough to within ½ inch of edge. Spoon on salsa and black beans. Scatter cheese over top.

• Bake at 475° for 15 to 17 minutes, or until bottom of pizza is brown and crispy.

• Scatter cilantro, lettuce and tomatoes over top and cut into 6 slices. Serve with Arugula-Carrot Salad, if desired.

PER SERVING 414 **CAL**; 9 g **FAT** (4 g **SAT**); 18 g **PRO**; 62 g **CARB**; 10 g **FIBER**; 794 mg **SODIUM**; 22 mg **CHOL**

Arugula-Carrot Salad

Whisk together 2 tablespoons olive oil, 1 tablespoon sherry wine vinegar, 1 teaspoon honey and ⅛ teaspoon each salt and pepper. Toss with 8 cups baby arugula and 2 cups shredded carrots.

RADICCHIO &
SHAVED FENNEL

SKILLET VEGGIE MEATBALLS
& CAVATAPPI

WHEAT BERRY &
EDAMAME SALAD

Wheat Berry & Edamame Salad

MAKES 6 servings **SOAK** overnight
PREP 15 minutes **COOK** 45 minutes
REFRIGERATE at least 1 hour

1	cup wheat berries
⅓	cup orange juice
3	tablespoons rice wine vinegar
2	tablespoons peanut oil
2	tablespoons reduced-sodium soy sauce
1	tablespoon sesame oil
1	teaspoon prepared mustard
2	cups shelled edamame
2	oranges, peeled and segments halved
1	cucumber, peeled and cut into ¼-inch dice
4	scallions, trimmed and chopped
1	head Bibb lettuce
½	cup unsalted peanuts, coarsely chopped

• Place wheat berries in a medium-size saucepan and add 4 cups water. Soak overnight.

• Drain wheat berries; add 4 cups water and bring to a boil. Reduce heat and simmer covered for 45 minutes or until tender. Drain.

• In a large bowl, whisk together orange juice, vinegar, peanut oil, soy sauce, sesame oil and mustard. Stir in wheat berries, edamame, oranges, cucumber and scallions. Cover and refrigerate at least 1 hour.

• To serve, stir well and spoon salad onto lettuce. Garnish each serving with peanuts.

PER SERVING 324 **CAL**; 15 g **FAT** (2 g **SAT.**); 12 g **PRO**; 38 g **CARB**; 9 g **FIBER**; 228 mg **SODIUM**; 0 mg **CHOL**

Sloppy Joe Casserole

MAKES 6 servings **PREP** 20 minutes **COOK** 17 minutes **BAKE** at 350° for 30 minutes

1	tablespoon olive oil
2	large onions, chopped
2	green peppers, cored, seeded and chopped
2	cloves garlic, chopped
1	package (12 ounces) soy crumbles
1	can (8 ounces) no-salt-added tomato sauce
3	tablespoons red wine vinegar
1	tablespoon reduced-sodium soy sauce
2	teaspoons sugar
1	package (11.75 ounces) Arnold Pocket Thins Italian Herb flatbreads (8 pocket halves), separated and split open
1	cup shredded cheddar cheese

• Heat oven to 350°. Coat a 13 x 9 x 2-inch baking dish with nonstick cooking spray.

• Heat oil in a large nonstick skillet over medium-high heat. Add onions, peppers and garlic. Cook 7 minutes, stirring so garlic doesn't burn. Stir in soy crumbles, tomato sauce, vinegar, soy sauce and sugar; cover and simmer on medium-low heat for 10 minutes.

• Line bottom of prepared dish with half the flatbreads; tear to fit if needed. Spread half the skillet mixture over breads; sprinkle with ½ cup of the cheese. Layer with remaining breads and skillet mixture. Cover with foil.

• Bake, covered, at 350° for 25 minutes. Top with remaining ½ cup cheese and bake uncovered 5 more minutes to melt cheese. Cool slightly before serving.

PER SERVING 355 **CAL**; 11 g **FAT** (4 g **SAT**); 24 g **PRO**; 47 g **CARB**; 12 g **FIBER**; 805 mg **SODIUM**; 20 mg **CHOL**

UP TO SPEED

Satisfying suppers that come together in 30 minutes MAX.

BEEF & BARLEY SOUP,
PAGE 133

STEAK SALAD WITH MAPLE
BALSAMIC, PAGE 134

QUICK RATATOUILLE

SMOKY CHICKEN QUESADILLAS

Smoky Chicken Quesadillas

MAKES 4 servings   **TOTAL TIME** 28 minutes

- **2** cups (about 7 ounces) Perdue Simply Smart Original Grilled Chicken Strips, frozen
- **1½** tablespoons olive oil, plus more for brushing
- **10** ounces cremini mushrooms, quartered
- **2** cloves garlic, minced
- **⅛** teaspoon pepper
- **4** 10-inch tortillas
- **8** ounces smoked cheddar cheese (such as Tillamook), grated
  Sour cream (optional)
  Chipotle salsa (optional)

• Coat a nonstick sauté pan with nonstick cooking spray over medium heat. Add frozen chicken and cook 5 to 7 minutes to heat through and slightly brown. Remove chicken from pan and set aside.

• Add olive oil to same pan. Stir in mushrooms and cook 5 to 7 minutes or until lightly browned; pan will be fairly dry. Stir in garlic and cook 1 to 2 more minutes. Season with pepper.

• Heat oven to 450°. Line two baking sheets with nonstick foil. Place a tortilla on each prepared sheet. Add one-fourth of the cheese to each tortilla, then layer each with half the chicken and mushrooms. Divide remaining cheese between tortillas. Cover with the last 2 tortillas and brush lightly with olive oil. Bake at 450° for 7 minutes or until slightly golden-brown and cheese has melted.

• Cut each quesadilla into 6 wedges. Serve with sour cream and chipotle salsa, if desired.

PER SERVING 490 **CAL**; 28 g **FAT** (12 g **SAT**); 40 g **PRO**; 30 g **CARB**; 8 g **FIBER**; 999 mg **SODIUM**; 111 mg **CHOL**

Beef & Barley Soup

MAKES 6 servings   **TOTAL TIME** 30 minutes

- **2** tablespoons vegetable oil
- **1** pound sirloin steak, trimmed and cut into ¾-inch chunks
- **3** carrots, peeled and sliced
- **2** ribs celery, trimmed and sliced
- **3** parsnips, peeled and sliced
- **1** medium onion, chopped
- **2** cans (14.5 ounces each) low-sodium beef broth
- **½** teaspoon dried thyme
- **1** cup quick-cook barley
- **½** teaspoon salt
- **¼** teaspoon pepper

• Heat oil in a large pot over high heat. Add beef and brown 1 minute. Turn and brown another minute. Remove to a bowl with a slotted spoon.

• Reduce heat under pot to medium. Add carrots, celery, parsnips and onion. Cook, stirring, 5 minutes. Add broth, 2 cups water and the dried thyme. Increase heat to high and bring to a boil.

• Add barley and reduce heat to medium. Cook 12 minutes or as per package instructions. Stir in beef and any accumulated juices, salt and pepper. Cook 2 minutes and serve.

PER SERVING 310 **CAL**; 8 g **FAT** (2 g **SAT**); 21 g **PRO**; 39 g **CARB**; 7 g **FIBER**; 735 mg **SODIUM**; 28 mg **CHOL**

Chicken-Apple Sausage Quinoa

MAKES 6 servings **TOTAL TIME** 25 minutes

- **1** **pound broccoli rabe, stems trimmed, cut into 2-inch pieces**
- **3** **tablespoons olive oil**
- **1** **cup uncooked quinoa**
- **½** **cup raisins**
- **1** **package (12 ounces) fully cooked chicken-apple sausages**
- **1** **sweet onion, chopped**
- **2** **cloves garlic, minced**
- **½** **cup sliced almonds, toasted**
- **¾** **teaspoon salt**
- **¼** **teaspoon pepper**

• Bring a large pot of lightly salted water to a boil. Add broccoli rabe and cook until tender, about 3 minutes. Drain and set aside.

• Meanwhile, bring 2 cups water and 1 tablespoon of the olive oil to a boil in a lidded, medium-size pot. Stir in quinoa and raisins. Turn down to a simmer and cover. Cook 20 minutes or until all liquid is absorbed.

• Heat 1 tablespoon of the olive oil in a large, lidded sauté pan on medium heat. Add sausages and cook 5 to 7 minutes, turning to brown all sides. Remove sausages to rest.

• To same pan, add remaining 1 tablespoon olive oil. Sauté onion 3 to 5 minutes or until softened. Add garlic and broccoli rabe and sauté 3 minutes. Meanwhile, slice sausage on the bias; add to pan along with quinoa mixture, almonds, salt and pepper. Stir to combine and cover. Cook 2 minutes or until heated through.

PER SERVING 401 **CAL**; 17 g **FAT** (3 g **SAT.**); 18 g **PRO**; 47 g **CARB**; 4 g **FIBER**; 645 mg **SODIUM**; 40 mg **CHOL**

Steak Salad with Maple Balsamic

MAKES 4 servings **TOTAL TIME** 15 minutes

- **3** **tablespoons balsamic vinegar**
- **½** **teaspoon Dijon mustard**
- **1½** **tablespoons pure maple syrup**
- **⅛** **plus ½ teaspoon salt**
- **⅛** **plus ¼ teaspoon pepper**
- **¼** **cup olive oil**
- **1** **pound skirt steak**
- **5** **ounces baby arugula blend**
- **1** **small red onion, sliced**
- **1** **package (16 ounces) grape tomatoes, halved**
- **4** **ounces blue cheese, crumbled**

• Combine vinegar, mustard, maple syrup, ⅛ teaspoon of the salt and ⅛ teaspoon of the pepper in a small bowl. Slowly whisk in olive oil until well blended. Set dressing aside.

• Heat a grill or grill pan on medium-high heat. Season steak on both sides with remaining ½ teaspoon salt and ¼ teaspoon pepper. Brush grill lightly with vegetable oil, then sear steak for 2 to 3 minutes on one side; flip and sear another 2 minutes for medium-rare. Place steak on a cutting board. Cover with aluminum foil and allow to rest for 5 minutes. Slice steak against the grain into thin strips.

• Arrange steak over arugula, onion and tomatoes. Sprinkle with cheese. Drizzle with dressing or serve on the side.

PER SERVING 471 **CAL**; 31 g **FAT** (11 g **SAT**); 32 g **PRO**; 15 g **CARB**; 2 g **FIBER**; 869 mg **SODIUM**; 86 mg **CHOL**

CHICKEN-APPLE
SAUSAGE QUINOA

Coconut Shrimp Curry

MAKES 6 servings TOTAL TIME 30 minutes

- 1 **cup uncooked jasmine rice**
- 2 **tablespoons vegetable oil**
- 2 **cloves garlic, minced**
- 1 **2-inch piece ginger, peeled and grated**
- 1 **tablespoon green curry paste (such as Thai Kitchen)**
- 1 **can (14.5 ounces) coconut milk**
- ½ **cup low-sodium chicken broth**
- 1 **large sweet potato (about ¾ pound), peeled and cut into 1-inch cubes**
- 2 **cups cauliflower florets**
- 1 **medium onion, diced**
- ¾ **pound raw shrimp, peeled and deveined**
- ¼ **cup fresh basil, chopped**
  Juice of 1 lime
- ½ **teaspoon salt**

• Bring 3 cups water to a boil in a medium saucepan. Stir in rice, reduce to a simmer and cover. Cook 20 minutes or until liquid is absorbed.

• Meanwhile, heat oil in a large, lidded skillet over medium heat. Add garlic and ginger; cook 1 minute. Add curry paste; cook 30 seconds. Whisk in coconut milk and chicken broth; bring to a boil. Mix in sweet potato and reduce heat to a simmer. Cover and cook 5 minutes. Add cauliflower and onion; cover and simmer 10 minutes or until tender. Stir in shrimp, basil, lime juice and salt; cook uncovered for 3 minutes. Serve over cooked jasmine rice.

PER SERVING 352 CAL; 20 g FAT (14 g SAT); 16 g PRO; 29 g CARB; 4 g FIBER; 507 mg SODIUM; 111 mg CHOL

Pork over Spaetzle

MAKES 4 servings TOTAL TIME 30 minutes

- 1 **box (10.5 ounces) spaetzle (or 8 ounces egg noodles)**
- ¼ **cup all-purpose flour**
- 2 **teaspoons fresh rosemary, chopped**
- ¾ **teaspoon salt**
- ¼ **teaspoon black pepper**
- 1 **pound pork tenderloin, cut into ¼-inch-thick medallions**
- 4 **tablespoons unsalted butter**
- 1 **container (10 ounces) Brussels sprouts, stems trimmed, sliced**
- 1 **head radicchio (about 8 ounces), cored and sliced**
- 1 **cup sliced fresh mushrooms**
- ½ **cup vegetable broth**

• Cook spaetzle for 25 minutes, as per package directions. (For noodles, cook 7 minutes or as per package directions.)

• Meanwhile, blend flour, 1 teaspoon of the rosemary, ¼ teaspoon of the salt and the pepper in a dish. Coat pork in flour mixture.

• Heat 2 tablespoons of the butter in a large nonstick skillet over medium heat. Add Brussels sprouts, radicchio, mushrooms, remaining rosemary and vegetable broth. Cook 8 to 10 minutes or until softened. Add remaining ½ teaspoon salt.

• In another large skillet, melt remaining 2 tablespoons butter over medium-high heat. Add half the pork and brown on both sides (1 to 2 minutes per side). Repeat with remaining pork.

• Drain spaetzle and stir into veggies. Serve pork over spaetzle mixture.

PER SERVING 602 CAL; 18 g FAT (9 g SAT); 39 g PRO; 68 g CARB; 6 g FIBER; 641 mg SODIUM; 160 mg CHOL

GOOD TO GO

Crowd-pleasing potluck picks from your slow cooker.

LASAGNA, PAGE 141

Creamy Broccoli Cheese Soup

MAKES 6 servings PREP 15 minutes
SLOW COOK on HIGH for 3 hours or LOW for 5 hours

- 1 **quart low-sodium chicken broth**
- 2 **cups 1% milk**
- 1 **package (20 ounces) frozen broccoli cuts, thawed**
- ½ **small onion, finely chopped**
- ¼ **teaspoon black pepper**
- 7 **ounces Velveeta, cut into ½-inch cubes (1 cup packed cubes)**
- 1⅓ **cups instant mashed potatoes**

• Combine broth, milk, broccoli, onion, pepper and 1 cup water in slow cooker bowl. Cover and cook on HIGH for 3 hours or LOW for 5 hours.

• Whisk Velveeta into slow cooker until smooth. Sprinkle instant potatoes over soup and whisk to combine. Serve immediately.

PER SERVING 188 CAL; 8 g FAT (5 g SAT); 13 g PRO; 17 g CARB; 3 g FIBER; 962 mg SODIUM; 34 mg CHOL

Italian-Style Chicken & Potatoes

MAKES 8 servings PREP 15 minutes SLOW COOK on HIGH for 4 hours or LOW for 6 hours

- 1 **package bone-in meaty chicken pieces (4 pounds), skin and excess fat removed**
- 3 **tablespoons all-purpose flour**
- 2 **cups thinly sliced mushrooms**
- 2 **carrots, peeled and chopped**
- 1 **large potato (12 ounces), peeled and cut into ½-inch pieces**
- 1 **large green pepper, seeded and chopped**
- 1 **large onion, chopped**
- 2 **cans (14.5 ounces each) diced tomatoes, drained**
- ½ **cup white wine**
- ¾ **teaspoon Italian seasoning**
- ⅔ **cup tomato sauce**
- ⅓ **cup chopped fresh basil leaves**
- ¼ **teaspoon salt**
- ¼ **teaspoon black pepper**

• Pat chicken dry with paper towels. Toss together chicken and flour.

• Place chicken in slow cooker bowl with mushrooms, carrots, potato, green pepper, onion, tomatoes, wine and Italian seasoning.

• Cover and cook on HIGH for 4 hours or LOW for 6 hours. Stir in tomato sauce, basil, salt and pepper and serve immediately.

PER SERVING 373 CAL; 7 g FAT (2 g SAT); 52 g PRO; 20 g CARB; 3 g FIBER; 613 mg SODIUM; 159 mg CHOL

Carolina Pulled-Pork Sandwiches

MAKES 8 servings **PREP** 15 minutes **COOK** 22 minutes **SLOW COOK** on HIGH for 6 hours or LOW for 8 hours

PORK
- **1** boneless pork shoulder roast or picnic roast, skin removed, trimmed (about 3½ pounds)
- **1** teaspoon seasoned salt
- **1** teaspoon paprika
- **2** tablespoons canola oil

SAUCE
- **1** tablespoon canola oil
- **1** small onion, diced
- **1** cup vinegar
- **¾** cup ketchup
- **⅓** cup packed light-brown sugar
- **2** tablespoons spicy brown mustard
- **8** seedless sandwich buns

• **Pork.** Rub pork all over with seasoned salt and paprika. Heat oil in a large nonstick skillet over medium-high heat. Brown pork on all sides, 12 minutes.

• **Sauce.** Heat oil in a large saucepan over medium heat. Add onion and cook 5 minutes. Stir in vinegar, ketchup, brown sugar and mustard. Bring to a boil, then reduce heat and simmer 5 minutes.

• Transfer pork to slow cooker; add sauce. Cover and cook on HIGH for 6 hours or LOW for 8 hours.

• Meanwhile, prepare **Coleslaw.**

• Remove pork from slow cooker and allow to cool slightly. With two forks or your hands, shred meat, discarding fat and bones. Stir pulled pork into sauce in cooker. Divide evenly among sandwich buns, topping with coleslaw, if desired.

PER SANDWICH 492 **CAL**; 19 g **FAT** (5 g **SAT**); 42 g **PRO**; 37 g **CARB**; 1 g **FIBER**; 817 mg **SODIUM**; 119 mg **CHOL**

Coleslaw

In a medium bowl, whisk together ¾ cup light mayo, 3 tablespoons cider vinegar, 1 tablespoon sugar, ¼ teaspoon each celery salt and black pepper. Stir in 1 bag (1 pound) deli shredded coleslaw mix. Refrigerate until serving.

Lasagna

MAKES 8 servings PREP 20 minutes
SLOW COOK on HIGH for 4 hours or LOW
for 5½ hours

1	medium-size onion, finely chopped
2	cloves garlic, minced
1	pound ground turkey
1	teaspoon dried oregano
½	teaspoon salt
¼	teaspoon black pepper
1	container (15 ounces) part-skim ricotta
1	package (8 ounces) reduced-fat Italian-blend shredded cheese
1	package (10 ounces) frozen chopped spinach, thawed and squeezed dry
12	lasagna noodles (12 ounces) broken in half
1	jar (24 ounces) chunky tomato sauce

• Coat slow cooker bowl with nonstick cooking spray. Stir together onion, garlic, turkey, oregano, salt and pepper; set aside.

• In a small bowl, stir together ricotta, 1 cup of the shredded cheese and the spinach.

• In slow cooker bowl, layer about 8 of the uncooked noodle halves, overlapping as necessary. Spread half of both the meat mixture and the ricotta mixture over noodles, then top with about 1 cup of the tomato sauce and ¼ cup water. Continue layering with remaining noodles, meat, ricotta mixture, 2 cups of the sauce and an additional ¼ cup water. Top layers with 8 noodle halves and remaining ½ cup tomato sauce.

• Cover and cook on HIGH for 4 hours or LOW for 5½ hours, or until internal temperature registers 160° on an instant-read thermometer. Sprinkle remaining 1 cup shredded cheese on top for last 30 minutes of cooking time or until melted.

PER SERVING 460 CAL; 18 g FAT (8 g SAT); 30 g PRO; 45 g CARB; 3 g FIBER; 863 mg SODIUM; 79 mg CHOL

Meatloaf

MAKES 8 servings PREP 15 minutes SLOW COOK on HIGH for 3 hours or LOW for 6 hours

2	pounds lean ground beef
1	small green pepper, finely chopped
1	small onion, finely chopped
½	cup plain bread crumbs
¼	cup plus 3 tablespoons ketchup
¼	cup chopped parsley
2	tablespoons 1% milk
2	tablespoons Worcestershire sauce
½	teaspoon salt
¼	teaspoon black pepper

• In a large bowl, stir together meat, green pepper, onion, bread crumbs, ¼ cup of the ketchup, parsley, milk, Worcestershire, salt and pepper until well blended.

• Fit a long piece of foil into oval slow cooker so ends are hanging over sides and press into place. Spoon meatloaf mixture onto foil and form into an oval-shape loaf. Spread remaining 3 tablespoons of ketchup over top of meat mixture.

• Cover and cook on HIGH for 3 hours or LOW for 6 hours, or until internal temperature registers 160° on an instant-read thermometer.

• To serve, carefully lift meatloaf out of slow cooker using foil handles. Slice using a serrated knife and serve immediately.

PER SERVING 206 CAL; 6 g FAT (3 g SAT); 26 g PRO; 11 g CARB; 1 g FIBER; 461 mg SODIUM; 71 mg CHOL

TIRAMISU ICE CREAM CAKE,
PAGE 168

JUNE

147

160

171

SALAD DAYS

Seven satisfying main-dish options—toss one together tonight.

MISO-GLAZED
SALMON SALAD,
PAGE 151

FARRO WITH CHICKEN
& CHERRIES,
PAGE 151

GRILLED STEAK SALAD WITH
CHIMICHURRI DRESSING

Grilled Steak Salad with Chimichurri Dressing

MAKES 6 servings **PREP** 15 minutes
GRILL 14 minutes **ROAST** at 425° for 25 minutes
LET REST 10 minutes

3	tablespoons plus 2 teaspoons olive oil
1½	tablespoons red wine vinegar
¾	cup fresh parsley
2	tablespoons fresh oregano
2	cloves garlic, roughly chopped
¼	teaspoon red pepper flakes
1	teaspoon salt
1	pound beef tenderloin
1	pound fingerling potatoes
3	medium red onions, sliced into ½-inch rounds
10	cups watercress (3 large bunches), trimmed
1	head Boston or butter lettuce, torn into bite-size pieces

• Heat oven to 425°. Heat grill or grill pan to medium-high.

• In a food processor, combine 3 tablespoons of the olive oil, the vinegar, parsley, oregano, garlic, pepper flakes and ½ teaspoon of the salt. Process until well combined. Rub 1 tablespoon of the chimichurri dressing on beef. Grill 2 minutes per side, turning 3 times, for a total of 8 minutes. Meanwhile, toss potatoes in remaining 2 teaspoons olive oil and remaining ½ teaspoon salt and place on a baking sheet.

• Transfer beef to a second baking sheet and roast with potatoes at 425° for 20 to 25 minutes. Beef should reach 135° for medium-rare and potatoes should be fork-tender. Allow beef to rest 10 minutes before slicing. Meanwhile, grill onion slices 2 to 3 minutes per side.

• Arrange watercress and lettuce on a plate with sliced beef, potatoes and onions. Pour remaining chimichurri over beef.

PER SERVING 314 **CAL**; 18 g **FAT** (5 g **SAT**); 18 g **PRO**; 21 g **CARB**; 3 g **FIBER**; 446 mg **SODIUM**; 49 mg **CHOL**

Shrimp & Tomatoes with Avocado-Basil Dressing

MAKES 4 servings **PREP** 20 minutes **GRILL** 8 minutes

1	avocado, peeled and pitted
½	cup buttermilk
½	cup packed fresh basil, plus more for garnish
2	tablespoons fresh lime juice
½	teaspoon salt
2	tablespoons olive oil
2½	pounds mixed tomatoes (cherry, plum, heirloom, etc.)
1	pound peeled and deveined shrimp
6	ounces French bread, cut into 4 pieces
	Fresh cracked pepper (optional)

• Heat grill to medium-high heat. In a blender, combine avocado, buttermilk, basil, ¼ cup water, lime juice, salt and 1 tablespoon of the olive oil. Blend until smooth. Transfer to a bowl, cover and set aside.

• Slice tomatoes as desired; arrange on a large platter. Skewer shrimp. Brush grill lightly with oil. Grill shrimp 2 to 3 minutes per side or until pink and cooked through. Halve each piece of French bread lengthwise; brush cut sides with remaining 1 tablespoon olive oil. Grill bread cut-side down for 2 minutes.

• Remove shrimp from skewers and scatter over sliced tomatoes. Drizzle half the avocado-basil dressing on tomatoes and shrimp; garnish with basil leaves and season with fresh cracked pepper, if desired. Serve remaining dressing on the side, along with grilled bread.

PER SERVING 453 **CAL**; 18 g **FAT** (3 g **SAT**); 33 g **PRO**; 43 g **CARB**; 8 g **FIBER**; 785 mg **SODIUM**; 174 mg **CHOL**

With chewy grains, leafy greens, eggs, and cheeses, even meatless main-dish salads can be hearty and satisfying.

Wild Rice Salad with Apricots, Fennel & Feta

MAKES 4 servings PREP 15 minutes
COOK 20 minutes LET STAND 5 minutes

1	cup RiceSelect Royal Blend with Flaxseed
½	teaspoon salt
¼	cup apricot nectar
2	tablespoons white wine vinegar
1	tablespoon coarse-grain mustard
1	clove garlic, minced
3	tablespoons extra virgin olive oil
4	fresh apricots, pitted and sliced into 8 wedges each
½	small fennel bulb, cored and thinly sliced (about 1½ cups)
¾	cup crumbled reduced-fat feta cheese
¼	cup chopped fresh parsley Fresh cracked black pepper (optional)

• In a medium lidded saucepan, combine rice, 2 cups water and ¼ teaspoon of the salt. Bring to a boil; stir once. Reduce heat to medium-low, cover and cook for 18 to 20 minutes, or until water is absorbed. Remove from heat and let stand 5 minutes.

• Meanwhile, in a large bowl, whisk together apricot nectar, vinegar, mustard, garlic and remaining ¼ teaspoon salt. Slowly whisk in olive oil until blended.

• Transfer hot cooked rice to bowl with apricot-mustard dressing; mix well. Allow to cool slightly, then stir in apricots, fennel, feta cheese and parsley. Top with cracked black pepper, if desired.

PER SERVING 365 CAL; 17 g FAT (4 g SAT); 11 g PRO; 44 g CARB; 5 g FIBER; 712 mg SODIUM; 8 mg CHOL

Poached Eggs & Mushrooms with Lemon-Tarragon Dressing

MAKES 4 servings PREP 10 minutes COOK 15 minutes

½	cup plain nonfat yogurt
2	tablespoons chopped fresh tarragon
1	tablespoon fresh lemon juice
¾	teaspoon salt
¼	teaspoon white pepper
2	tablespoons unsalted butter
1½	pounds sliced cremini mushrooms
8	eggs
8	cups (5 ounces) frisée, roughly chopped
4	large slices pumpernickel bread

• Combine yogurt, 1 tablespoon of the tarragon, the lemon juice, 1 tablespoon water, ¼ teaspoon of the salt and ⅛ teaspoon of the pepper in a small bowl. Set aside.

• Melt butter in a large skillet over medium-high heat. Add mushrooms and cook 5 to 7 minutes or until slightly softened, stirring occasionally. Stir in remaining ½ teaspoon salt, remaining ⅛ teaspoon pepper and remaining 1 tablespoon tarragon. Set aside; cover with a lid or aluminum foil to keep warm.

• Meanwhile, bring a large skillet three-quarters full of water to a low simmer. Crack 4 eggs into separate measuring cups; pour into water one by one. Poach eggs for 3 to 4 minutes or until whites are just set. Remove with a slotted spoon and set aside. Repeat with remaining 4 eggs. Reheat first batch of eggs in simmering water if necessary.

• Distribute frisée and cooked mushrooms evenly among 4 plates. Top each with 2 poached eggs and drizzle with dressing. Serve each with a slice of pumpernickel.

PER SERVING 308 CAL; 17 g FAT (7 g SAT); 21 g PRO; 19 g CARB; 4 g FIBER; 716 mg SODIUM; 440 mg CHOL

WILD RICE SALAD
WITH APRICOTS,
FENNEL & FETA

Grilled Peaches, Beans & Arugula with Warm Bacon Dressing

MAKES 4 servings **PREP** 10 minutes **GRILL** 4 minutes **COOK** 10 minutes

4	peaches, halved and pitted
5	slices bacon
1	large shallot, finely diced
2	tablespoons white balsamic vinegar
1½	teaspoons Dijon mustard
¼	teaspoon black pepper
1	package (5 ounces) arugula
2	cans (15 ounces each) cannellini beans, drained and rinsed

• Heat grill or grill pan to medium-high. Brush lightly with oil. Grill peaches cut-side down for 4 minutes; cut into wedges and set aside.

• Meanwhile, cook bacon in a large skillet over medium heat for 8 minutes. Remove bacon with tongs to a paper towel–lined plate. Reduce heat to low. Pour off all but 3 tablespoons of the bacon drippings. Add shallot and sauté 1 to 2 minutes or until slightly softened. Whisk in vinegar, mustard and pepper.

• Crumble bacon and toss in bowl with arugula, beans, grilled peaches and warm dressing. Serve immediately.

PER SERVING 388 **CAL**; 16 g **FAT** (6 g **SAT**); 15 g **PRO**; 45 g **CARB**; 10 g **FIBER**; 629 mg **SODIUM**; 23 mg **CHOL**

Farro with Chicken & Cherries

MAKES 4 servings **PREP** 20 minutes
COOK 50 minutes **REFRIGERATE** at least 2 hours

- **1   cup uncooked farro**
- **1⅛ teaspoons salt**
- **¼   cup dark cherry balsamic vinegar (such as Lucini)**
- **1   tablespoon honey**
      Pinch of black pepper
- **2   tablespoons extra virgin olive oil**
- **2   cups shredded roasted chicken**
- **1½ cups fresh sweet cherries (about 20), pitted and halved**
- **½   cup sliced almonds, toasted**
- **¼   cup chopped fresh mint**

• Combine farro, 3 cups water and ½ teaspoon of the salt in a medium lidded pot. Bring to a boil; reduce heat to a low simmer, cover and cook 50 minutes or as per package directions. Drain and pour into a bowl.

• Meanwhile, whisk together 2 tablespoons of the balsamic vinegar, the honey, ⅛ teaspoon of the salt and the pepper in a medium bowl. In a slow stream, whisk in olive oil until well combined. Pour over hot, drained farro. Mix well and cover bowl with plastic wrap. Refrigerate at least 2 hours or overnight.

• Stir in chicken, cherries, almonds, mint, remaining ½ teaspoon salt and remaining 2 tablespoons vinegar.

PER SERVING 460 **CAL**; 16 g **FAT** (2 g **SAT**); 30 g **PRO**; 49 g **CARB**; 6 g **FIBER**; 722 mg **SODIUM**; 60 mg **CHOL**

Miso-Glazed Salmon Salad

MAKES 4 servings **PREP** 20 minutes **ROAST** at 400° for 15 minutes

- **1¼ pounds salmon cut into 4 pieces, or four 5-ounce fillets**
- **2   tablespoons white miso paste (see Note)**
- **2   tablespoons peanut oil**
- **½   teaspoon sesame oil**
- **2   tablespoons rice vinegar**
- **1   tablespoon honey**
- **½   cup thinly sliced scallions**
- **1   package (5 ounces) baby spinach**
- **8   ounces fresh snow peas (about 3 cups), trimmed**
- **1   cup thinly sliced radishes**

• Heat oven to 400°. Place salmon fillets on a foil-lined baking sheet. Mix 1 tablespoon of the miso with 1 tablespoon water until well combined. Whisk in 1 tablespoon of the peanut oil and ¼ teaspoon of the sesame oil. Brush mixture on salmon and roast at 400° for 15 minutes or until fish flakes easily with a fork.

• Blend remaining 1 tablespoon miso with 1 tablespoon water until well combined. Whisk in remaining 1 tablespoon peanut oil and remaining ¼ teaspoon sesame oil followed by the vinegar and honey. Stir in 2 tablespoons of the scallions.

• Divide spinach, snow peas and radishes among 4 plates. Top each with a salmon fillet; garnish with remaining scallions.

Note Find miso in your market's refrigerated section near the tofu or in the Asian aisle.

PER SERVING 343 **CAL**; 17 g **FAT** (3 g **SAT**); 32 g **PRO**; 16 g **CARB**; 4 g **FIBER**; 575 mg **SODIUM**; 78 mg **CHOL**

FIRE POWER

10 hot new grill recipes—talk about sizzle!

TURKEY SLIDERS,
PAGE 159

CHILI CHEESE DOGS,
PAGE 160

CHICAGO-STYLE
RELISH DOGS,
PAGE 160

RED SLAW DOGS,
PAGE 160

MOJITO-MARINATED SWORDFISH
WITH AVOCADO CHOPPED SALAD

Mojito-Marinated Swordfish with Avocado Chopped Salad

MAKES 4 servings **PREP** 20 minutes
MARINATE 15 minutes **GRILL** 8 minutes

SWORDFISH

- ⅓ **cup fresh lime juice**
- ½ **cup mint leaves, chopped**
- 1 **tablespoon sugar**
- 2 **teaspoons lime zest**
- ¼ **cup olive oil**
- ¼ **teaspoon salt**
- ⅛ **teaspoon pepper**
- 1½ **pounds fresh or frozen swordfish, thawed if frozen**

AVOCADO CHOPPED SALAD

- 2 **avocados, pitted, peeled and diced**
- 3 **ribs celery, trimmed and sliced**
- ½ **small red onion, chopped**

• Heat grill to medium-high heat or medium-hot coals.

• **Swordfish.** In a medium-size bowl, combine lime juice, mint, ¼ cup water, sugar and lime zest. Whisk in oil, salt and pepper until blended. Pour ⅓ cup of the marinade into a resealable plastic bag and add fish. Marinate in the refrigerator for 15 minutes.

• Meanwhile, prepare **Avocado Chopped Salad.** Gently stir together avocados, celery, red onion and ⅓ cup of the remaining dressing.

• Remove fish from bag (discard marinade) and grill 6 to 8 minutes, depending on thickness, turning once. Transfer fish to a platter and drizzle with remaining dressing. Serve with Avocado Chopped Salad.

PER SERVING 519 **CAL**; 35 g **FAT** (6 g **SAT**); 37 g **PRO**; 17 g **CARB**; 8 g **FIBER**; 334 mg **SODIUM**; 66 mg **CHOL**

Shrimp, Chicken & Pineapple Kabobs

MAKES 6 servings **PREP** 20 minutes **MARINATE** 30 minutes to 1 hour **COOK** 5 minutes **GRILL** 8 minutes

- ¼ **cup teriyaki sauce**
- ¼ **cup rice vinegar**
- 3 **tablespoons olive oil**
- 1 **tablespoon fish sauce**
- ½ **teaspoon Sriracha or other hot sauce**
- 3 **tablespoons packed dark brown sugar**
- ½ **teaspoon grated fresh ginger**
- 1 **pound boneless, skinless chicken breasts, cut into 1-inch pieces**
- ¾ **pound raw cleaned and deveined shrimp**
- 2 **cups fresh pineapple chunks (about 18 pieces)**
- ½ **teaspoon cornstarch**

• In a small bowl, combine teriyaki sauce, vinegar, oil, fish sauce, Sriracha, 1 tablespoon of the brown sugar and the grated ginger. Combine in a resealable plastic bag with chicken pieces and shrimp. Marinate in the refrigerator at least 30 minutes to 1 hour.

• Heat grill to medium-high heat. Thread a piece of chicken, a shrimp and a pineapple chunk onto a skewer. Repeat, reserving marinade.

• Transfer reserved marinade to a small saucepan. Add remaining 2 tablespoons brown sugar and the cornstarch. Bring to a boil. Reduce heat and cook 5 minutes.

• Lightly oil grill grate. Grill skewers for 3 to 4 minutes. Flip over and grill 3 to 4 minutes more or until chicken and shrimp are cooked. Place on a platter and drizzle with some of the cooked marinade. Serve extra alongside.

PER SERVING 265 **CAL**; 9 g **FAT** (1 g **SAT**); 30 g **PRO**; 16 g **CARB**; 1 g **FIBER**; 820 mg **SODIUM**; 130 mg **CHOL**

Real Barbecued Chicken

MAKES 4 servings PREP 10 minutes
COOK 5 minutes GRILL 1 hour, 10 minutes

- **1** teaspoon vegetable oil, plus more for grill
- **1** onion, finely chopped
- **2** cloves garlic, finely chopped
- **3** tablespoons cider vinegar
- **¾** cup ketchup
- **2** tablespoons pickle relish
- **2** teaspoons spicy brown mustard
- **1** tablespoon Worcestershire sauce
- **1** tablespoon molasses
- **2** teaspoons hot sauce
- **3½** pounds meaty chicken pieces
- **½** teaspoon salt
- **¼** teaspoon pepper

• Lightly brush grill rack with vegetable oil. Prepare grill with coals stacked to one side or heat gas grill to medium-low heat.

• Sauté onion and garlic in oil in skillet until softened, 5 minutes. Mix onion, garlic, vinegar, ketchup, pickle relish, mustard, Worcestershire, molasses and hot sauce in a small bowl. Season chicken with salt and pepper.

• Grill chicken, uncovered, directly over coals for 5 minutes, until browned. Turn over; spoon sauce on chicken. Grill 5 minutes. Turn over; spoon on more sauce. Move to cooler side of grate. Cover grill. Grill 10 minutes. Spoon on sauce. Turn every 5 to 10 minutes, until internal temperature registers 165°, about 50 minutes more. Do not spoon on sauce during last 10 minutes.

PER SERVING 493 CAL; 26 g FAT (7 g SAT); 52 g PRO; 11 g CARB; 1 g FIBER; 734 mg SODIUM; 166 mg CHOL

Chili Flank Steak

MAKES 4 servings PREP 5 minutes MARINATE 8 hours or overnight GRILL 12 minutes LET REST 5 minutes

- **⅔** cup brown sugar
- **⅔** cup reduced-sodium soy sauce
- **⅔** cup V8 juice
- **½** cup olive oil
- **2** tablespoons chili powder
- **4** cloves garlic, chopped
- **¼** teaspoon ground cumin
- **1** flank steak (about 1½ pounds)
  Sweet peppers, cored and sliced; zucchini, trimmed and sliced; red onion, sliced; and on-the-vine cherry tomatoes (optional)
  Corn tortillas (optional)

• In a large resealable plastic bag, combine brown sugar, soy sauce, V8 juice, olive oil, chili powder, garlic and cumin.

• Add steak and marinate in refrigerator at least 8 hours or overnight.

• Remove steak from bag and discard marinade.

• Heat a gas grill to medium-high or a charcoal grill to medium-hot coals. Grill steak for 5 to 6 minutes per side, until internal temperature registers 140° on an instant-read thermometer. Remove steak from grill and cover with foil. Let rest 5 minutes before thinly slicing against the grain. Meanwhile, grill peppers, zucchini, onion and tomatoes, if desired. Serve sliced steak with warmed corn tortillas and grilled vegetables, if desired.

PER SERVING 471 CAL; 23 g FAT (7 g SAT); 48 g PRO; 14 g CARB; 1 g FIBER; 344 mg SODIUM; 94 mg CHOL

REAL BARBECUED CHICKEN

BBQ BACON PIZZAS

BBQ Bacon Pizzas

MAKES 6 servings PREP 15 minutes
THAW overnight COOK 16 minutes
GRILL 12 minutes

1	pound frozen pizza dough, thawed overnight
12	slices bacon
3	tablespoons olive oil
½	cup barbecue sauce
1	sweet yellow pepper, cored and diced
1½	cups shredded cheddar cheese
2	scallions, trimmed and sliced

• Remove thawed dough from refrigerator and let sit until at room temperature. Cook half of the bacon in a large nonstick skillet over medium heat for 8 minutes or until crispy. Repeat with remaining bacon. Drain on paper towel-lined plate.

• Heat gas grill to medium heat or light charcoal grill to medium coals.

• On a lightly floured surface, divide dough into 6 pieces. Roll out 3 pieces to 6- to 7-inch circles. Brush one side of each with some oil. Place oil-side down on heated grill. Cover and grill 3 minutes. Uncover, brush with a little more oil and flip over. Spread each with a heaping tablespoon of barbecue sauce, 2 slices of bacon, crumbled, some of the diced pepper and ¼ cup of the cheese. Cover and grill 3 more minutes. Transfer to a cutting board and tent with foil. Repeat with remaining dough, oil, sauce, bacon, diced pepper and cheese. Sprinkle pizzas with scallions before serving.

PER PIZZA 394 CAL; 18 g FAT (8 g SAT); 17 g PRO; 45 g CARB; 1 g FIBER; 935 mg SODIUM; 44 mg CHOL

Turkey Sliders

MAKES 4 servings PREP 20 minutes BAKE at 400° for 12 minutes GRILL 9 minutes

6	medium mushrooms (about ¼ pound), trimmed and cleaned
1	package (20.8 ounces) ground turkey
1	small onion, grated
2	teaspoons fresh oregano, chopped
½	teaspoon salt
¼	teaspoon black pepper
1	package (12 ounces) frozen ciabatta rolls (such as Alexia)
8	slices (3 ounces) Cracker Barrel Mediterranean-flavor cheddar cheese
1	plum tomato, cored and sliced Sweet potato fries (optional)

• Heat grill to medium-high heat. Heat oven to 400°. Pulse mushrooms in food processor or finely chop them by hand.

Transfer to a bowl and add ground turkey, grated onion, oregano, salt and pepper. Mix gently and shape into 8 patties, each about 3 inches in diameter.

• Bake rolls at 400° for 12 minutes or as per package directions. Split in half. Grill patties 3 to 4 minutes. Flip over and grill an additional 3 to 4 minutes. Top each with a slice of cheese and grill 1 minute.

• Transfer burgers to split rolls and top each with a slice of tomato. Serve with sweet potato fries, if desired.

PER SERVING (2 SLIDERS) 556 CAL; 25 g FAT (8 g SAT); 40 g PRO; 42 g CARB; 3 g FIBER; 983 mg SODIUM; 130 mg CHOL

Topped Dogs

MAKES 8 servings   PREP 20 minutes   GRILL 6 minutes

• Heat grill to medium-high heat. Grill 8 hot dogs for 6 minutes, turning frequently. Place each hot dog on a bun and add desired topping.

Chili Cheese Dogs

• Heat 1 teaspoon oil in a medium nonstick skillet over medium heat. Add 1 clove garlic, chopped; cook 1 minute. Add 1 tablespoon chili powder and cook 1 minute. Stir in 1 can (8 ounces) tomato sauce, 1 tablespoon sugar and 1 teaspoon onion flakes. Crumble in 1 pound lean ground beef. Bring to a simmer; cook 10 minutes. Spoon ¼ cup chili on each dog. Sprinkle with grated cheddar.

PER ¼ CUP 128 CAL; 6 g FAT (3 g SAT); 14 g PRO; 4 g CARB; 1 g FIBER; 240 mg SODIUM; 43 mg CHOL

Chicago-Style Relish Dogs

• Combine ½ of a medium peeled cucumber, diced; 1 plum tomato, seeded and diced; 2 dill pickles, diced; 1 teaspoon olive oil; 1 teaspoon grainy mustard; 1 teaspoon vinegar; and a pinch each of sugar and pepper. Stir to coat. Spoon 3 tablespoons on each hot dog.

PER 3 TABLESPOONS 12 CAL; 1 g FAT (0 g SAT); 0 g PRO; 1 g CARB; 0 g FIBER; 184 mg SODIUM; 0 mg CHOL

Red Slaw Dogs

• Blend 2 tablespoons oil, 3 tablespoons cider vinegar, 1 teaspoon honey, 1 teaspoon Dijon mustard and ¼ teaspoon salt. Toss with 3 cups shredded red cabbage or coleslaw mix. Spoon ¼ cup on each hot dog.

PER ¼ CUP 42 CAL; 3 g FAT (0 g SAT); 0 g PRO; 3 g CARB; 1 g FIBER; 95 mg SODIUM; 0 mg CHOL

Pork Chops with Bourbon-Blueberry Glaze

MAKES 4 servings   PREP 10 minutes
COOK 24 minutes   GRILL 12 minutes
LET REST 5 minutes

2	tablespoons olive oil
1	small onion, diced
2	cloves garlic, minced
3	teaspoons fresh rosemary, chopped
½	cup bourbon
2	cups fresh blueberries
¼	cup packed dark brown sugar
2	tablespoons white wine vinegar
¾	teaspoon salt
⅛	teaspoon red pepper flakes
⅛	teaspoon black pepper
4	boneless center-cut pork chops (about 1½ pounds)
2	leeks, trimmed, halved lengthwise and rinsed

• Heat grill to medium-high heat. Heat 1 tablespoon of the oil in a medium saucepan over medium heat. Add onion and cook 4 to 5 minutes, until softened. Add garlic and 1 teaspoon of the rosemary. Cook 1 minute. Carefully stir in bourbon and simmer 3 minutes, until almost all liquid has evaporated.

• Stir in blueberries, sugar, vinegar, ½ teaspoon of the salt and the pepper flakes. Simmer, stirring occasionally, 15 minutes.

• Meanwhile, combine remaining tablespoon oil, 2 teaspoons rosemary, ¼ teaspoon salt and the black pepper. Brush onto both sides of the pork.

• Separate leeks into layers. Grill leeks about 4 minutes, until soft and flat. Transfer to a platter. Grill pork 8 minutes, turning once, until internal temperature registers 145°. Let rest 5 minutes, then place over leeks and top with sauce.

PER SERVING 471 CAL; 15 g FAT (4 g SAT); 37 g PRO; 31 g CARB; 3 g FIBER; 513 mg SODIUM; 106 mg CHOL

PORK CHOPS WITH
BOURBON-BLUEBERRY GLAZE

GRILLED SAUSAGE &
PEPPER PASTA SALAD

Grilled Sausage & Pepper Pasta Salad

MAKES 6 servings **PREP** 20 minutes
COOK 7 minutes **GRILL** 22 minutes

DRESSING

- ⅓ **cup white wine vinegar**
- 1 **teaspoon sugar**
- 1 **teaspoon Dijon mustard**
- ⅓ **cup olive oil**
- ½ **cup fresh basil, sliced**
- ¼ **teaspoon salt**
- ¼ **teaspoon pepper**

PASTA SALAD

- 1 **pound fiori pasta (honeycomb shape)**
- 1 **sweet onion, cut into ½-inch slices**
- 2 **sweet red peppers, cored and cut into 4 pieces**
- 1 **green bell pepper, cored and cut into 4 pieces**
- 1½ **pounds mild pork sausage links**
- ¼ **teaspoon salt**

• Heat grill to medium-high heat. Make **Dressing.** Whisk together vinegar, sugar and mustard. While whisking, add oil in a thin stream. Whisk in basil, salt and pepper.

• **Pasta Salad.** Heat a pot of lightly salted water to boiling. Add pasta; cook 7 minutes. Drain and transfer to a large bowl. Toss with half the dressing.

• Secure onion slices with toothpicks. Grill onion and peppers for 10 to 12 minutes, turning. Remove toothpicks and chop veggies. Stir into pasta. Reduce grill temp to medium.

• Grill sausages on medium heat or the cooler part of a charcoal grill for 9 to 10 minutes, turning often, until internal temperature registers 150°. Slice into coins. Toss with pasta, salt, peppers, onions and remaining dressing.

PER SERVING 608 **CAL**; 30 g **FAT** (8 g **SAT**); 22 g **PRO**; 65 g **CARB**; 5 g **FIBER**; 921 mg **SODIUM**; 33 mg **CHOL**

Chicken Quesadillas

MAKES 8 servings **PREP** 15 minutes **COOK** 1 minute **GRILL** 24 minutes

MARINADE

- 3 **tablespoons lime juice**
- 2 **tablespoons olive oil**
- ½ **teaspoon chili powder**
- ¼ **teaspoon ground cumin**
- ¼ **teaspoon salt**

QUESADILLAS

- 1¼ **pounds thin-sliced chicken breasts**
- 2 **ears corn on the cob, shucked**
- 1 **can (15.5 ounces) black beans, drained and rinsed**
- 8 **burrito-size tortillas**
- 2 **cups Mexican cheese blend**
  Sour cream and salsa (optional)

• Bring a pot of lightly salted water to a boil. Prepare **Marinade.** In a medium-size bowl, whisk lime juice, olive oil, chili powder, cumin and salt. Set aside 2 tablespoons and pour remaining mixture into a large resealable plastic bag.

• **Quesadillas.** Add chicken to marinade in bag. Refrigerate while heating grill to medium-high heat.

• Add corn to boiling water. Cook 1 minute. Remove from heat; drain.

• Once grill is heated, place corn on grill and cook 12 minutes, turning, until some of the kernels are a little charred. Remove from grill and cut kernels from cobs. Combine in bowl with beans and reserved marinade.

• Remove chicken from bag, discard marinade and grill about 2 minutes per side. Slice into thin strips. Place 2 tortillas on grill. Top half of each with 2 tablespoons of the cheese, some of the chicken strips, a heaping ¼ cup of the corn mixture and 2 tablespoons more cheese. Fold in half and grill 1 minute. Turn over and grill another minute. Repeat with all ingredients. Serve quesadillas with sour cream and salsa, if desired.

PER SERVING 514 **CAL**; 20 g **FAT** (8 g **SAT**); 32 g **PRO**; 50 g **CARB**; 6 g **FIBER**; 948 mg **SODIUM**; 66 mg **CHOL**

DESSERTS THAT TAKE THE CAKE

5 ways to end any celebration on a sweet note.

Chocolate-Hazelnut Layer Cake

MAKES 16 servings **PREP** 20 minutes **MICROWAVE** 1 minute **BAKE** at 325° for 38 minutes **CHILL** 30 minutes

- **2 cups cake flour (not self-rising)**
- **1½ teaspoons baking soda**
- **½ teaspoon salt**
- **¾ cup (1½ sticks) unsalted butter, softened**
- **1½ cups sugar**
- **2 teaspoons vanilla extract**
- **4 eggs**
- **4 ounces unsweetened chocolate, chopped**
- **2 teaspoons vegetable oil**
- **1½ cups buttermilk**
- **8 ounces bittersweet chocolate, chopped**
- **1 cup heavy cream**
- **½ cup Nutella**
- **½ cup chopped hazelnuts, plus more for garnish (optional)**

• Heat oven to 325°. Coat two 9 x 2-inch round baking pans with nonstick cooking spray. Line bottoms with wax paper; coat paper.

• In a medium-size bowl, whisk together flour, baking soda and salt.

• In a large bowl, beat butter until creamy. Add sugar and beat until fluffy, about 2 minutes. Add vanilla and beat in eggs, 1 at a time, beating well after each addition.

• Place unsweetened chocolate and vegetable oil in a small microwave-safe dish and microwave until melted, about 1 minute. Stir until smooth. Beat into butter mixture.

• On low speed, beat flour mixture into butter mixture in 3 additions, alternating with buttermilk. Beat on medium 1 minute. Divide batter between pans.

• Bake at 325° for 35 to 38 minutes, until toothpicks inserted in centers come out clean. Cool on wire racks 15 minutes. Turn cakes out onto racks; remove wax paper. Cool completely. Trim cakes with serrated knife if necessary.

• Place chopped bittersweet chocolate in a medium-size bowl. Bring cream to a boil and pour over chocolate. Whisk until smooth. Cool to room temperature; cover and chill until good spreading consistency, about 30 minutes.

• Place 1 cake layer on a serving plate. Spread Nutella over cake layer; sprinkle ½ cup chopped nuts evenly over Nutella. Place remaining cake layer on top. Spread chocolate mixture over top and sides of cake.

• Garnish with additional hazelnuts, if desired. Let stand at room temperature until set.

PER SERVING 436 **CAL**; 30 g **FAT** (15 g **SAT**); 7 g **PRO**; 43 g **CARB**; 3 g **FIBER**; 247 mg **SODIUM**; 97 mg **CHOL**

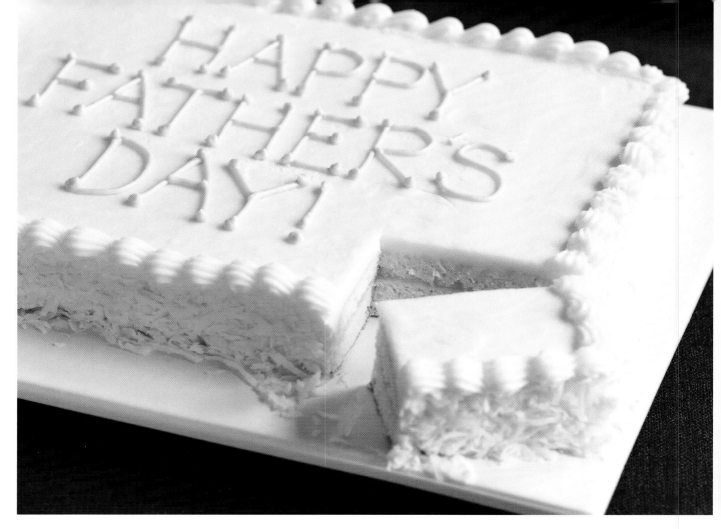

Coconut Sheet Cake with Meyer Lemon Frosting

MAKES 24 servings **PREP** 25 minutes **BAKE** at 350° for 30 minutes

CAKE

- **3** cups all-purpose flour
- **1** tablespoon baking powder
- **½** teaspoon salt
- **1¼** cups 2% milk
- **1** teaspoon vanilla extract
- **1** teaspoon coconut extract
- **4** egg whites, at room temperature
- **1½** cups sugar
- **½** cup (1 stick) butter, softened
- **½** cup jarred lemon curd

FROSTING

- **1** cup (2 sticks) unsalted butter, softened
- **2** boxes (16 ounces each) confectioners' sugar
- **¼** cup Meyer (or regular) lemon juice
- **¼** cup 2% milk
- **1** teaspoon vanilla extract
- **½** teaspoon coconut extract
- **1** cup shredded coconut
  Food coloring (optional)

• **Cake**. Heat oven to 350°. Coat a 13 x 9-inch baking pan with nonstick cooking spray. Line bottom with wax paper. Coat paper.

• In a large bowl, whisk together flour, baking powder and salt. Combine milk and extracts. In a medium-size bowl, beat egg whites until frothy and then beat in ¼ cup of the sugar until stiff peaks form.

• In a second large bowl, beat remaining 1¼ cups sugar with butter on low. Beat in flour mixture, alternating with milk mixture. Beat 1 minute. Fold in beaten egg white mixture in 2 batches.

• Spoon batter into prepared pan and spread evenly. Bake at 350° for 30 minutes, until a toothpick inserted in center comes out clean. Cool in pan for 15 minutes. Turn out onto wire rack and cool completely.

• **Frosting**. In a large bowl, beat together butter, confectioners' sugar, lemon juice, milk and extracts until smooth.

• Place toothpicks around the edge of cake, halfway up sides. Using picks as a guide, slice cake in half horizontally. Using two large spatulas, lift off top layer and place on a cutting board. Spread lemon curd on cut side of bottom layer. Gently replace top layer.

• Reserve 1½ cups of the frosting for piping a border and message. Spread cake with remaining frosting. Press coconut onto sides. Transfer 1 cup of the reserved frosting to a piping bag fitted with #21 star tip. Pipe shell pattern on top edge of cake. Tint remaining ½ cup frosting with food coloring, if desired. Transfer to bag fitted with writing tip and inscribe.

PER SERVING 405 **CAL**; 14 g **FAT** (9 g **SAT**); 3 g **PRO**; 70 g **CARB**; 1 g **FIBER**; 135 mg **SODIUM**; 31 mg **CHOL**

Mocha Bundt Cake

MAKES 12 servings **PREP** 15 minutes **BAKE** at 325° for 60 minutes

- 3½ **cups cake flour**
- ¾ **cup unsweetened cocoa powder**
- 2 **teaspoons baking powder**
- 1 **teaspoon espresso powder**
- ½ **teaspoon baking soda**
- ½ **teaspoon salt**
- ½ **teaspoon cinnamon**
- 1 **cup (2 sticks) unsalted butter, softened**
- 1½ **cups sugar**
- 4 **eggs**
- 2 **teaspoons vanilla extract**
- 1 **cup 2% milk**

• Heat oven to 325°. Generously coat a 10-cup Bundt pan with Baker's Joy nonstick spray for baking.

• In a medium-size bowl, combine flour, cocoa powder, baking powder, espresso powder, baking soda, salt and cinnamon.

• In a large bowl, beat butter until smooth. Beat in sugar until fluffy. Add eggs 1 at a time, beating well after each addition. Beat in vanilla. On low, beat in flour mixture, alternating with milk. Beat 1 minute. Scrape into prepared pan.

• Bake at 325° for 60 minutes or until toothpick inserted in cake comes out clean. Cool in pan on wire rack for 20 minutes. Carefully trim cake level. Run a thin knife around edge of cake, invert onto rack and remove pan. Cool completely. Serve with Strawberry-Ancho Chile Sauce.

Strawberry-Ancho Chile Sauce

• In a medium-size saucepan, heat 2 tablespoons vegetable oil. Add ¼ teaspoon each ancho chile powder and cinnamon; cook 1 minute. Stir in 2 tablespoons sugar and 1 pound strawberries, hulled and coarsely chopped. Simmer 3 to 5 minutes until slightly thickened. Cool.

PER SERVING 405 **CAL**; 18 g **FAT** (11 g **SAT**); 8 g **PRO**; 58 g **CARB**; 3 g **FIBER**; 253 mg **SODIUM**; 112 mg **CHOL**

Tiramisu Ice Cream Cake

MAKES 12 servings **PREP** 30 minutes **FREEZE** overnight

- **22   soft ladyfingers**
- **25   Nabisco thin chocolate wafer cookies, finely crushed (plus more for garnish)**
- **2   tablespoons unsalted butter, melted**
- **1   pint coffee ice cream**
- **1   pint vanilla ice cream**
- **1   pint java chip ice cream**
- **1   container (8 ounces) thawed whipped topping**

• Coat a 9-inch springform pan with nonstick cooking spray. Line side with wax paper.

• Place ladyfinger halves along side of pan, flat sides facing in. Combine cookie crumbs and butter; press into bottom of pan. Freeze.

• Allow ice cream to stand on countertop until softened. Transfer coffee ice cream to a bowl and stir until good spreading consistency. Remove pan from freezer; spread coffee ice cream on bottom. Repeat softening and spreading with vanilla and java chip ice creams. Top with thawed whipped topping.

• Freeze overnight. Remove side of pan and wax paper. Decorate top of cake with crushed cookies.

PER SERVING 367 **CAL**; 20 g **FAT** (13 g **SAT**); 6 g **PRO**; 40 g **CARB**; 1 g **FIBER**; 210 mg **SODIUM**; 112 mg **CHOL**

Orange Layer Cake

MAKES 16 servings PREP 30 minutes BAKE at 350° for 32 minutes CHILL 30 minutes

CAKE

3½	**cups cake flour**
1	**tablespoon baking powder**
½	**teaspoon salt**
¼	**teaspoon baking soda**
¾	**cup (1½ sticks) unsalted butter, softened**
1¾	**cups sugar**
4	**eggs**
¾	**cup 2% milk**
¼	**cup orange juice**
1	**container (6 ounces) orange-flavor yogurt**
1	**tablespoon orange zest**
1	**teaspoon vanilla extract**

FROSTING

1	**cup (2 sticks) unsalted butter, softened**
2	**boxes (1 pound each) confectioners' sugar**
¼	**cup orange juice**
¼	**cup 2% milk**
1	**teaspoon vanilla extract**
1	**teaspoon orange extract**
	Orange food coloring (optional)

• **Cake**. Heat oven to 350°. Coat three 9 x 2-inch baking pans with nonstick cooking spray. Line bottoms with wax paper. Coat paper.

• In a large bowl, whisk together flour, baking powder, salt and baking soda. Set aside.

• In a second large bowl, beat butter until creamy. Add sugar and beat until fluffy, about 2 minutes. Add eggs, 1 at a time, beating well after each addition. In a medium-size bowl, mix together milk, juice, yogurt, zest and vanilla.

• On low, beat flour mixture into butter mixture in 3 additions, alternating with orange juice mixture. Beat on medium 2 minutes. Divide batter among prepared pans.

• Bake at 350° for 30 to 32 minutes, until toothpicks inserted in centers come out clean. Cool cakes on wire rack 10 minutes. Turn cakes out onto rack; remove wax paper. Cool completely. Trim cakes with serrated knife if necessary.

• **Frosting**. Beat butter in a large bowl until fluffy, about 1 minute. Add confectioners' sugar, orange juice, milk and extracts. Beat on low 1 minute until blended. Beat 1 minute until smooth. Add 1 to 2 more tablespoons of milk, if necessary, for good spreading consistency. Beat in a few drops of orange food coloring, if desired.

• Place 1 cake layer on a serving plate. Spread about 1 cup of the frosting over top. Place another cake layer on frosted layer and spread with another 1 cup of the frosting. Cover with remaining cake layer. Frost top and sides with remaining frosting.

• Chill at least 30 minutes before decorating.

PER SERVING 505 **CAL**; 17 g **FAT** (11 g **SAT**); 4 g **PRO**; 85 g **CARB**; 0 g **FIBER**; 100 mg **SODIUM**; 86 mg **CHOL**

RACK'EM UP

Slow cooker ribs that are worth the wait.

ASIAN-STYLE RIBS

Summer is rib season. When you can't be home to tend the grill, try the slow cooker. Long simmering makes the meat fall off the bone.

Asian-Style Ribs

MAKES 15 ribs **PREP** 15 minutes
SLOW COOK on HIGH for 6 hours
COOK 2 minutes

- ⅔ **cup light brown sugar**
- ½ **cup low-sodium soy sauce**
- 2 **tablespoons sesame oil**
- 2 **tablespoons rice vinegar**
- 2 **tablespoons minced fresh ginger**
- 4 **cloves garlic, crushed**
- ½ **teaspoon red pepper flakes**
- 1 **rack pork ribs (about 3 pounds) cut into sections of 3 to 4 ribs**
- 2 **tablespoons cornstarch**
- 3 **scallions, trimmed and thinly sliced**
- 1 **teaspoon sesame seeds**

• In a small bowl, blend sugar, soy sauce, sesame oil, vinegar, ginger, garlic and red pepper.

• Place ribs in slow cooker bowl; add sauce. Cover; cook on HIGH for 6 hours or until meat is tender.

• Transfer ribs to a platter. Strain sauce and discard excess fat. Combine cornstarch and ¼ cup water; blend with sauce in a saucepan. Bring to a boil over high heat and cook for 2 minutes, stirring, until thickened. Top ribs with ½ cup of the sauce, the scallions and sesame seeds; serve with remaining sauce alongside.

PER SERVING 324 **CAL**; 23 g **FAT** (8 g **SAT**); 15 g **PRO**; 12 g **CARB**; 0 g **FIBER**; 395 mg **SODIUM**; 73 mg **CHOL**

Country-Style Barbecue Ribs

MAKES 6 servings **PREP** 15 minutes
SLOW COOK on HIGH for 6 hours or LOW for 9 hours

- 1 **cup ketchup**
- 3 **tablespoons molasses**
- 1 **tablespoon cider vinegar**
- 1 **tablespoon Worcestershire sauce**
- 1 **tablespoon dark brown sugar**
- 1½ **teaspoons Dijon mustard**
- ½ **teaspoon hot pepper sauce (such as Tabasco)**
- ¼ **teaspoon liquid smoke**
- 4 **pounds country-style pork ribs**

• In a small bowl, stir together ketchup, molasses, vinegar, Worcestershire sauce, sugar, mustard, hot sauce and liquid smoke.

• Place pork ribs in the slow cooker insert and pour 1 cup of the sauce over top, reserving the rest for later. Cover and cook on HIGH for 6 hours or LOW for 9 hours, or until very tender.

• Remove ribs from slow cooker and brush with reserved sauce.

PER SERVING 393 **CAL**; 16 g **FAT** (6 g **SAT**); 38 g **PRO**; 21 g **CARB**; 0 g **FIBER**; 705 mg **SODIUM**; 127 mg **CHOL**

Moroccan Ribs

MAKES 4 servings   PREP 20 minutes   SLOW COOK on HIGH for 6 hours or LOW for 11 hours, plus 10 minutes on HIGH

½   **pound carrots, peeled and chopped (1¼ cups)**

½   **pound parsnips, peeled and chopped (1 cup)**

1   **onion, coarsely chopped (1½ cups)**

1   **cup (6-ounce package) dried apricots, each apricot halved**

½   **cup (3½ ounces) pitted prunes, each prune halved**

2   **cloves garlic, minced**

1   **3-inch cinnamon stick**

4   **whole cloves**

4   **whole allspice berries**

1   **6-inch square of cheesecloth**

3   **pounds country-style pork ribs**

1½ **cups chicken broth**

½   **cup orange juice**

2   **tablespoons balsamic vinegar**

1   **teaspoon salt**

⅛   **teaspoon black pepper**

¼   **cup all-purpose flour**
    Hot cooked couscous (optional)

• Layer the carrots, parsnips, onion, apricots, prunes and garlic in a 5- to 5½-quart slow cooker. Place cinnamon stick, cloves and allspice on the piece of clean cheesecloth. Tie ends together with kitchen twine to form a little bundle. Place pork ribs and spice packet on top of vegetables.

• Stir together 1 cup of the chicken broth, the orange juice, balsamic vinegar, salt and pepper in a 2-cup measure until well blended; pour evenly over ribs.

• Cover and cook on HIGH for 5 to 6 hours or LOW for 10 to 11 hours, until the vegetables and pork ribs are tender.

• Remove ribs; cover with foil to keep warm. Remove spice packet.

• Stir together remaining ½ cup chicken broth and the flour in a 1-cup measure until well blended and smooth. Stir into liquid in slow cooker. Cover and cook on HIGH for 5 to 10 minutes or until liquid is thickened. Spoon vegetable mixture from pot around the ribs on the platter. Serve with couscous on the side for soaking up the juices, if desired.

PER SERVING 622 **CAL**; 23 g **FAT** (8 g **SAT**); 45 g **PRO**; 61 g **CARB**; 9 g **FIBER**; 1,094 mg **SODIUM**; 133 mg **CHOL**

Sweet Spiced Short Ribs

MAKES 8 servings **PREP** 15 minutes
SLOW COOK on LOW for 9 hours

- **1   medium-size onion, finely chopped**
- **2   cloves garlic, minced**
- **1   teaspoon cinnamon**
- **1   can (8 ounces) tomato sauce**
- **1   tablespoon plus 2 teaspoons red wine vinegar**
- **1   tablespoon plus 1 teaspoon packed light brown sugar**
- **¼   teaspoon salt**
- **¼   teaspoon black pepper**
- **4   pounds beef short ribs**
- **3   cups cooked egg noodles (optional)**

• Blend onion, garlic, cinnamon, tomato sauce, 1 tablespoon of the vinegar, 1 tablespoon of the brown sugar, the salt and pepper in a bowl. Place ribs in slow cooker and pour sauce over top. Cover and cook on LOW for 9 hours.

• Transfer ribs to a platter. Skim and discard excess fat from liquid. Stir in remaining 2 teaspoons vinegar and 1 teaspoon brown sugar. Top ribs with sauce. Serve with cooked noodles, if desired.

PER SERVING 416 **CAL**; 23 g **FAT** (10 g **SAT**); 44 g **PRO**; 6 g **CARB**; 1 g **FIBER**; 371 mg **SODIUM**; 134 mg **CHOL**

Korean Short Ribs

MAKES 6 servings **PREP** 10 minutes **SLOW COOK** on HIGH for 6 hours or LOW for 9 hours
COOK 2 minutes

- **½   cup low-sodium soy sauce**
- **⅓   cup packed light brown sugar**
- **2   tablespoons sesame oil**
- **2   tablespoons rice vinegar**
- **2   tablespoons minced fresh ginger**
- **4   cloves garlic, crushed**
- **½   teaspoon red pepper flakes**
- **5   pounds beef short ribs**
- **3   tablespoons cornstarch**
- **1½ cups shredded carrots**
- **3   scallions, trimmed and thinly sliced**
- **1   tablespoon sesame seeds**
- **3   cups cooked white rice**

• Combine soy sauce, sugar, oil, vinegar, ginger, garlic and red pepper in a bowl.

• Place ribs in a 5-quart slow cooker; add sauce. Cover and cook on HIGH for 6 hours or LOW for 9 hours, until meat is tender.

• Transfer ribs to a platter. Skim and discard excess fat from liquid. Combine cornstarch and 3 tablespoons water; blend with liquid in a saucepan. Bring to a boil over high heat and cook for 2 minutes, stirring, until thickened. Stir in carrots. Top ribs with sauce, scallions and sesame seeds. Serve with cooked rice.

PER SERVING 518 **CAL**; 23 g **FAT** (8 g **SAT**); 33 g **PRO**; 43 g **CARB**; 2 g **FIBER**; 829 mg **SODIUM**; 92 mg **CHOL**

PORK & VEGGIE SKEWERS,
PAGE 184

JULY

181

191

195

MEAL DEALS

Great-tasting, affordable dinners.

Lemony Vegetable Risotto

MAKES 4 servings **PREP** 15 minutes **COOK** 34 minutes

2	**cans (14.5 ounces each) vegetable broth**
½	**pound asparagus, ends trimmed, cut into 1-inch pieces**
1	**pound fresh English pea pods, shelled (1 cup peas), or thawed frozen peas**
1	**tablespoon olive oil**
1	**tablespoon unsalted butter**
⅓	**cup finely diced shallots**
1	**cup arborio rice**
½	**cup dry white wine**
1	**tablespoon lemon zest**
½	**lemon, juiced (about 2 tablespoons)**
½	**cup grated Parmesan**
¼	**teaspoon salt**

• Bring broth and ½ cup water to a simmer in a medium lidded pot. Add asparagus and cook 3 minutes or until crisp-tender. Remove asparagus to a colander with a slotted spoon and run under cold water; set aside. Repeat with fresh peas, but cook only 1 minute. (If using frozen peas, skip this step.) Reduce heat to low and cover broth.

• Heat oil and butter in a large sauté pan over medium heat. Add shallots and cook 2 minutes. Stir in rice and cook 1 minute. Pour in wine and cook until liquid is almost absorbed, about 2 minutes. Add ½ cup of the reserved hot broth and stir; when most of the liquid has been absorbed, add another ½ cup broth. Continue until broth is gone and rice is tender, stirring well with each addition, about 20 to 25 minutes total.

• Stir in lemon zest and juice, Parmesan, salt, frozen peas (if using) and reserved vegetables. Serve immediately.

PER SERVING 401 CAL; 10 g FAT (4 g SAT); 13 g PRO; 60 g CARB; 4 g FIBER; 893 mg SODIUM; 16 mg CHOL

ALL FIRED UP

Turn up the heat and get grilling with 7 good-for-you summer suppers.

CAPRESE-STYLE GRILLED
CHICKEN BREASTS, PAGE 185

MAHOGANY GRILLED
TURKEY BREAST,
PAGE 185

BEEF PORTOBELLO STACKS

Beef Portobello Stacks

MAKES 4 servings   PREP 15 minutes
GRILL 8 minutes

- ¼   **cup fat-free plain Greek yogurt**
- 2   **tablespoons reduced-fat mayonnaise**
- 2   **tablespoons ketchup**
- 2   **tablespoons sweet relish**
- 2   **teaspoons dried minced onion**
- 4   **large portobello mushroom caps**
- ½   **pound lean ground beef**
- 6   **sesame hamburger rolls, split**
     Pickle slices, tomato slices, cucumber slices and shredded lettuce (optional)

• Heat a gas grill to medium-high or the coals in a charcoal grill to medium-hot.

• Combine yogurt, mayonnaise, ketchup, relish and dried onion in a small bowl. Refrigerate until serving.

• Lightly coat grill rack with oil or nonstick cooking spray. Grill mushrooms 4 minutes per side or until tender. Meanwhile, form beef into 4 thin patties, each about 3½ inches in diameter. Grill about 2 minutes per side for medium.

• To serve, set aside 4 bun tops. Spread 4 bun bottoms with 1 tablespoon of the yogurt mixture. Place a beef patty on each. Top each with a bun half and repeat layering with yogurt mixture, portobello cap and, if desired, pickles, tomato cucumber and lettuce. Top each with a reserved bun top. Serve with any remaining yogurt mixture.

PER SERVING 339 CAL; 9 g FAT (3 g SAT); 23 g PRO; 44 g CARB; 3 g FIBER; 682 mg SODIUM; 38 mg CHOL

Grilled Tuna Salad with Garden Dressing

MAKES 4 servings   PREP 15 minutes   GRILL 6 minutes

- 6   **tablespoons reduced-fat mayonnaise**
- 6   **tablespoons reduced-fat sour cream**
- 1   **tablespoon white vinegar**
- 1   **tablespoon lemon juice**
- 2   **scallions, chopped**
- 2   **tablespoons chopped parsley**
- 1   **tablespoon snipped chives**
- ¼   **teaspoon salt**
- ⅛   **teaspoon black pepper**
- 2   **tuna steaks, about 12 ounces each, cut vertically in half into 4 steaks**
- 8   **teaspoons lemon pepper seasoning**
- 2   **medium tomatoes, cut in half, seeds removed**
- 12 **cups mixed salad greens**

• Heat a gas grill to medium-high or the coals in a charcoal grill to medium-hot.

• Combine mayonnaise, sour cream, vinegar, lemon juice, scallions, parsley, chives, ⅛ teaspoon of the salt and the pepper in a medium bowl.

• Lightly coat grill rack with oil or nonstick cooking spray. Season tuna with remaining salt and 7 teaspoons of the lemon pepper. Grill about 3 minutes per side for medium. Meanwhile, season tomato halves with remaining 1 teaspoon lemon pepper and grill, cut-sides down, about 5 minutes, until slightly charred.

• Toss greens with 6 tablespoons of the dressing. Serve with tuna, tomato halves and remaining dressing.

PER SERVING 295 CAL; 12 g FAT (4 g SAT); 39 g PRO; 5 g CARB; 1 g FIBER; 646 mg SODIUM; 99 mg CHOL

Beef Tenderloin "Skirt" Steak

MAKES 4 servings **PREP** 15 minutes **GRILL** 12 minutes

¼	cup balsamic vinegar
2	tablespoons olive oil
1	tablespoon brown sugar
1	teaspoon chopped fresh thyme
1	teaspoon chopped fresh oregano
⅛	teaspoon plus ½ teaspoon salt
1	pound beef tenderloin
4	large sweet potatoes (about 2 pounds), peeled and cut into ½-inch slices
¼	teaspoon black pepper

• Heat a gas grill to medium-high or the coals in a charcoal grill to medium-hot.

• In a small bowl, whisk together vinegar, oil, brown sugar, thyme, oregano and ⅛ teaspoon of the salt.

• Cut beef in a circular motion so it becomes a long flat strip of steak ½ to ¾ inch thick. Pound slightly.

• Lightly coat grill rack with oil or nonstick cooking spray. Brush sweet potato slices with balsamic mixture and season with ¼ teaspoon of the remaining salt and ⅛ teaspoon of the pepper. Grill for 6 minutes per side or until fork-tender. Meanwhile, brush beef with remaining balsamic mixture and season with remaining ¼ teaspoon salt and ⅛ teaspoon pepper. Grill 2 minutes per side for medium-rare.

• Slice meat into ½-inch slices and serve with sweet potatoes.

PER SERVING 411 **CAL**; 17 g **FAT** (5 g **SAT**); 26 g **PRO**; 38 g **CARB**; 5 g **FIBER**; 732 mg **SODIUM**; 70 mg **CHOL**

Apricot-Lime Glazed Shrimp

MAKES 4 servings **PREP** 15 minutes **COOK** 15 minutes **GRILL** 6 minutes

1	cup rice
½	pound snow peas, trimmed
1	tablespoon olive oil
½	cup cilantro, chopped
½	cup apricot preserves
3	tablespoons reduced-sodium soy sauce
3	tablespoons lime juice
¼	teaspoon red pepper flakes
1½	pounds jumbo shrimp (about 24), shelled and deveined

• Cook rice following package directions, about 15 minutes. Meanwhile, bring a medium pot of lightly salted water to a boil; add snow peas and cook 4 minutes. Drain and toss with cooked rice, olive oil and cilantro.

• Combine apricot preserves, soy sauce, lime juice and red pepper flakes. Stir 4 tablespoons of the mixture into rice. Cover and refrigerate until ready to serve.

• Heat a gas grill to medium-high or the coals in a charcoal grill to medium-hot. Lightly coat grill rack with oil or nonstick cooking spray. Reserve 2 tablespoons of the apricot mixture. Brush remaining mixture on shrimp and grill 2 to 3 minutes per side or until cooked through.

• Serve shrimp with rice and reserved sauce.

PER SERVING 487 **CAL**; 5 g **FAT** (1 g **SAT**); 33 g **PRO**; 72 g **CARB**; 2 g **FIBER**; 752 mg **SODIUM**; 252 mg **CHOL**

BEEF TENDERLOIN
"SKIRT" STEAK

Pork & Veggie Skewers

MAKES 4 servings **PREP** 25 minutes **MARINATE** 2 to 4 hours **COOK** 10 minutes **GRILL** 8 minutes

- **3** tablespoons rosemary-infused olive oil
- **2** tablespoons red wine vinegar
- **2** sun-dried tomatoes, chopped
- **2** cloves garlic, chopped
- **½** teaspoon salt
- **¼** teaspoon black pepper
- **1** pound boneless pork tenderloin, cut into 1-inch pieces
- **1** pound small red, white and purple potatoes (about 1 inch diameter)
- **2** sweet red peppers, cored, seeded and cut into 1-inch pieces
- **3** summer squash (about ¾ pound), halved lengthwise and cut into ½-inch moons

• Whisk together olive oil, vinegar, sun-dried tomatoes, garlic, ¼ teaspoon of the salt and ⅛ teaspoon of the black pepper.

• Place pork and 2 tablespoons of the oil and vinegar mixture in a resealable plastic bag. Shake to coat pork, and refrigerate 2 to 4 hours.

• Place potatoes in a medium saucepan and cover with water. Bring to boiling and simmer 10 minutes; drain.

• Heat a gas grill to medium-high or the coals in a charcoal grill to medium-hot. Thread pork onto 2 skewers, potatoes onto 2 skewers and vegetables onto separate skewers. Brush generously with oil and vinegar mixture.

• Lightly coat grill rack with oil or nonstick cooking spray. Grill vegetables 5 to 6 minutes and potatoes about 4 minutes, turning a few times and brushing with oil and vinegar mixture. Grill pork 3 to 4 minutes per side or until internal temperature reaches 145°. Brush with remaining oil and vinegar mixture. Sprinkle remaining ½ teaspoon salt and ⅛ teaspoon pepper over skewers before serving.

PER SERVING 355 **CAL**; 16 g **FAT** (4 g **SAT**); 29 g **PRO**; 21 g **CARB**; 5 g **FIBER**; 493 mg **SODIUM**; 62 mg **CHOL**

RASPBERRY PAVLOVA,
PAGE 190

Blueberry-Blue Cheese Salad

MAKES 6 side-dish servings **PREP** 15 minutes

2	tablespoons balsamic vinegar
1	tablespoon blueberry preserves
1	teaspoon Dijon mustard
⅛	teaspoon salt
⅛	teaspoon pepper
2	tablespoons extra virgin olive oil
2	tablespoons snipped chives
5	ounces (10 cups) baby spinach
12	ounces (approximately 2 cups) blueberries
¾	cup walnuts, toasted and roughly chopped
½	cup crumbled blue cheese

• In a small bowl, stir together vinegar, blueberry preserves, mustard, salt and pepper. Slowly whisk in olive oil until well combined. Mix in chives. Set aside.

• Toss together spinach, blueberries, walnuts and blue cheese. Mix in dressing, or serve it on the side.

PER SERVING 220 **CAL**; 16 g **FAT** (4 g **SAT**); 5 g **PRO**; 16 g **CARB**; 3 g **FIBER**; 265 mg **SODIUM**; 8 mg **CHOL**

The natural acidity and sweet-tart flavor of berries makes them pair beautifully with rich foods such as blue cheese and steak.

Strawberry Salsa

MAKES 1⅔ cups (6 servings) PREP 15 minutes

1	pound strawberries, hulled and diced
¼	cup thinly sliced scallions
1	jalapeño, seeded and diced
¼	cup cilantro, chopped
2	tablespoons fresh lime juice
1	tablespoon agave syrup or honey
⅛	teaspoon salt

• Gently mix ingredients together in a bowl. Serve with tortilla chips or over fish or chicken.

PER SERVING 34 CAL; 0 g FAT (0 g SAT); 1 g PRO; 9 g CARB; 0 g FIBER; 50 mg SODIUM; 0 mg CHOL

Grilled Sirloin with Blackberry Sauce

MAKES 6 servings PREP 5 minutes GRILL 10 minutes LET REST 10 minutes COOK 15 minutes

1½	pounds sirloin steak, about 1 inch thick
1	teaspoon salt
¼	teaspoon plus ⅛ teaspoon pepper
⅓	cup balsamic vinegar
¼	cup finely diced shallots
1½	cups fresh blackberries
2	teaspoons chopped fresh thyme
2	tablespoons honey
1	tablespoon unsalted butter

• Heat grill to medium-high. Allow steak to come to room temperature; season with ½ teaspoon of the salt and ¼ teaspoon of the pepper. Grill steak 4 to 5 minutes per side, or until the internal temperature reaches 135° for medium-rare. Set aside to rest for 10 minutes.

• Meanwhile, combine vinegar and shallots in a medium saucepan set over medium heat. Bring to a simmer and reduce liquid by half, about 5 minutes. Stir in blackberries, thyme, honey and 1 tablespoon water. Bring to a simmer and cook until berries burst and sauce thickens, about 10 minutes.

• Slice meat thinly against the grain. Pour any accumulated drippings into sauce. Remove sauce from heat and stir in butter to melt. Add ¼ teaspoon of the salt and remaining ⅛ teaspoon pepper. Sprinkle remaining ¼ teaspoon salt over sliced meat. Serve with sauce.

PER SERVING 206 CAL; 7 g FAT (3 g SAT); 23 g PRO; 13 g CARB; 2 g FIBER; 439 mg SODIUM; 47 mg CHOL

Raspberry Pavlova

MAKES 8 servings **PREP** 20 minutes
BAKE at 250° for 1 hour **COOL** in oven for 1 hour
COOK 3 minutes

1	**cup superfine sugar**
2	**teaspoons cornstarch**
⅛	**teaspoon salt**
3	**egg whites**
¼	**teaspoon cream of tartar**
½	**teaspoon vanilla extract**
2	**cups fresh raspberries**
	Fresh mint and whipped cream (optional)

• Heat oven to 250°. Line a baking sheet with parchment paper. Draw a 7-inch circle on the parchment; flip paper. (For a crunchier Pavlova, opt for an 8-inch circle.)

• In a small bowl, combine ¾ cup of the sugar, the cornstarch and salt; set aside. Beat egg whites and cream of tartar on medium speed until soft peaks form, about 2 minutes. Increase speed to high; add sugar mixture 1 tablespoon at a time. Add vanilla and beat until mixture is glossy and sugar is incorporated, about 5 minutes.

• Transfer egg-sugar mixture to parchment paper. Carefully spread within the circle, creating a slight dip in the middle (where raspberry sauce will rest). Bake at 250° on middle rack for 1 hour. Turn off oven, crack door and cool inside for 1 hour.

• Meanwhile, make raspberry sauce. In a small pot, combine 1 cup of the raspberries, remaining ¼ cup sugar and 1 tablespoon water over medium heat. Bring to a simmer and cook 3 minutes, until sugar is dissolved. Stir in remaining 1 cup raspberries and pour into bowl to cool.

• Transfer Pavlova to a plate; pour raspberry sauce on top and, if desired, garnish with mint. Whipped cream can also be spread on the Pavlova before sauce is poured on top.

PER SERVING 116 **CAL**; 0 g **FAT** (0 g **SAT**); 2 g **PRO**; 28 g **CARB**; 2 g **FIBER**; 58 mg **SODIUM**; 0 mg **CHOL**

Strawberry-Basil Lemonade

MAKES 8 servings **PREP** 15 minutes **STEEP** 10 minutes

2	**cups strawberries, hulled and diced, plus extra for garnish (optional)**
1	**cup plus 2 tablespoons sugar**
	Rind of 1 lemon (carefully removed with a peeler, making sure not to include the white pith)
½	**cup fresh tightly packed basil leaves, plus extra for garnish (optional)**
1½	**cups fresh lemon juice (from about 6 lemons)**
1	**cup vodka (optional)**

• Combine strawberries and 2 tablespoons of the sugar. Set aside.

• In a small, lidded pot, combine 1 cup water, remaining 1 cup sugar, the lemon rind and basil over medium-high heat. Stir until sugar dissolves. Cover, remove from heat and steep 10 minutes. Strain and cool.

• In a pitcher, stir together strawberries, lemon juice, lemon-basil syrup, 2 cups ice and 2 cups cold water. (For an adult tweak, replace 1 cup of the water with 1 cup vodka.) Fill 8 glasses with ice and pour lemonade into each. Garnish with extra strawberries and basil, if desired.

PER SERVING 131 **CAL**; 0 g **FAT** (0 g **SAT**); 0 g **PRO**; 35 g **CARB**; 1 g **FIBER**; 1 mg **SODIUM**; 0 mg **CHOL**

Very Berry Ice Cream

MAKES 6 cups (twelve ½-cup servings) **PREP** 10 minutes **COOK** 13 minutes **PROCESS** according to manufacturer's directions **FREEZE** at least 1 hour

- **⅓ cup fresh blueberries**
- **⅓ cup fresh blackberries**
- **½ cup chopped and hulled fresh strawberries**
- **1 tablespoon lemon juice**
- **½ cup plus 1 tablespoon sugar**
- **4 egg yolks**
- **2 cups whole milk**
- **1 cup heavy cream**
- **⅛ teaspoon salt**
- **½ teaspoon vanilla extract**

• Combine berries, lemon juice and 1 tablespoon of the sugar in a small saucepan over medium heat. Cook 5 minutes or until berries burst and become a bit syrupy. Cool.

• In a bowl, whisk together egg yolks and ¼ cup of the sugar. Heat milk, cream, salt and remaining ¼ cup sugar in a medium pot until barely simmering. Remove from heat and slowly whisk into egg-sugar mixture to temper. Pour mixture back into pot and set over medium-low heat. Stir constantly until mixture coats the back of a wooden spoon (170° to 180°), about 4 to 8 minutes. Pour through strainer into a new bowl; cool over ice bath or in refrigerator.

• Whisk vanilla extract and berries into cooled creamy egg mixture. Process in an ice cream maker according to manufacturer's directions. Transfer to a lidded container and freeze at least 1 hour.

PER SERVING 154 **CAL**; 10 g **FAT** (6 g **SAT**); 3 g **PRO**; 14 g **CARB**; 0 g **FIBER**; 51 mg **SODIUM**; 100 mg **CHOL**

TEN SUPERCHARGED SMOOTHIES

Heart-healthy. Immune-boosting. Vitamin-packed. Delicious!

Carrot-Peach Smoothie

MAKES 6 servings **PREP** 10 minutes

• In a blender, combine 1 pound frozen peach slices (about 2 cups), 1½ cups tangerine or orange sections (peeled and pitted), 2 cups carrot juice (such as Bolthouse Farms), 2 cups orange-tangerine juice and 2 teaspoons grated fresh ginger. Blend until smooth.

PER SERVING 113 **CAL**; 0 g **FAT** (0 g **SAT**); 2 g **PRO**; 27 g **CARB**; 2 g **FIBER**; 51 mg **SODIUM**; 0 mg **CHOL**

Green Machine Smoothie

MAKES 6 servings **PREP** 10 minutes
FREEZE 3 hours

• Remove 1¼ pounds green grapes from their stems. Freeze at least 3 hours.

• In a blender, combine half of the frozen grapes; 3 cups packed baby spinach; 1 Granny Smith apple, peeled, cored and chopped; and 3 cups pear nectar or apple juice. Blend until smooth, adding remaining grapes while blender is running.

PER SERVING 160 **CAL**; 0 g **FAT** (0 g **SAT**); 1 g **PRO**; 42 g **CARB**; 3 g **FIBER**; 26 mg **SODIUM**; 0 mg **CHOL**

Coconut-Pineapple Smoothie

MAKES 4 servings **PREP** 15 minutes
FREEZE 3 hours

• Place 2 cups fresh pineapple chunks (12 ounces) in a resealable plastic bag and freeze at least 3 hours.

• In a blender, combine frozen pineapple, 1 container (17 ounces) chilled Vita Coco coconut water, 2 containers (6 ounces each) pineapple yogurt (such as Chobani), 1 cup sweetened flake coconut and 1 small can (6 ounces) pineapple juice. Blend until creamy and smooth.

PER SERVING 298 **CAL**; 8 g **FAT** (7 g **SAT**); 5 g **PRO**; 53 g **CARB**; 3 g **FIBER**; 249 mg **SODIUM**; 6 mg **CHOL**

Raspberry Smoothie

MAKES 4 servings **PREP** 10 minutes

• Combine 2 cups cranberry-raspberry or pomegranate juice, 2 cups 2% low-fat milk, 1 bag (12 ounces) frozen raspberries and 1 container (6 ounces) raspberry or cherry yogurt in a blender. Cover and blend until smooth but still thick.

PER SERVING 194 **CAL**; 1 g **FAT** (0 g **SAT**); 7 g **PRO**; 41 g **CARB**; 4 g **FIBER**; 95 mg **SODIUM**; 4 mg **CHOL**

Peanut Butter Cup Smoothie

MAKES 4 servings **PREP** 15 minutes

• Combine 3 cups vanilla-flavor soy milk, ½ cup reduced-fat peanut butter, ⅓ cup unsweetened cocoa powder, 2 cups ice, ¼ cup honey and ¼ teaspoon salt in a blender. Run blender until ice is crushed and mixture is smooth.

PER SERVING 366 **CAL**; 14 g **FAT** (2 g **SAT**); 15 g **PRO**; 50 g **CARB**; 4 g **FIBER**; 388 mg **SODIUM**; 0 mg **CHOL**

COCONUT-PINEAPPLE SMOOTHIE

PEANUT BUTTER CUP SMOOTHIE

RASPBERRY SMOOTHIE

GREEN MACHINE SMOOTHIE

CARROT-PEACH SMOOTHIE

Banana-Nut Smoothie

MAKES 6 servings **PREP** 15 minutes **FREEZE** 3 hours

• Pour 2 cups almond milk into ice cube trays. Peel 2 bananas and wrap in plastic wrap. Freeze at least 3 hours.

• In blender, combine almond milk ice cubes, frozen bananas, 2 more cups almond milk, 1/3 cup almond butter, 1/4 cup maple syrup, 1 teaspoon vanilla extract and 1/2 teaspoon ground cinnamon. Blend until ice is crushed and mixture is smooth.

PER SERVING 201 **CAL**; 10 g **FAT** (1 g **SAT**); 3 g **PRO**; 27 g **CARB**; 2 g **FIBER**; 166 mg **SODIUM**; 0 mg **CHOL**

Melon-Cucumber Smoothie

MAKES 6 servings **PREP** 10 minutes **FREEZE** 3 hours

• Combine 1 1/2 cups water and 2 tablespoons turbinado sugar in a small saucepan. Bring to a boil and add 1 cup loosely packed mint leaves. Remove from heat; let stand 5 minutes. Strain into ice cube trays. Freeze 3 hours.

• In a blender, combine 4 cups watermelon cubes; 1 cucumber, peeled, seeded and chopped; 1/2 cup pomegranate or cranberry juice; and the mint-flavor ice cubes. Blend until smooth.

PER SERVING 57 **CAL**; 0 g **FAT** (0 g **SAT**); 1 g **PRO**; 17 g **CARB**; 1 g **FIBER**; 7 mg **SODIUM**; 0 mg **CHOL**

Papaya-Mango Smoothie

MAKES 6 servings **PREP** 10 minutes

• Combine 3 cups mango nectar or juice; 1 apricot-mango yogurt (such as Voskos); 1 mango, peeled, pitted and cut into chunks (1 1/2 cups); 1/2 small papaya, peeled, seeded and cut into chunks (2 cups); 2 tablespoons lime juice; and 1/4 cup ground flaxseed (if desired) in a blender. Cover and blend until smooth.

• Add 2 cups ice and 2 tablespoons honey and blend until smooth and a little frothy. Pour into glasses and serve.

PER SERVING 188 **CAL**; 1 g **FAT** (0 g **SAT**); 4 g **PRO**; 43 g **CARB**; 4 g **FIBER**; 54 mg **SODIUM**; 2 mg **CHOL**

Kiwi-Honeydew Smoothie

MAKES 6 servings **PREP** 15 minutes

• Combine 4 cups honeydew melon chunks (1/2 medium melon), 3 cups white cranberry juice, 2 cups ice and 4 peeled and coarsely chopped kiwifruit (2 cups) in a blender. Pulse until smooth and ice is crushed.

PER SERVING 126 **CAL**; 0 g **FAT** (0 g **SAT**); 1 g **PRO**; 30 g **CARB**; 2 g **FIBER**; 45 mg **SODIUM**; 0 mg **CHOL**

Berry Blast Smoothie

MAKES 6 servings **PREP** 10 minutes

• Combine 1 package (10 ounces) frozen blackberries, 1 cup fresh blueberries, 3 cups blueberry-pomegranate juice, 2 cups ice, 1 container (6 ounces) blueberry yogurt, 2 tablespoons fresh lemon juice, 2 tablespoons agave syrup and 2 tablespoons wheat germ in a blender. Cover and blend until smooth.

PER SMOOTHIE 166 **CAL**; 1 g **FAT** (0 g **SAT**); 3 g **PRO**; 39 g **CARB**; 3 g **FIBER**; 35 mg **SODIUM**; 2 mg **CHOL**

With these tasty powerhouse smoothies that can easily be whipped up at home, skip the smoothie shop stop—and keep your dollars.

BANANA-NUT SMOOTHIE

MELON-CUCUMBER SMOOTHIE

PAPAYA-MANGO SMOOTHIE

KIWI-HONEYDEW SMOOTHIE

BERRY BLAST SMOOTHIE

DISH IT OUT!

Three crowd-pleasing potluck picks.

Peach-Bacon Baked Beans

MAKES 8 servings **PREP** 15 minutes **SLOW COOK** on HIGH for 3 hours

- **6 slices bacon, diced**
- **2 cans (15.5 ounces each) dark kidney beans, drained and rinsed**
- **2 cans (15.5 ounces each) red beans, drained and rinsed**
- **2 fresh peaches, peeled and sliced, or 1 bag (16 ounces) sliced frozen peaches, thawed**
- **1 cup diced sweet onion**
- **1 can (8 ounces) tomato sauce**
- **½ cup peach preserves**
- **⅓ cup molasses**
- **⅓ cup cider vinegar**
- **2 teaspoons chili powder**
- **1 teaspoon dried mustard**
- **¾ teaspoon salt**

● Cook bacon in a skillet over medium heat until crisp, about 5 to 7 minutes. Transfer to a paper towel-lined plate to drain.

● Combine kidney beans, red beans, peaches, onion and cooked bacon in a slow cooker. In a small bowl, mix together tomato sauce, preserves, molasses, vinegar, chili powder, dried mustard and salt. Pour over bean mixture and stir well. Cook on HIGH for 3 hours.

PER SERVING 321 **CAL**; 3 g **FAT** (1 g **SAT**); 14 g **PRO**; 62 g **CARB**; 14 g **FIBER**; 895 mg **SODIUM**; 5 mg **CHOL**

Warm Greek Dip

MAKES 5 cups PREP 15 minutes
SLOW COOK on LOW for 2 hours

2	packages (8 ounces each) low-fat cream cheese, at room temperature
⅔	cup light mayonnaise
½	cup 2% milk
1	tablespoon fresh lemon juice
1	box (10 ounces) frozen chopped spinach, thawed, squeezed dry
1	cup crumbled feta cheese
1	teaspoon dried oregano
¼	teaspoon pepper
¼	cup pitted Kalamata olives, sliced
¼	cup diced cucumber
¼	cup diced red onion
¼	cup halved grape tomatoes
	Pita bread (optional)

• In a bowl, stir together cream cheese, mayonnaise, milk and lemon juice until well combined. Mix in spinach, feta, oregano and pepper. Transfer to the bowl of a 4-quart slow cooker. Cover and cook on LOW for 2 hours.

• Reduce slow cooker to WARM. Scatter olives, cucumber, onion and tomatoes on top of the warm dip. Serve with pita bread, if desired.

PER TABLESPOON 30 CAL; 2 g FAT (1 g SAT); 1 g PRO; 1 g CARB; 0 g FIBER; 75 mg SODIUM; 7 mg CHOL

Summer Succotash

MAKES 8 servings PREP 15 minutes SLOW COOK on HIGH for 4 hours

4	corn cobs, kernels removed (about 2½ cups kernels)
3	large sweet peppers (any combination of red, orange and yellow), diced into 1-inch pieces
3	cloves garlic, chopped
½	cup vegetable broth
1	teaspoon salt
2	cups frozen lima beans, thawed
2	tablespoons unsalted butter
½	cup packed fresh basil, chopped
¼	cup sliced scallions
¼	teaspoon pepper

• Combine corn kernels, sweet peppers, garlic, vegetable broth and ½ teaspoon of the salt in the base of a slow cooker. Cover and cook on HIGH for 3 hours. Stir in thawed lima beans and cook 1 more hour.

• Stir in butter until melted. Mix in basil, scallions, pepper and remaining ½ teaspoon salt.

PER SERVING 130 CAL; 4 g FAT (2 g SAT); 5 g PRO; 21 g CARB; 4 g FIBER; 418 mg SODIUM; 8 mg CHOL

FRIED CHICKEN,
PAGE 215

AUGUST

202

217

220

GARDEN OF EATING

Serving up veggies has never been easier, thanks to this bumper crop of recipes.

FLANK STEAK WITH TOMATO,
CUCUMBER & WATERMELON
SALAD, PAGE 201

CREAMY CORN
& SHRIMP,
PAGE 202

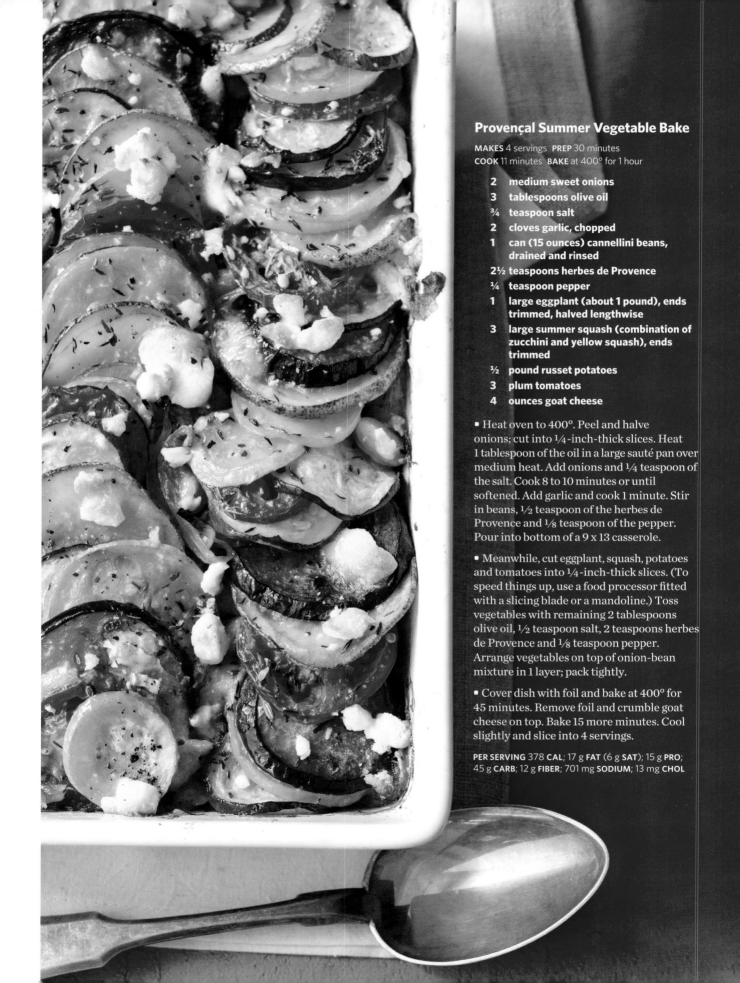

Provençal Summer Vegetable Bake

MAKES 4 servings **PREP** 30 minutes
COOK 11 minutes **BAKE** at 400° for 1 hour

2	medium sweet onions
3	tablespoons olive oil
¾	teaspoon salt
2	cloves garlic, chopped
1	can (15 ounces) cannellini beans, drained and rinsed
2½	teaspoons herbes de Provence
¼	teaspoon pepper
1	large eggplant (about 1 pound), ends trimmed, halved lengthwise
3	large summer squash (combination of zucchini and yellow squash), ends trimmed
½	pound russet potatoes
3	plum tomatoes
4	ounces goat cheese

• Heat oven to 400°. Peel and halve onions; cut into ¼-inch-thick slices. Heat 1 tablespoon of the oil in a large sauté pan over medium heat. Add onions and ¼ teaspoon of the salt. Cook 8 to 10 minutes or until softened. Add garlic and cook 1 minute. Stir in beans, ½ teaspoon of the herbes de Provence and ⅛ teaspoon of the pepper. Pour into bottom of a 9 x 13 casserole.

• Meanwhile, cut eggplant, squash, potatoes and tomatoes into ¼-inch-thick slices. (To speed things up, use a food processor fitted with a slicing blade or a mandoline.) Toss vegetables with remaining 2 tablespoons olive oil, ½ teaspoon salt, 2 teaspoons herbes de Provence and ⅛ teaspoon pepper. Arrange vegetables on top of onion-bean mixture in 1 layer; pack tightly.

• Cover dish with foil and bake at 400° for 45 minutes. Remove foil and crumble goat cheese on top. Bake 15 more minutes. Cool slightly and slice into 4 servings.

PER SERVING 378 **CAL**; 17 g **FAT** (6 g **SAT**); 15 g **PRO**; 45 g **CARB**; 12 g **FIBER**; 701 mg **SODIUM**; 13 mg **CHOL**

Flank Steak with Tomato, Cucumber & Watermelon Salad

MAKES 4 servings **PREP** 20 minutes
MARINATE 30 minutes **GRILL** 14 minutes
LET REST 10 minutes

- **2** tablespoons extra virgin olive oil
- **2** tablespoons fresh lime juice
- **1** teaspoon lime zest
- **½** cup cilantro, chopped
- **½** cup sliced scallions
- **¼** cup fresh mint, chopped
- **¼** teaspoon cayenne
- **1** teaspoon salt
- **1½** pounds flank steak
- **4** tomatoes on the vine, seeded and diced
- **2** cucumbers, diced
- **3** cups diced watermelon

• Whisk together oil, lime juice, zest, half the cilantro, half the scallions, half the mint, the cayenne and ½ teaspoon of the salt to make a dressing. Pour half into a large resealable plastic bag; add steak and coat well. Marinate in refrigerator for 30 minutes.

• Meanwhile, heat grill to medium-high. Toss tomatoes, cucumbers and watermelon with remaining dressing, cilantro, scallions and mint, and ¼ teaspoon of the salt.

• Remove steak from marinade and grill 5 to 7 minutes per side or until internal temperature reaches 140°. Cover with foil and let rest 10 minutes, or until temperature increases to 145°. Slice steak against the grain; sprinkle with remaining ¼ teaspoon salt. Serve with salad.

PER SERVING 375 **CAL**; 17 g **FAT** (4 g **SAT**); 39 g **PRO**; 20 g **CARB**; 3 g **FIBER**; 689 mg **SODIUM**; 56 mg **CHOL**

Cod with Eggplant Caponata

MAKES 4 servings **PREP** 10 minutes **COOK** 26 minutes **BAKE** at 400° for 15 minutes

- **3** tablespoons olive oil
- **1** medium sweet onion, diced
- **2** celery ribs, diced
- **3** cloves garlic, chopped
- **1** large eggplant (about 1 pound), cut into ½-inch cubes
- **3** plum tomatoes, diced (don't remove seeds)
- **1** can (8 ounces) tomato sauce
- **3** tablespoons white balsamic vinegar
- **½** cup golden raisins
- **¼** cup pine nuts
- **3** tablespoons capers, drained
- **¼** teaspoon plus ⅛ teaspoon salt
- **¼** teaspoon pepper
- **4** cod fillets (about 5 ounces each)
  Chopped parsley (optional)
  Toasted baguette (optional)

• Heat oven to 400°. Heat 1 tablespoon of the oil in a large nonstick sauté pan over medium heat. Add onion and celery; cook 5 minutes. Add garlic; cook 1 minute. Pour in another 1 tablespoon of the oil and add eggplant; mix well and cook 5 minutes. Add tomatoes, tomato sauce, vinegar, raisins, pine nuts and capers. Cook 5 minutes, then reduce heat to medium-low and cook 10 more minutes. Stir in ¼ teaspoon of the salt and ⅛ teaspoon of the pepper.

• Meanwhile, place cod fillets skin-side down on a rimmed baking sheet lined with aluminum foil. Brush with remaining 1 tablespoon oil and season with remaining ⅛ teaspoon salt and remaining ⅛ teaspoon pepper. Bake at 400° for 12 to 15 minutes or until fish flakes easily with a fork.

• Serve cod with eggplant caponata. Garnish with chopped parsley and serve with toasted baguette slices, if desired.

PER SERVING 400 **CAL**; 17 g **FAT** (2 g **SAT**); 28 g **PRO**; 38 g **CARB**; 7 g **FIBER**; 800 mg **SODIUM**; 54 mg **CHOL**

Summer produce peaks in August, when gardens and farmers' markets burst with a bounty of corn, squash, peppers and tomatoes.

Creamy Corn & Shrimp

MAKES 4 servings **PREP** 20 minutes
COOK 22 minutes **GRILL** 4 minutes

5	slices bacon, diced
4	ears corn, kernels removed
1	medium yellow onion, diced
1	tablespoon all-purpose flour
1	cup 1% milk
1	tablespoon honey
3	tablespoons snipped fresh chives
½	teaspoon salt
¼	teaspoon pepper
1¼	pounds shrimp, peeled and deveined

• Heat grill to medium-high. Cook bacon in a large sauté pan over medium heat for 8 to 10 minutes or until crisp. Remove with a slotted spoon; set aside.

• In the same pan, remove all but 2 tablespoons of the bacon fat (compensate with olive oil to reach 2 tablespoons, if necessary). Add corn and onion. Cook over medium heat for 8 to 10 minutes, until softened. Add flour and cook 1 minute, stirring constantly. Stir in milk. Bring to a simmer; cook 1 minute. Turn off heat. Stir in honey, 2 tablespoons of the chives, ¼ teaspoon of the salt and ⅛ teaspoon of the pepper.

• Meanwhile, skewer shrimp. Coat with nonstick cooking spray and season with remaining ¼ teaspoon salt and remaining ⅛ teaspoon pepper. Grill 2 minutes per side or until cooked through. Serve shrimp skewers over corn. Distribute remaining 1 tablespoon chives over each serving.

PER SERVING 402 **CAL**; 15 g **FAT** (4 g **SAT**); 38 g **PRO**; 31 g **CARB**; 3 g **FIBER**; 721 mg **SODIUM**; 233 mg **CHOL**

Chicken & Shaved Squash Salad

MAKES 6 servings **PREP** 20 minutes **MARINATE** 30 minutes **GRILL** 8 minutes

¼	cup fresh lemon juice
¼	cup extra virgin olive oil
¾	teaspoon salt
⅛	teaspoon pepper
1½	pounds boneless, skinless chicken breasts (6 small breasts, about 4 ounces each)
3	pounds summer squash (mixed zucchini and yellow squash)
½	cup sliced almonds, toasted
½	cup shaved Pecorino Romano cheese
1	cup fresh basil, chopped

• Whisk together lemon juice, olive oil, ½ teaspoon of the salt and the pepper. Pour half the dressing into a large resealable plastic bag. Add chicken to bag and coat well. Marinate in refrigerator for 30 minutes.

• Meanwhile, heat grill to medium-high. Using a vegetable peeler, remove large, lengthwise strips from yellow squash and zucchini. Toss with remaining dressing, the almonds, cheese and basil, and remaining ¼ teaspoon salt.

• Remove chicken from marinade and grill 4 minutes per side, or until internal temperature reaches 165° on an instant-read thermometer. Serve chicken over squash salad.

PER SERVING 371 **CAL**; 18 g **FAT** (4 g **SAT**); 42 g **PRO**; 10 g **CARB**; 3 g **FIBER**; 500 mg **SODIUM**; 102 mg **CHOL**

Orecchiette with Roasted Red Pepper Sauce

MAKES 6 servings **PREP** 5 minutes **ROAST** at 450° for 40 minutes **COOK** 11 minutes

1 **tablespoon plus 1 teaspoon olive oil**
4 **large sweet red peppers**
1 **small yellow onion, peeled and halved**
1 **head garlic**
1 **package (12 ounces) sweet Italian chicken sausage (such as Al Fresco)**
¾ **teaspoon salt**
⅛ **teaspoon pepper**
2 **tablespoons heavy cream or half-and-half**
1 **pound orecchiette pasta**
Fresh chopped parsley (optional)
Grated Parmesan cheese (optional)

• Heat oven to 450°. Rub 1 tablespoon of the olive oil on red peppers and onion halves; place on a rimmed baking sheet. Cut off top quarter of the garlic and rub remaining 1 teaspoon olive oil on it; wrap garlic in aluminum foil and place on same baking sheet. Roast at 450° for 40 minutes, turning red peppers every 10 minutes. Place sausages on a separate baking sheet. During the last 10 minutes of cooking, place sausages in oven.

• When cool enough to touch, remove stem, seeds and skin from peppers. Squeeze head of garlic to remove cloves.

Place peppers, g[...] a blender with s[...] Blend until sm[...] coins; set aside[...]

• Meanwhile, bring a pot of lightly salted water to boiling. Cook orecchiette 11 minutes or according to package directions. Drain and return to pot. Stir in sauce and sliced sausage. Garnish with parsley and cheese, if desired.

PER SERVING 461 **CAL**; 11 g **FAT** (3 g **SAT**); 21 g **PRO**; 71 g **CARB**; 4 g **FIBER**; 621 mg **SODIUM**; 47 mg **CHOL**

CHICKEN DELIGHT

Rule the roost with our terrific new takes.

FRIED CHICKEN,
PAGE 215

CHICKEN BURGERS WITH
CARAMELIZED ONIONS,
PAGE 212

CURRIED CHICKEN
SALAD-STUFFED TOMATOES

Curried Chicken Salad-Stuffed Tomatoes

MAKES 6 servings **PREP** 15 minutes
COOK 12 minutes **MICROWAVE** 3½ minutes

3	**teaspoons curry powder**
1	**pound boneless, skinless chicken breasts**
6	**medium-large heirloom tomatoes**
½	**cup light mayonnaise**
½	**cup golden raisins**
⅓	**cup sliced almonds**
¼	**plus ⅛ teaspoon salt**
¼	**teaspoon black pepper**

• Bring 2 inches of water and 1½ teaspoons of the curry powder to a simmer in a medium straight-sided pan. Add chicken and poach for 12 minutes or until cooked through. Cool slightly, then chop into ½-inch pieces. Cool completely.

• Meanwhile, slice tops off tomatoes and set aside. Scoop out tomatoes and turn upside down onto paper towels to drain.

• Place remaining 1½ teaspoons curry powder in a small glass bowl. Microwave 1 minute, until fragrant. Combine with chicken, mayonnaise and raisins. Place almonds in a second small glass bowl. Microwave 2½ minutes to toast, stirring every 45 seconds or so. Add to chicken mixture, along with ¼ teaspoon of the salt and the pepper. Flip over tomatoes and sprinkle with remaining ⅛ teaspoon salt. Fill with chicken salad and replace tops, if desired.

PER SERVING 263 **CAL**; 11 g **FAT** (2 g **SAT**); 21 g **PRO**; 22 g **CARB**; 4 g **FIBER**; 388 mg **SODIUM**; 51 mg **CHOL**

Stuffed Chicken Breasts

MAKES 4 servings **PREP** 20 minutes **COOK** 9 minutes

1½	**pounds thinly sliced chicken breast halves**
⅓	**cup crumbled blue cheese**
⅓	**cup chopped dried Mission figs**
¼	**cup shelled pistachios, chopped**
¼	**teaspoon each salt and pepper**
1	**tablespoon unsalted butter**
1	**tablespoon olive oil**
	Salad greens (optional)

• Spread chicken onto a large cutting board. In a medium bowl, stir together blue cheese, dried figs and pistachios.

• Spoon 1 to 2 tablespoons filling onto center of each piece of chicken, compacting slightly. Roll chicken around filling to enclose completely. Secure with a toothpick.

• Season chicken with salt and pepper. Heat butter and oil in a large, lidded stainless skillet over medium-high heat. Add chicken and cook 4 minutes without turning. Carefully flip over and cook, covered, an additional 4 to 5 minutes, until internal temperature registers 165°.

• Remove chicken to a clean cutting board and remove toothpicks. Slice on a slight diagonal and serve with salad greens, if desired.

PER SERVING 368 **CAL**; 15 g **FAT** (5 g **SAT**); 44 g **PRO**; 13 g **CARB**; 2 g **FIBER**; 414 mg **SODIUM**; 115 mg **CHOL**

Chicken Chili Nachos

MAKES 8 servings **PREP** 10 minutes
COOK 17 minutes **BAKE** at 400° for 8 minutes

2	tablespoons olive oil
1	medium onion, chopped
2	cloves garlic, minced
1	pound ground chicken
3	tablespoons chili powder
½	teaspoon salt
½	teaspoon ground cumin
1	can (14.5 ounces) diced tomatoes with zesty green chiles
1	tablespoon tomato paste
8	cups corn tortilla chips (from a 9-ounce bag)
1	bag (7.5 ounces) blue corn tortilla chips
1½	cups Mexican cheese blend
	Sliced canned jalapeño peppers, sour cream, prepared guacamole, diced tomatoes and fresh cilantro (optional)

• Heat oven to 400°. Heat oil in a large, lidded nonstick skillet over medium heat. Add onion and cook 5 minutes. Stir in garlic and cook an additional minute. Add ground chicken and increase heat to medium-high. Stir in chili powder, salt and cumin and cook for 6 to 7 minutes.

• Stir in diced tomatoes and tomato paste. Cover and simmer over low heat for 5 minutes.

• Meanwhile, arrange half of the tortilla chips on an oven-safe platter or rimmed baking sheet. Spoon half the chicken chili over chips and top with ¾ cup of the cheese. Repeat layering. Bake at 400° for 8 minutes or until cheese has melted. Garnish with jalapeños, sour cream, guacamole, tomatoes and cilantro, if desired.

PER SERVING 462 **CAL**; 24 g **FAT** (8 g **SAT**); 20 g **PRO**; 45 g **CARB**; 5 g **FIBER**; 813 mg **SODIUM**; 87 mg **CHOL**

Saltimbocca Sandwiches

MAKES 6 servings **PREP** 5 minutes **TOAST** 3 minutes **COOK** 16 minutes

6	slices bacon, halved
6	slices roasted garlic bread or other rustic bread
2	tablespoons plus ¼ teaspoon Dijon mustard
1	tablespoon olive oil
1	tablespoon white wine vinegar Pinch each of salt and pepper
6	thin-sliced chicken cutlets (about 1¼ pounds)
12	fresh sage leaves
6	slices provolone cheese

• Heat broiler. Cook bacon in a large stainless skillet over medium heat 8 minutes, turning once. Transfer to a paper towel-lined plate.

• Meanwhile, spread bread onto a baking sheet. Toast under broiler 2 minutes.

Flip over and toast 1 minute. Spread each slice with 1 teaspoon of the Dijon mustard. Keep warm.

• In a small bowl, whisk remaining ¼ teaspoon mustard with oil, vinegar, salt and pepper. Brush onto cutlets.

• Carefully drain all but 1 tablespoon of the bacon drippings from skillet and heat over medium-high heat. Cook 3 of the cutlets in drippings in skillet for 2 minutes. Flip over and top each with 2 sage leaves, 1 piece (2 halves) bacon and 1 slice provolone. Cover and cook 1 to 2 minutes more. Remove to 3 of the toast pieces and repeat with remaining cutlets, sage, bacon and provolone. Serve warm.

PER SERVING 362 **CAL**; 14 g **FAT** (6 g **SAT**); 32 g **PRO**; 23 g **CARB**; 1 g **FIBER**; 770 mg **SODIUM**; 77 mg **CHOL**

CHICKEN CHILI NACHOS

ORANGE-GARLIC
BUTTERFLIED CHICKEN

Orange-Garlic Butterflied Chicken

MAKES 4 servings **PREP** 15 minutes
BAKE at 425° for 20 minutes, then at 400° for 25 minutes

1	whole chicken (about 4 pounds)
¼	cup sweet orange marmalade
¼	cup orange juice
6	cloves garlic, sliced
2	tablespoons ponzu sauce
¼	teaspoon salt
¼	teaspoon pepper
1	orange, quartered

• Heat oven to 425°. Remove chicken from packaging, saving giblets for another use. Turn chicken so it is breast-side down on cutting board. With kitchen shears, cut along both sides of backbone. Set aside with giblets. Flip over chicken and press down until breast cracks and bird lies flat on cutting board. Tuck wings under breast, if desired.

• In a small bowl, stir together marmalade, orange juice, garlic, ponzu, salt, pepper and orange quarters. Place chicken on a rack in a roasting pan. Pour sauce over chicken and add 1 cup water to pan. Roast at 425° for 20 minutes. Reduce oven temperature to 400°, cover chicken with foil and continue to roast for 25 minutes or until chicken registers 165° on instant-read thermometer.

• Remove to a platter and pour pan drippings into a fat separator. Slice chicken and serve with defatted drippings alongside.

PER SERVING 350 **CAL**; 9 g **FAT** (3 g **SAT**); 42 g **PRO**; 23 g **CARB**; 1 g **FIBER**; 452 mg **SODIUM**; 125 mg **CHOL**

Grilled Tandoori Chicken Legs

MAKES 4 servings **PREP** 20 minutes **MARINATE** overnight **GRILL** 20 minutes

4	chicken leg quarters (about 3¼ pounds)
1	cup plain low-fat yogurt
3	tablespoons lemon juice
1	tablespoon grated ginger
2	cloves garlic, minced
2	teaspoons curry powder
1	teaspoon ground cumin
1	teaspoon salt
½	teaspoon cayenne pepper
¼	teaspoon black pepper
	Cooked couscous (optional)

RAITA

¾	cup plain low-fat yogurt
⅓	cup grated cucumber
1	large clove garlic, grated
1	tablespoon lemon juice
½	teaspoon salt

• Remove skin from chicken legs (use a paper towel to get a grip on the skin). Make a few slash marks in legs so marinade can soak in. Place legs in a glass dish or resealable plastic bag.

• In a medium bowl, combine yogurt, lemon juice, ginger, garlic, curry powder, cumin, salt, cayenne and black pepper. Pour over chicken and turn to coat. Refrigerate overnight.

• Heat gas grill to medium-high; for charcoal grill, bank coals to one side. Remove chicken from dish and scrape off as much marinade as possible. Coat with nonstick cooking spray and grill, bone-side down, 4 minutes. Flip over; reduce heat to medium. If cooking over charcoal, move legs to side without coals. Grill, covered, 16 minutes more, until legs register 165°.

• Meanwhile, prepare **Raita.** Blend yogurt, cucumber, garlic, lemon juice and salt. Serve chicken over couscous, if desired, with raita alongside.

PER SERVING 350 **CAL**; 14 g **FAT** (4 g **SAT**); 46 g **PRO**; 6 g **CARB**; 1 g **FIBER**; 571 mg **SODIUM**; 156 mg **CHOL**

The mild flavor of chicken makes it adaptable to a world of flavors, including an American-style burger or spiced Middle Eastern pita sandwich.

Chicken Shawarma

MAKES 6 sandwiches PREP 20 minutes
BROIL 10 minutes

6	**pieces naan or lavash bread**
1	**teaspoon ground coriander**
1	**teaspoon ground cumin**
1	**teaspoon paprika**
½	**teaspoon ground cinnamon**
¼	**teaspoon salt**
¼	**teaspoon pepper**
2	**tablespoons fresh lemon juice**
2	**cloves garlic, grated**
1	**package (about 1½ pounds) boneless, skinless chicken thighs**
¾	**cup prepared hummus**
2	**plum tomatoes, sliced**
½	**large cucumber, sliced**

• Heat oven to broil. Wrap bread in foil and warm in bottom of oven. Coat a broiler pan with nonstick cooking spray.

• In a small bowl, combine coriander, cumin, paprika, cinnamon, salt and pepper. Stir in lemon juice and garlic to make a paste. Rub all over chicken thighs.

• Place chicken thighs on prepared broiler pan and broil 2 to 3 inches from heat for 5 minutes. Flip over and broil another 5 minutes, or until thighs register 165° on an instant-read thermometer. Transfer to a cutting board and slice into strips.

• Spread 2 tablespoons of the hummus onto each piece of bread. Top with some of the tomatoes, cucumber and chicken. Fold in half and serve.

PER SERVING 546 CAL; 19 g FAT (4 g SAT); 35 g PRO; 49 g CARB; 11 g FIBER; 1,098 mg SODIUM; 120 mg CHOL

Chicken Burgers with Caramelized Onions

MAKES 4 servings PREP 15 minutes COOK 30 minutes

1	**tablespoon unsalted butter**
1	**large Vidalia onion, thinly sliced**
1¼	**pounds ground chicken**
½	**cup part-skim ricotta cheese**
1¾	**teaspoons Worcestershire sauce**
1¾	**teaspoons Dijon mustard**
¼	**teaspoon salt**
¼	**teaspoon black pepper**
1	**tablespoon vegetable oil**
4	**hamburger buns**
4	**romaine lettuce leaves**

• Melt butter in a large skillet over medium-high heat. Add onion and cook 15 minutes or until well browned; set aside.

• In a large bowl, combine chicken, ricotta, Worcestershire sauce, mustard, salt and pepper. Stir until well combined. Form into 4 equal-size patties and flatten.

• Heat oil in a large nonstick skillet over medium heat. Cook burgers about 5 minutes per side. Partially cover, reduce heat to medium and cook another 5 minutes or until instant-read thermometer registers 160°.

• Place burgers on buns and top each with some of the onions and a lettuce leaf.

PER SERVING 478 CAL; 26 g FAT (9 g SAT); 33 g PRO; 30 g CARB; 2 g FIBER; 567 mg SODIUM; 188 mg CHOL

CHICKEN SHAWARMA

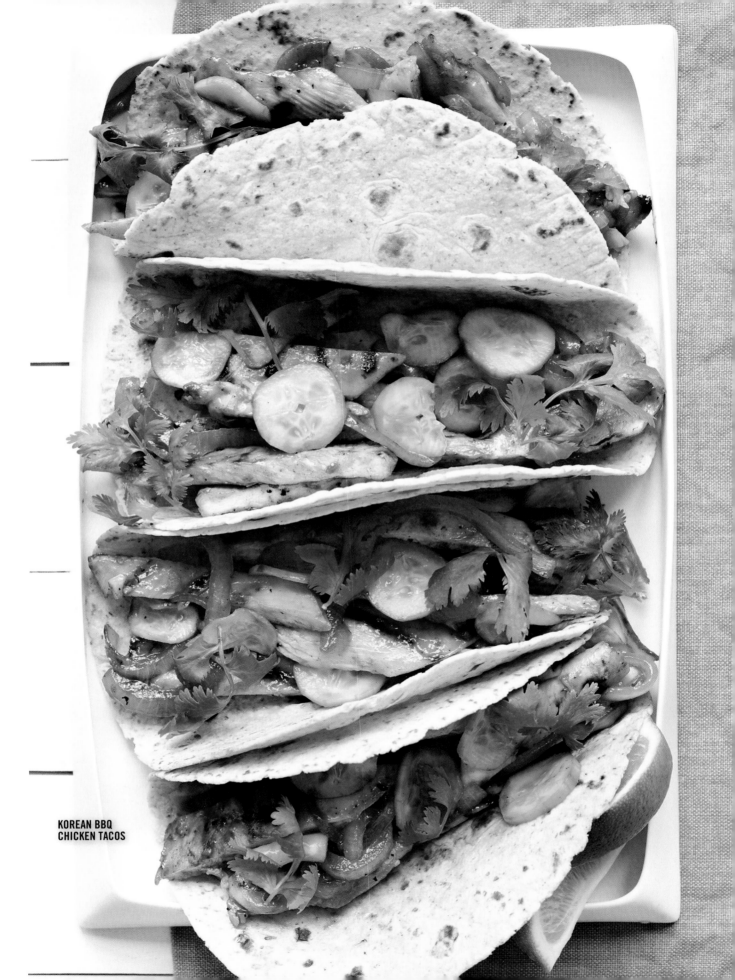

KOREAN BBQ
CHICKEN TACOS

Korean BBQ Chicken Tacos

MAKES 8 soft tacos **PREP** 15 minutes
LET STAND 15 minutes **GRILL** 6 minutes
COOK 7 minutes

- ¼ **cup mirin (Asian cooking wine)**
- ¼ **cup plus 1 tablespoon rice vinegar**
- 1 **tablespoon plus 1 teaspoon sugar**
  Pinch of salt
- 1 **cucumber, peeled and thinly sliced**
- 1¼ **pounds thinly sliced chicken cutlets**
- 5 **tablespoons Korean teriyaki stir-fry sauce (such as House of Tsang)**
- 1 **tablespoon canola oil**
- 1 **onion, halved and thinly sliced**
- 1 **package small flour tortillas (8 per package)**
- ⅓ **cup cilantro leaves**

• In a glass or plastic bowl, combine mirin, ¼ cup of the vinegar, 1 tablespoon of the sugar and the salt. Whisk until sugar is dissolved. Add cucumber and let stand 15 minutes.

• Heat a grill or grill pan to medium-high. Lightly coat grill rack with oil. Place chicken on a sheet of wax paper or plastic wrap. Brush both sides with 3 tablespoons of the sauce. Grill until cooked through, 2 to 3 minutes per side. Transfer to a cutting board.

• Meanwhile, heat oil in a large nonstick skillet over medium heat. Add onion and cook 5 to 7 minutes. Add remaining 2 tablespoons sauce. Cut chicken into strips and add to skillet.

• To serve, spoon about ¼ cup of the chicken mixture onto a tortilla. Add some of the marinated cucumbers and cilantro.

PER TACO 297 **CAL**; 7 g **FAT** (1 g **SAT**); 21 g **PRO**; 35 g **CARB**; 1 g **FIBER**; 584 mg **SODIUM**; 41 mg **CHOL**

Fried Chicken

MAKES 10 pieces **PREP** 15 minutes **FRY** at 350° for 13 minutes per batch **KEEP WARM** in 200° oven

- 5 **cups peanut oil**
- 2 **cups buttermilk**
- 1 **large egg**
- 1½ **cups all-purpose flour**
- 2 **teaspoons garlic salt**
- 1 **teaspoon onion powder**
- 1 **teaspoon black pepper**
- ¼ **teaspoon baking soda**
- ⅛ **teaspoon cayenne pepper**
- 1 **whole chicken, cut into 10 pieces (2 thighs, 2 drumsticks, 2 wings, each breast half cut in half)**

• Heat oil in a 12-inch stainless lidded skillet (cast iron, if desired) over medium heat to 350° on a deep-fry thermometer. Oil should be 1½ to 2 inches deep. Heat oven to 200°.

• In a medium bowl, whisk together buttermilk and egg. In a second bowl or shallow dish, combine flour, garlic salt, onion powder, black pepper, baking soda and cayenne.

• Pat chicken dry. Coat a few of the chicken pieces with flour mixture. Dip in buttermilk mixture, allowing excess to drip back into the bowl. Return to flour mixture to coat. Place on a wire rack over a baking sheet while you coat remaining chicken pieces.

• Carefully place 4 to 5 pieces of chicken skin-side down in hot oil (don't let pieces touch). Fry 4 minutes. Flip pieces over with tongs and fry 4 more minutes. Try to keep temperature around 350°; you will have to adjust heat under pan. Flip chicken one more time and cover pan. Cook 4 to 5 more minutes or until pieces register 165° on an instant-read thermometer. Transfer to a baking pan fitted with a wire rack and keep warm in 200° oven. Repeat with all chicken pieces.

PER PIECE 357 **CAL**; 24 g **FAT** (5 g **SAT**); 18 g **PRO**; 17 g **CARB**; 1 g **FIBER**; 336 mg **SODIUM**; 77 mg **CHOL**

JUICY SALMON BURGERS

CHEDDAR BURGERS

CHICKEN BURGERS WITH CARAMELIZED ONIONS, PAGE 212

Juicy Salmon Burgers

MAKES 4 burgers **PREP** 15 minutes
GRILL 10 minutes

1¼	**pounds salmon fillet**
2	**scallions, trimmed and roughly chopped**
2	**tablespoons chopped fresh dill**
1	**teaspoon lemon zest**
⅓	**cup panko bread crumbs**
¼	**teaspoon salt**
¼	**teaspoon pepper**
¼	**cup tartar sauce**
1½	**cups shredded lettuce**
6	**whole wheat hamburger buns**

• Remove skin from salmon fillet: With a sharp knife, cut a small corner of the skin away from the flesh. Gently pull and slice off remaining skin, removing as little flesh as possible. Discard skin; coarsely chop salmon.

• Heat gas grill to medium-high or coals in charcoal grill to medium-hot. Transfer salmon to a food processor, along with scallions, 1 tablespoon of the dill, the lemon zest, panko, salt and pepper. Pulse until salmon is the consistency of ground beef but still has some shape. Do not overprocess.

• Form mixture into 4 patties, each about 3½ inches in diameter. Coat patties with nonstick cooking spray. Grill patties 5 minutes. Flip over and continue to grill another 5 minutes. Meanwhile, stir remaining 1 tablespoon dill into tartar sauce. Divide lettuce evenly among buns. Top each with a burger patty and 1 tablespoon tartar sauce.

PER BURGER 485 **CAL**; 18 g **FAT** (3 g **SAT**); 39 g **PRO**; 42 g **CARB**; 6 g **FIBER**; 720 mg **SODIUM**; 95 mg **CHOL**

Cheddar Burgers

MAKES 6 burgers **PREP** 20 minutes
GRILL 7 minutes

2½	**pounds ground beef (90% lean)**
1	**tablespoon dried minced onion**
1	**tablespoon Worcestershire sauce**
¾	**teaspoon garlic salt**
½	**teaspoon Italian seasoning**
¼	**teaspoon black pepper**
6	**hamburger buns**
12	**leaves fresh arugula or other leafy green, cleaned**
6	**slices sharp cheddar cheese**
6	**slices tomato**

• Heat gas grill to medium-high or prepare charcoal grill with medium-hot coals. In a large bowl, mix together ground beef, onion, Worcestershire sauce, garlic salt, Italian seasoning and black pepper until well combined.

• Shape seasoned beef into 6 patties.

• Split rolls in half and toast cut-side down on grill, about 1 minute. Transfer to a large platter. Top buns with arugula leaves.

• Transfer hamburger patties to grill and cook 2 minutes. Flip and cook 2 additional minutes or until cooked through. Top burgers with cheese. Grill until slightly melted, 1 to 2 minutes.

• Transfer burgers to lettuce-topped buns and place a tomato slice on each. Serve warm.

PER BURGER 513 **CAL**; 26 g **FAT** (12 g **SAT**); 45 g **PRO**; 23 g **CARB**; 1 g **FIBER**; 612 mg **SODIUM**; 141 mg **CHOL**

PLAY IT COOL

20 no-cook weeknight dinners.

THAI SALAD WITH CHICKEN

CHICKEN

Thai Salad with Chicken

MAKES 4 servings **PREP** 15 minutes

• Whisk together ½ cup smooth peanut butter, ½ cup hot water, 3 tablespoons reduced-sodium soy sauce, juice of 1 lime and 2 cloves chopped garlic. Evenly distribute 1 head shredded iceberg lettuce, 2 cups cooked shredded chicken, 1 sliced peeled cucumber and ½ sliced red pepper among 4 plates. Top each serving with some of the peanut dressing, sliced scallions and crispy Asian noodles, if desired. Serve remaining dressing on the side.

PER SERVING 482 **CAL**; 25 g **FAT**

Chicken Gyros

MAKES 4 servings; **PREP** 10 minutes

• Combine 1 container (7 ounces) 2% Greek yogurt and ⅓ cup crumbled feta cheese. Cut 4 pita flatbreads into 8 halves. Into each half, spoon an equal amount of yogurt mixture, ¼ cup shredded rotisserie chicken, shredded iceberg lettuce and slices of cucumber, tomato and red onion.

PER SERVING 366 **CAL**; 7 g **FAT**

MEATLESS VARIATION

Veggie Gyros

• Eliminate shredded chicken and increase amount of tomato and cucumber. Replace plain feta cheese with ⅔ cup tomato-basil-flavor feta.

Mediterranean Bulgur & Chicken

MAKES 4 servings **PREP** 15 minutes

• In a microwave-safe bowl, combine 1½ cups water and ½ cup orange juice. Cover with plastic wrap and microwave 4 minutes until simmering. Stir in 1 cup bulgur, ¼ cup sweetened dried cranberries, ¾ teaspoon salt and ⅛ teaspoon black pepper. Cover with plastic and let stand 35 minutes, stirring once. Stir in 2 cups diced cooked chicken, ½ cup walnuts and 3 tablespoon chopped mint. Serve chilled or at room temp.

PER SERVING 371 **CAL**; 13 g **FAT**

Honey-Dijon Chicken & Spinach Wraps

MAKES 4 servings **PREP** 10 minutes

• In a large bowl, whisk together ½ cup reduced-fat mayonnaise and 2 tablespoons each honey-Dijon mustard and milk. Stir in 2 cups cubed rotisserie chicken, 1 cup each chopped celery and halved red seedless grapes and ½ cup chopped walnuts. Wrap 4 whole wheat tortillas in damp paper towels and microwave for 30 seconds. Scatter baby spinach over each tortilla and spoon about ¾ cup of the chicken mixture down the center. Roll up tightly and cut diagonally in half.

PER SERVING 488 **CAL**; 25 g **FAT**

MUFFALETTA

BEEF

Beef & Chickpea Toss

MAKES 4 servings PREP 10 minutes

• Drain and rinse 2 cans (15 ounces each) chickpeas. Combine with 3 tablespoons each olive oil and raspberry balsamic vinegar, 2 tablespoons mayonnaise, 1/2 teaspoon fresh chopped thyme and 1/8 teaspoon each salt and pepper. Serve in Bibb lettuce cups with 1/2 pound roast beef, sliced into ribbons. Top each serving with 2 tablespoons crumbled blue cheese.

PER SERVING 474 CAL; 23 g FAT

Fajita Salad

MAKES 4 servings PREP 10 minutes

• Place 2 diced ripe avocados in a medium bowl; fold in 1/3 cup chopped red onion, 3 tablespoons chopped cilantro, 1 tablespoon lime juice and 1/8 teaspoon each salt and pepper. Line 4 plates with red leafy lettuce. On each plate arrange 2 slices roast beef, 2 slices pepper Jack cheese and a quarter of the avocado mixture. Serve with 1 tablespoon reduced-fat ranch dressing.

PER SERVING 490 CAL; 34 g FAT

Wasabi Beef Pockets

MAKES 4 servings PREP 10 minutes

• In a small bowl, dissolve 1 teaspoon wasabi powder in 1 tablespoon warm water. Add 1/3 cup reduced-fat mayonnaise, 2 tablespoons chopped parsley, 1 tablespoon lemon juice; stir until smooth. Split open 8 sandwich thins (such as Arnold) and spread cut sides with wasabi mayonnaise. Place 2 slices roast beef (about 2 ounces) on each bottom half; top with alfalfa sprouts and other bread half.

PER SERVING 500 CAL; 17 g FAT

Muffaletta

MAKES 8 servings PREP 10 minutes

• Drain 1 jar (4¾ ounces) pimento-stuffed olives and chop; combine with 2 chopped seeded plum tomatoes, 1/4 cup olive oil, 1 tablespoon red wine vinegar and 1/2 teaspoon each garlic salt and dried oregano. Cut a round crusty Italian or Portuguese loaf (about 20 ounces) in half crosswise. Spread bottom of cut side with half of olive mixture. Layer on 1/2 pound each sliced mozzarella, sliced roast beef and provolone. Spread remaining olive mixture over provolone and top with other half of bread. Wrap tightly in plastic and weight down with a heavy pot filled with canned goods for at least 1 hour. To serve, remove plastic wrap and cut into 8 wedges.

PER SERVING 468 CAL; 23 g FAT

MEATLESS VARIATION
Veggie Muffaletta

• Replace roast beef and provolone cheese with sliced pepper Jack cheese and a layer each of sliced tomato and sliced cucumber.

SHRIMP

Vietnamese Shrimp Lettuce Wraps

MAKES 4 servings   **PREP** 15 minutes

• In a small bowl, combine 2 tablespoons each fish sauce and lime juice, 2 teaspoons sugar, 1 teaspoon Asian chili paste and 2 chopped cloves of garlic. In a medium-size bowl, combine 1 pound coarsely chopped cooked shrimp and 1 tablespoon each soy sauce and rice vinegar. Serve shrimp wrapped in Boston lettuce leaves along with plain coleslaw mix, cilantro, mint and chopped peanuts. Serve fish sauce mixture for dipping.
PER SERVING 266 **CAL**; 11 g **FAT**

Layered Shrimp & Avocado Salad

MAKES 6 servings   **PREP** 15 minutes

• In a 14-cup trifle bowl, layer 6 cups torn romaine lettuce, 2 cups chopped tomatoes, 3 diced avocados, 1 pound cooked shrimp, 1 sliced red onion and 1 package (10 ounces) thawed frozen peas. Spread 1 cup jarred Thousand Island dressing evenly over the top. Scatter 6 pieces crumbled fully cooked microwavable bacon over dressing.
PER SERVING 481 **CAL**; 33 g **FAT**

VIETNAMESE SHRIMP LETTUCE WRAPS

Shrimp Spinach Salad

MAKES 4 servings   **PREP** 15 minutes

• In a medium-size bowl, whisk together 1/3 cup Miracle Whip, 2 tablespoons lemon juice, 1 tablespoon mustard and 1/2 teaspoon Old Bay seasoning. Stir in 1 pound coarsely chopped cooked shrimp and 1 cup chopped celery. Line each of 4 soup bowls with 2 cups of baby spinach. On each serving, spoon a fourth of the shrimp salad, 1 hard-cooked egg, cut into wedges, 1/4 cup pickled sliced beets and carrot sticks.
PER SERVING 330 **CAL**; 15 g **FAT**

Greek Shrimp & Feta

MAKES 4 servings   **PREP** 10 minutes

• Whisk together 3 tablespoons olive oil, 2 tablespoon red wine vinegar, 1/2 teaspoon dried Greek seasoning and 1/8 teaspoon black pepper. Place 8 cups mixed salad greens in a large salad bowl and toss with dressing. Fold in 1 pound cooked shrimp and 1/4 cup each chopped pitted Kalamata olives and crumbled feta cheese. Serve with garlic herb pita chips (such as Stacy's), if desired.
PER SERVING 281 **CAL**; 16 g **FAT**

Shrimp Taco Bowl

MAKES 4 servings   **PREP** 10 minutes

• Mix together 1/2 cup jarred salsa, 1/4 cup sour cream and 2 tablespoons chopped cilantro. Line 4 bowls with tortilla chips. Chop 1 yellow sweet pepper and 2 tomatoes; scatter over chips. Top each bowl with 1/4 pound cooked shrimp and serve with salsa mixture. Garnish with additional cilantro and lime wedges, if desired.
PER SERVING 360 **CAL**; 12 g **FAT**

TURKEY

Bean, Corn & Turkey Salad

MAKES 6 servings   PREP 10 minutes

• Whisk together 3 tablespoons olive oil, ⅓ cup orange juice, 2 tablespoons red wine vinegar, ¾ teaspoon ground cumin, ¼ teaspoon salt and ⅛ teaspoon black pepper. Combine 1 can (15 ounces) each, drained and rinsed, kidney beans, black beans and corn. Stir in the olive oil mixture, 3 cups cubed turkey, ⅓ cup chopped red onion and 2 tablespoons chopped cilantro.
PER SERVING 434 CAL; 9 g FAT

Sundried Tomato Pesto Turkey Salad

MAKES 4 servings   PREP 15 minutes

• Combine 2 cups diced cooked turkey, 1 cup chopped celery, ½ cup reduced-fat mayonnaise and 2 tablespoons sundried tomato pesto. Cut tops off 4 large tomatoes and remove most of seeds and pulp. Stuff each tomato with one-quarter of the turkey mixture. Sprinkle each with 1 tablespoon pine nuts and garnish with basil.
PER SERVING 348 CAL; 17 g FAT

Curried Turkey Couscous

MAKES 4 servings   PREP 15 minutes

• In a glass bowl, combine 2 cups reduced-sodium chicken broth, ½ cup water, ¾ teaspoon curry and ¼ teaspoon salt. Microwave 4 minutes until boiling. Stir in 1¼ cups couscous and cover with plastic. After 5 minutes, fluff with fork and fold in 2 cups chopped cooked turkey, 1 cup green grapes, quartered, and 3 sliced scallions. Microwave ⅓ cup Major Grey's chutney for 15 seconds; drizzle over the couscous. Sprinkle with ¼ cup sliced almonds.
PER SERVING 491 CAL; 7 g FAT

Dinner Antipasto with Turkey

MAKES 4 servings   PREP 15 minutes

• Drain liquid from 1 jar (6 ounces) marinated artichokes into a blender; chop artichokes and reserve. Into blender, add ½ cup basil leaves, 2 cloves chopped garlic and ⅛ teaspoon black pepper; pulse until combined. Line a large serving platter with 10 cups torn romaine lettuce. Top with 2 cups shredded cooked turkey, ¼ pound sliced fresh mozzarella cheese, half a jar (4 ounces) of chopped roasted red peppers and the chopped artichokes. Drizzle the artichoke-basil mixture over the top.
PER SERVING 312 CAL; 10 g FAT

Turkey Pita Club

MAKES 4 servings   PREP 10 minutes

• Heat 12 slices fully cooked bacon in microwave for 1 minute. On each of 4 pita breads, spread 2 tablespoons spicy ranch dressing. Layer each with iceberg lettuce leaves, ½ cup carved turkey breast strips, 3 slices bacon and 3 slices plum tomato.
PER SERVING 477 CAL; 24 g FAT

TURKEY PITA CLUB

CHUTNEY PORK
CHOPS & COUSCOUS,
PAGE 228

SEPTEMBER

225

231

243

SUPPER SOLUTIONS

Savor these healthy, kid-friendly meals from the moms on the Family Circle® *staff.*

SLOW COOKER BRISKET
BBQ CHILI, PAGE 227

Rotini with Sautéed Chicken Sausage & Vegetables

MAKES 6 servings **PREP** 15 minutes **COOK** 17 minutes

½	**pound green beans, trimmed**
1	**head broccoli, cut into florets**
1	**box (13.25 ounces) whole wheat rotini pasta**
3	**tablespoons olive oil**
4	**sweet Italian-style fully cooked chicken sausages (such as Al Fresco), cut into ¼-inch coins**
4	**cloves garlic, chopped**
½	**cup reduced-sodium chicken broth**
1	**cup grape tomatoes, halved**
½	**teaspoon dried oregano**
½	**teaspoon salt**
⅛	**teaspoon black pepper**
½	**cup basil, sliced**
2	**tablespoons grated Parmesan**

• Bring a large pot of lightly salted water to boiling. Add green beans and broccoli; cook 3 minutes or until crisp-tender. Remove to a bowl with a slotted spoon.

• To same pot, add rotini; cook following package directions, about 14 minutes. Reserve 1 cup of the cooking liquid and drain.

• Meanwhile, heat 1 tablespoon of the olive oil in a large nonstick skillet over medium-high heat. Add sausage and cook 5 minutes, turning once, until browned. Remove to a plate. Add remaining 2 tablespoons olive oil, green beans, broccoli and garlic; cook 2 minutes. Stir in sausage, broth, tomatoes, oregano, salt and pepper; simmer 2 minutes.

• Toss pasta with sausage and vegetables, adding reserved cooking liquid as needed to create a sauce. To serve, stir in basil and top with Parmesan.

PER SERVING 450 **CAL**; 17 g **FAT** (4 g **SAT**); 21 g **PRO**; 55 g **CARB**; 9 g **FIBER**; 763 mg **SODIUM**; 56 mg **CHOL**

Smoky Chicken and Potatoes

MAKES 4 servings **PREP** 15 minutes
BAKE at 450° for 30 minutes

- 1½ **pounds boneless, skinless chicken thighs, cut into 1-inch pieces**
- 1½ **pounds baking potatoes, unpeeled, cut into ½-inch pieces**
- 1 **sweet onion, cut into 8 wedges**
- 1 **green pepper, cored, seeded and cut into ½-inch strips**
- 4 **cloves garlic, sliced**
- 2 **tablespoons olive oil**
- 2 **teaspoons smoked paprika**
- 1 **teaspoon salt**
- ½ **teaspoon black pepper**
- 1 **lemon, cut into wedges, plus more for serving (optional)**
- ½ **cup parsley, chopped**

• Heat oven to 450°. Coat a 13 x 9 x 2-inch baking dish with nonstick cooking spray.

• Add chicken, potatoes, onion, green pepper and garlic. Toss with olive oil and season with paprika, salt and pepper. Squeeze lemon wedges over top and scatter wedges over casserole.

• Bake at 450° for 30 minutes or until chicken reaches 160°. Stir once after 20 minutes.

• Scatter parsley over top. Serve with additional lemon, if desired.

PER SERVING 454 CAL; 16 g **FAT** (3 g **SAT**); 37 g **PRO**; 43 g **CARB**; 5 g **FIBER**; 721 mg **SODIUM**; 166 mg **CHOL**

Cuts like brisket, chuck, short ribs and stew are ideal for meals that slow cook for 10 hours.

Slow Cooker Brisket BBQ Chili

MAKES 8 servings **PREP** 15 minutes
SLOW COOK on LOW for 10½ hours

- 1 beef brisket or chuck roast (about 2 pounds), cut into 2-inch pieces
- 1 onion, chopped
- 3 cloves garlic, chopped
- 1 can (16 ounces) stewed tomatoes
- 1 cup ketchup
- ⅓ cup brown sugar
- ¼ cup molasses
- ¼ cup reduced-sodium Worcestershire sauce
- ¼ cup chili powder
- 1 tablespoon dry mustard
- 1 tablespoon cumin
- 1 can (15 ounces) kidney beans, drained and rinsed
- 1 can (15 ounces) butter beans, drained and rinsed
- 2 cups cooked white rice
- ¼ cup chopped scallion
   Lime wedges (optional)

• Coat slow cooker bowl with nonstick cooking spray.

• Add brisket, onion and garlic. In a medium bowl, combine tomatoes, ketchup, brown sugar, molasses, Worcestershire sauce, chili powder, mustard and cumin. Stir into beef and onions. Cover and cook on LOW for 10 hours.

• Stir in beans and cook for 30 minutes. Serve with rice. Garnish with scallion and, if desired, lime wedges.

PER SERVING 436 **CAL**; 7 g **FAT** (2 g **SAT**); 33 g **PRO**; 62 g **CARB**; 9 g **FIBER**; 778 mg **SODIUM**; 49 mg **CHOL**

Asian Beef & Lentil Sloppy Joes

MAKES 6 servings **PREP** 15 minutes **COOK** 12 minutes

- ¾ pound lean ground beef
- 1½ cups cooked lentils
- 1 sweet pepper, cored, seeded and thinly sliced
- 3 cloves garlic, chopped
- 1 can (8 ounces) reduced-sodium tomato sauce
- 2 tablespoons hoisin sauce
- 2 tablespoons reduced-sodium teriyaki sauce
- 1 tablespoon rice vinegar
- 1 teaspoon sugar
- ½ teaspoon ground ginger
- ½ teaspoon Asian chili paste
- 6 soft whole wheat rolls
- 3 scallions, sliced

• Heat a large nonstick skillet over medium-high heat. Coat with nonstick cooking spray and crumble in ground beef. Cook 4 minutes or until beef is no longer pink.

• Stir in lentils, sweet pepper, garlic, tomato sauce, hoisin, teriyaki, vinegar, sugar, ginger and chili paste. Simmer, uncovered, for 8 minutes, stirring occasionally.

• Spoon about ⅔ cup beef and lentil mixture into each roll and sprinkle with scallions.

PER SERVING 304 **CAL**; 6 g **FAT** (2 g **SAT**); 21 g **PRO**; 44 g **CARB**; 8 g **FIBER**; 621 mg **SODIUM**; 35 mg **CHOL**

Chutney Pork Chops & Couscous

MAKES 4 servings PREP 10 minutes
COOK 12 minutes

1	tablespoon vegetable oil
4	bone-in pork chops (about 5 ounces each)
½	teaspoon salt
¼	teaspoon black pepper
1	tablespoon all-purpose flour
¾	cup apple juice
⅓	cup jarred chutney
1	tablespoon Dijon mustard
1	cup reduced-sodium chicken broth
1	cup chopped sweet onion
1	cup couscous
1	cup frozen peas, thawed
	Mixed green salad

• In a large nonstick skillet, heat oil over medium-high heat. Season pork chops with ¼ teaspoon of the salt and the pepper. Cook 4 to 5 minutes per side until temperature reaches 145°. Remove chops to a plate.

• Sprinkle flour over bottom of skillet and cook 30 seconds. Stir in apple juice and chutney. Simmer 1 minute until smooth and thickened; stir in mustard.

• Meanwhile, pour broth into a medium saucepan and bring to a simmer. Add onion; simmer 2 minutes. Stir in couscous, peas and remaining ¼ teaspoon salt. Cover and let stand 5 minutes.

• Fluff couscous gently with a fork. Serve with pork chops, chutney sauce and, if desired, mixed green salad.

PER SERVING 478 CAL; 14 g FAT (3 g SAT); 31 g PRO; 56 g CARB; 5 g FIBER; 664 mg SODIUM; 62 mg CHOL

Baked Flounder with Herbed Panko

MAKES 4 servings PREP 15 minutes BAKE at 425° for 18 minutes MICROWAVE 12 minutes

4	flounder fillets (about 6 ounces each)
¾	teaspoon salt
¼	teaspoon black pepper
½	cup parsley, chopped
1	teaspoon chopped thyme
¾	cup panko bread crumbs
1	cup grape tomatoes, halved
2	pounds sweet potatoes (about 4 medium), scrubbed and patted dry
3	tablespoons cream cheese with chives
1	tablespoon chopped chives

• Heat oven to 425°. Coat bottom of a 13 x 9 x 2-inch baking dish with nonstick cooking spray.

• Place flounder skinned-side up on a work surface and season with ¼ teaspoon of the salt and ⅛ teaspoon of the black pepper. Scatter ¼ cup of the parsley and ½ teaspoon of the thyme over fish and fold in half. Combine panko with remaining parsley and thyme; spoon evenly over flounder and place in prepared baking dish.

• Place tomatoes in dish around fish. Season with ¼ teaspoon of the salt and remaining ⅛ teaspoon black pepper. Bake at 425° for 18 minutes or until fish is cooked through and flakes easily.

• Meanwhile, microwave sweet potatoes on high for 12 minutes or until tender. Cool slightly and scoop flesh into a bowl. Season with remaining ¼ teaspoon salt and add cream cheese. Mash until smooth.

• Serve fish with sweet potatoes. Garnish with chives.

PER SERVING 400 CAL; 7 g FAT (4 g SAT); 39 g PRO; 43 g CARB; 5 g FIBER; 741 mg SODIUM; 97 mg CHOL

CHUTNEY PORK CHOPS
& COUSCOUS

PASTA PERFECT

10 creative takes on the Italian classic.

SPAGHETTI CARBONARA PIE,
PAGE 239

Mini Meatball Lasagna

MAKES 12 servings PREP 45 minutes COOK 30 minutes BAKE at 350° for 45 minutes LET STAND 20 minutes

MEATBALLS

¾	**pound lean ground beef**
¾	**pound Italian sausage, casings removed**
¼	**cup plain bread crumbs**
1	**egg**
2	**tablespoons milk**
2	**tablespoons grated Parmesan**
2	**tablespoons olive oil**

LASAGNA

16	**traditional lasagna noodles**
1	**medium onion, diced**
4	**cloves garlic, chopped**
1	**can (28 ounces) fire-roasted crushed tomatoes**
1	**can (28 ounces) fire-roasted diced tomatoes**
½	**cup basil leaves, finely chopped**
1	**container (15 ounces) ricotta cheese**
1	**egg**
¼	**cup grated Parmesan**
1	**bag (8 ounces) shredded mozzarella**
8	**ounces Fontina cheese, grated**

• Heat oven to 350°. Make **Meatballs**. In a large bowl, combine ground beef, sausage, bread crumbs, egg, milk and Parmesan. With wet hands, shape into 60 mini meatballs, using 2 teaspoons of mixture for each.

• Heat oil in a large skillet over medium-high heat. Add half the meatballs and cook for 5 minutes, shaking pan to turn meatballs while maintaining their shape. Remove to a plate; repeat with remaining meatballs. Reserve drippings in pan.

• Meanwhile, to make **Lasagna**, bring a large pot of lightly salted water to boiling. Add noodles, 1 at a time, and cook for 10 minutes. Drain and rinse with cool water.

• Place skillet from meatballs over medium heat. Add onion and cook, stirring occasionally, 4 minutes. Add garlic; cook 1 minute. Stir in both crushed and diced tomatoes. Simmer 15 minutes. Remove from heat and stir in half the chopped basil. Set aside ¾ cup of the sauce.

• In a medium bowl, blend ricotta, remaining basil, the egg and 2 tablespoons of the Parmesan.

• Spread 1 cup tomato sauce in bottom of a 13 x 9 x 2-inch baking dish. Top with 4 noodles. Scatter half the meatballs over noodles. Pour half the remaining tomato sauce over meatballs. Top with 4 more noodles and spread with ricotta mixture and 1 cup each mozzarella and Fontina. Add 4 more noodles and remaining meatballs. Pour remaining tomato sauce over meatballs. Top with final 4 noodles. Spread with reserved ¾ cup sauce. Top with remaining 1 cup each mozzarella and Fontina and remaining 2 tablespoons Parmesan.

• Bake at 350° for 45 minutes until bubbly and slightly browned. Let stand 15 to 20 minutes before serving.

PER SERVING 503 CAL; 23 g FAT (11 g SAT); 31 g PRO; 42 g CARB; 3 g FIBER; 845 mg SODIUM; 111 mg CHOL

Gnocchi all'Amatriciana

MAKES 6 servings PREP 10 minutes
COOK 27 minutes BAKE at 350° for 25 minutes

- **4** ounce pancetta, diced
- **1** large onion, diced
- **4** cloves garlic, sliced
- **½** to 1 teaspoon red pepper flakes
- **1** can (28 ounces) crushed tomatoes
- **¼** cup plus 2 tablespoons grated or shredded Pecorino Romano cheese
- **1** teaspoon chopped fresh thyme
- **2** packages (17.5 ounces each) potato gnocchi (such as De Cecco)

• Heat oven to 350°. Bring a large pot of lightly salted water to boiling.

• In a skillet over medium heat, cook pancetta until crispy, about 8 to 10 minutes. Remove pancetta with a slotted spoon. Pour off all but 2 tablespoons of the pancetta fat. Stir onion into same pan and sauté 4 to 5 minutes over medium heat until softened. Add garlic and red pepper flakes; cook 2 minutes. Stir in tomatoes, 2 tablespoon of the cheese, the thyme and cooked pancetta. Bring to a simmer and cook 10 minutes.

• Meanwhile, add gnocchi to lightly salted boiling water. Allow water to return to a boil and cook gnocchi 1 minute. Drain, reserving ½ cup of the pasta water. Return gnocchi to pot. Stir in tomato sauce and reserved pasta water. Transfer to a 13 x 9 x 2-inch baking dish. Sprinkle with remaining ¼ cup cheese and bake at 350° for 20 to 25 minutes, or until cheese has melted and sauce is bubbling.

PER SERVING 460 CAL; 13 g FAT (6 g SAT); 15 g PRO; 72 g CARB; 8 g FIBER; 1,081 mg SODIUM; 24 mg CHOL

Shrimp & Crab al Forno

MAKES 4 servings PREP 15 minutes COOK 9 minutes BAKE at 350° for 30 minutes
BROIL on HIGH for 2 minutes

- **8** ounces (1⅓ cups) orzo
- **2** tablespoons unsalted butter
- **3** shallots, finely diced (about ½ cup)
- **4** cloves garlic, chopped
- **2** tablespoons all-purpose flour
- **2** cups 1% milk
- **1** tablespoon fresh lemon juice
- **1** tablespoon lemon zest
- **1** cup grated Parmesan
- **½** pound peeled and deveined raw shrimp
- **8** ounces lump or claw crabmeat
- **½** cup fresh parsley, chopped
- **½** teaspoon salt
- **⅛** teaspoon ground cayenne

• Heat oven to 350°. Bring a large pot of lightly salted water to boiling. Cook orzo 2 minutes less than package directions, about 8 minutes. Drain.

• Meanwhile, melt butter in a large skillet over medium heat. Add shallots and sauté 2 minutes. Add garlic and cook 1 minute. Stir in flour; cook 2 minutes. Whisk in milk, lemon juice and zest. Bring to a simmer and cook 3 to 4 minutes or until thickened. Stir in ¾ cup of the Parmesan until melted. Turn off heat and stir in cooked orzo, shrimp, crabmeat, parsley, salt and cayenne.

• Pour mixture into an 8 x 8-inch baking dish. Top with remaining ¼ cup Parmesan. Bake at 350° for 25 to 30 minutes, until bubbly. Turn broiler on HIGH and broil 2 minutes, until lightly browned.

PER SERVING 549 CAL; 16 g FAT (8 g SAT); 44 g PRO; 58 g CARB; 3 g FIBER; 903 mg SODIUM; 182 mg CHOL

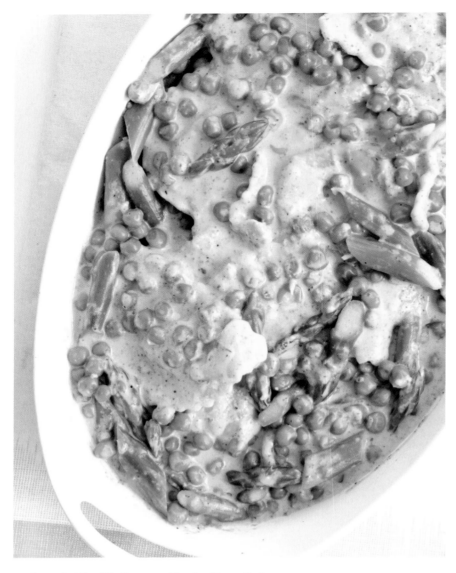

Baked Pumpkin & Sausage Rigatoni

MAKES 8 servings PREP 10 minutes
COOK 11 minutes BAKE at 350° for 20 minutes
BROIL on HIGH for 2 minutes

4	links (12 ounces) uncooked hot Italian sausage, casings removed
1	tablespoon chopped fresh sage
1	can (29 ounces) solid-pack pumpkin
1½	cups 1% milk
4	ounces Neufchâtel cheese, softened
2	egg yolks, beaten
1	cup plus 2 tablespoons grated Asiago cheese
¼	teaspoon nutmeg
¾	teaspoon pumpkin pie spice
½	teaspoon salt
1	pound mezzi rigatoni
⅓	cup panko bread crumbs

• Heat oven to 350°. Bring a large pot of lightly salted water to boiling.

• Add sausage to a large skillet set over medium heat. Cook 8 to 10 minutes or until browned, breaking apart with a wooden spoon. Stir in sage and cook 1 minute. Remove with a slotted spoon; set aside. Pour off and discard drippings.

• In same skillet, whisk pumpkin, milk, Neufchâtel, egg yolks, 1 cup of the Asiago, the nutmeg, pumpkin pie spice and salt. Stir over medium heat until cheeses are melted.

• Meanwhile, cook rigatoni in boiling water 1 minute less than package directions, about 9 minutes. Drain, reserving 1 cup of the pasta water. Return pasta to pot. Stir in sausage, pumpkin mixture and reserved pasta water. Mix well to combine. Transfer to a 13 x 9 x 2-inch dish and top with panko and remaining 2 tablespoons Asiago. Bake at 350° for 20 minutes. Turn broiler on HIGH and broil 1 to 2 minutes or until top is lightly browned.

PER SERVING 453 CAL; 17 g FAT (8 g SAT); 21 g PRO; 55 g CARB; 7 g FIBER; 654 mg SODIUM; 90 mg CHOL

Agnolotti with Creamy Pesto, Peas & Asparagus

MAKES 6 servings PREP 5 minutes COOK 10 minutes BAKE at 350° for 30 minutes

3	tablespoons butter
3	cloves garlic, chopped
3	tablespoons all-purpose flour
3	cups 1% milk
½	cup prepared pesto
½	teaspoon salt
2	packages (9 ounces each) Buitoni Wild Mushroom Agnolotti
1	pound asparagus, trimmed and cut into 1-inch pieces
1	box (10 ounces) frozen peas, thawed

• Heat oven to 350°. Bring a large pot of lightly salted water to boiling.

• In a medium saucepan, melt butter over medium heat. Add garlic and sauté 1 minute. Stir in flour and cook 1 minute more. Whisk in milk, pesto and salt; bring to a simmer and cook 6 to 8 minutes or until thickened.

• Meanwhile, add agnolotti to pot of boiling water and cook 2 minutes. Stir in asparagus and cook another minute. Add thawed peas and cook 1 minute more. Drain agnolotti mixture; return to pot. Stir in pesto sauce and transfer mixture to a 2-quart oven-safe dish. Bake at 350° for 25 to 30 minutes, until bubbling.

PER SERVING 485 CAL; 24 g FAT (11 g SAT); 22 g PRO; 45 g CARB; 6 g FIBER; 935 mg SODIUM; 75 mg CHOL

BAKED PUMPKIN &
SAUSAGE RIGATONI

Beef Stroganoff Casserole

MAKES 6 servings   **PREP** 20 minutes
COOK 21 minutes   **BAKE** at 350° for 20 minutes

- **2** **tablespoons vegetable oil**
- **½** **teaspoon each salt and black pepper**
- **1** **pound sirloin or beef tips, cut into 1-inch pieces**
- **1** **medium onion, diced**
- **1** **package (10 ounces) cremini mushrooms, cleaned, trimmed and sliced**
- **3** **tablespoons all-purpose flour**
- **1** **can (14.5 ounces) beef broth**
- **2** **tablespoons dry sherry (optional)**
- **1** **bag (12 ounces) egg noodles**
- **1** **cup sour cream**
- **⅔** **cup french-fried onions**

• Heat oven to 350°. Bring a large pot of salted water to boiling. Coat a 13 x 9 x 2-inch baking dish with nonstick cooking spray.

• Heat oil in a large skillet over medium-high heat. Season steak with ¼ teaspoon each of the salt and pepper. Add steak to skillet in single layer. Cook 3 to 4 minutes, turning once. Remove to a plate.

• Reduce heat to medium and add onion. Cook 3 minutes. Stir in mushrooms and sauté 5 minutes. Add remaining ¼ teaspoon each salt and pepper. Sprinkle with flour. Cook 1 minute. Whisk in broth. Bring to a simmer and add sherry, if using. Simmer 3 minutes.

• Cook noodles in boiling water for 5 minutes. Drain. Remove sauce from heat and slowly stir in meat and sour cream. Add noodles and spoon into prepared dish. Cover with foil; bake at 350° for 20 minutes. Uncover and top with fried onions.

PER SERVING 522 **CAL**; 21 g **FAT** (8 g **SAT**); 27 g **PRO**; 50 g **CARB**; 2 g **FIBER**; 665 mg **SODIUM**; 120 mg **CHOL**

Pastitsi
MAKES

Stuffed Shells

MAKES 8 servings   **PREP** 25 minutes   **COOK** 17 minutes   **BAKE** at 350° for 40 minutes

- **1** **pound broccoli rabe, tough stems trimmed, roughly chopped**
- **1** **box (12 ounces) jumbo pasta shells**
- **1** **tablespoon olive oil**
- **1** **to 1¼ pounds spicy chicken sausage, casings removed, crumbled (uncooked)**
- **2** **packages (5.3 ounces each) Chavrie goat cheese with basil and roasted garlic**
- **4** **ounces Neufchâtel cheese, softened**
- **2** **egg yolks**
- **1** **jar (24 ounces) cabernet marinara sauce**
- **1** **bag (8 ounces) shredded mozzarella**

• Heat oven to 350°. Bring a large pot of salted water to boiling. Add broccoli rabe and return to a boil. Cook 1 minute, remove with a strainer and let cool. Add pasta to boiling water; cook 10 minutes. Drain.

• Heat oil in a large skillet. Crumble in sausage and cook over medium-high heat until browned, 5 minutes. Meanwhile, squeeze as much water out of broccoli rabe as possible and chop. Add to sausage in skillet and cook 1 minute. Remove to a large bowl with a slotted spoon.

• In a medium bowl, stir together goat cheese, Neufchâtel and egg yolks. Fold into sausage mixture.

• Spread ⅓ cup marinara into bottoms of two 9 x 9-inch or 11 x 7-inch dishes. Spoon about 1 tablespoon filling into each shell; place in a dish. Repeat with all shells and filling.

• Divide remaining sauce between dishes. Sprinkle 1 cup mozzarella over each dish. Cover with foil and bake at 350° for 20 minutes. Uncover; bake 20 minutes more.

PER SERVING 552 **CAL**; 27 g **FAT** (14 g **SAT**); 35 g **PRO**; 44 g **CARB**; 1 g **FIBER**; 982 mg **SODIUM**; 135 mg **CHOL**

¼   cup olive oil
1   medium onion, diced
1   pound ground lamb or beef
4   cloves garlic, chopped
1   cup dry red wine
1   can (14.5 ounces) diced tomatoes
1   can (8 ounces) tomato sauce
1   teaspoon ground cinnamon
¾   teaspoon salt
½   cup fresh mint leaves, chopped
3   teaspoons fresh oregano, chopped
1   pound ziti
3   tablespoons all-purpose flour
3   cups 1% milk
1   cup reduced-fat crumbled feta
     cheese
2   eggs, beaten

• Heat oven to 350°. Bring a large pot of lightly salted water to boiling.

• In a large, straight-sided skillet, heat 1 tablespoon of the oil over medium-high heat. Add onion and cook 3 minutes, until slightly softened. Add lamb and cook 8 to 10 minutes, until meat is browned, breaking it up with a wooden spoon. Stir in garlic and cook 1 minute. Add wine; bring to a simmer and cook 3 minutes, scraping brown bits off the bottom of the skillet. Stir in tomatoes, tomato sauce, cinnamon and ½ teaspoon of the salt. Bring to a simmer and cook 6 minutes, or until sauce has thickened. Stir in mint and oregano; set aside.

• Meanwhile, cook ziti 2 minutes less than package directions in boiling water. Drain and stir into meat sauce.

• Heat remaining 3 tablespoons oil in a medium pot set over medium heat. Add flour; whisk for 1 minute. Whisk in milk; bring to a simmer and cook 5 to 7 minutes, until thickened. Stir in cheese and remaining ¼ teaspoon salt. Remove from heat, cool 1 minute and slowly whisk in eggs.

• To assemble: Transfer meat and noodle mixture to a 13 x 9 x 2-inch oven-safe baking dish. Press noodles with the back of a spatula to make a flat layer. Pour cheese-egg mixture on top. Bake at 350° for 50 to 55 minutes, or until top layer is set.

PER SERVING 582 CAL; 25 g FAT (9 g SAT); 27 g PRO; 56 g CARB; 4 g FIBER; 820 mg SODIUM; 104 mg CHOL

Spaghetti Carbonara Pie

MAKES 6 servings **PREP** 15 minutes
COOK 10 minutes **BAKE** at 375° for 35 minutes

6	slices thick-cut bacon, cut into ½-inch pieces
1	box (1 pound) spaghetti
4	eggs
2	egg yolks
⅔	cup plus 2 tablespoons grated Parmesan
1	cup whole milk
½	cup half-and-half
2	tablespoons chopped parsley
½	teaspoon salt
¼	teaspoon pepper

• Heat oven to 375°. Coat a 2-quart baking dish with nonstick cooking spray. Bring a large pot of lightly salted water to boiling.

• Cook bacon in a nonstick skillet over medium heat until just crisp, 10 minutes. Drain on a paper towel-lined plate.

• Meanwhile, cook spaghetti 9 minutes in boiling water. Drain and return to pot.

• In a large bowl, whisk together eggs and yolks. Add ⅔ cup of the cheese, the milk, half-and-half, parsley, salt and pepper. Toss sauce with pasta in pot along with bacon. Transfer to prepared dish and top with remaining 2 tablespoons Parmesan.

• Bake at 375° for 35 minutes. Cool 10 minutes, then cut into wedges.

PER SERVING 504 **CAL**; 17 g **FAT** (8 g **SAT**); 24 g **PRO**; 60 g **CARB**; 3 g **FIBER**; 683 mg **SODIUM**; 243 mg **CHOL**

Mac & Cheese with Cauliflower

MAKES 6 servings **PREP** 30 minutes **COOK** 13 minutes **BAKE** at 375° for 25 minutes, then at 350° for 20 minutes

1	head (1½ pounds) cauliflower, trimmed and cut into florets (4 cups)
2	tablespoons olive oil
1¼	teaspoons salt
¼	teaspoon garlic powder
⅛	teaspoon black pepper
1	slice white bread
3	tablespoons unsalted butter
1	box (16 ounces) pasta blend or your favorite shape
2	tablespoons all-purpose flour
2	cups 2% milk
¼	teaspoon smoked paprika
8	ounces Gouda, shredded

• Heat oven to 375°. Toss cauliflower, oil, ¼ teaspoon of the salt, ⅛ teaspoon of the garlic powder and the pepper in a large bowl. Spread onto a baking sheet; bake at 375° for 25 minutes. Reduce heat to 350°.

• Bring a large pot of salted water to boiling.

• Pulse bread in a chopper until crumbs are formed. Melt 1 tablespoon of the butter in a small skillet. Add bread crumbs; cook over medium-high heat, 2 to 3 minutes.

• Add pasta to boiling water. Cook 10 minutes. Drain and return to pot. Meanwhile, make sauce: Melt remaining 2 tablespoons butter in saucepan over medium heat. Add flour and whisk for 2 minutes. Whisk in milk, remaining 1 teaspoon salt, the smoked paprika and remaining ⅛ teaspoon garlic powder and bring to a simmer. Cook 3 minutes, whisking occasionally. Remove from heat and whisk in Gouda.

• Stir cauliflower and sauce into pasta. Spoon into a 13 x 9 x 2-inch dish. Top with bread crumbs. Bake at 350° for 20 minutes.

PER SERVING 588 **CAL**; 24 g **FAT** (12 g **SAT**); 25 g **PRO**; 70 g **CARB**; 5 g **FIBER**; 707 mg **SODIUM**; 65 mg **CHOL**

A+ SNACKS

6 healthy recipes to fuel your kids without spoiling their appetites.

PB&J BITES

Layered Hummus Dip

MAKES 34 servings (¼ cup each) **PREP** 15 minutes

1	**box (8 ounces) 5-minute tabbouleh**
2	**tablespoons extra virgin olive oil**
1	**cup diced cucumber**
2	**medium tomatoes, seeded and diced**
2	**teaspoons fresh lemon juice**
½	**teaspoon salt**
¼	**cup fresh parsley, chopped**
1	**container (17 ounces) plain hummus**
6	**ounces crumbled feta cheese**
	Whole wheat pitas, sliced cucumbers or carrots for dipping (optional)

• Bring 1¼ cups water to a boil. Pour over tabbouleh in a bowl; cover with plastic wrap for 5 minutes. Uncover and add oil, cucumber, tomatoes, lemon juice, salt and parsley; gently fluff with a fork, incorporating all ingredients.

• Spread hummus into the bottom of a 13 x 9 x 2-inch dish. Scatter 1 cup of the feta on top. Layer with tabbouleh mixture. Sprinkle remaining ½ cup feta on top.

PER SERVING 78 **CAL**; 6 g **FAT** (1 g **SAT**); 3 g **PRO**; 6 g **CARB**; 1 g **FIBER**; 201 mg **SODIUM**; 4 mg **CHOL**

PB&J Bites

MAKES 24 servings **PREP** 20 minutes **BAKE** at 350° for 30 minutes

1	**cup chunky natural peanut butter**
⅓	**cup pure maple syrup**
4	**cups old-fashioned oats**
½	**cup unsalted sunflower seeds**
½	**cup quinoa**
1	**jar (12 ounces) strawberry preserves**

• Mix peanut butter, maple syrup and ⅓ cup water in a saucepan over medium-low heat. Stir until peanut butter is melted and ingredients are combined.

• In a large bowl, mix together oats, sunflower seeds and quinoa. Stir in peanut butter mixture until well combined.

• Line two 12-cup muffin tins with paper wrappers. Scoop 2 tablespoons of the peanut butter-oats mixture into each wrapper, pressing down well with a spatula. Spread 2 teaspoons of the preserves over peanut butter-oats mixture in each cup. Add 2 more tablespoons peanut butter–oats mixture to cover preserves, pressing down well with a spatula.

• Bake at 350° for 25 to 30 minutes, until bites begin to brown. Cool in muffin tins 10 minutes; remove from tins to a wire rack and cool to room temperature. Store in an airtight container.

PER SERVING 193 **CAL**; 8 g **FAT** (1 g **SAT**); 5 g **PRO**; 27 g **CARB**; 2 g **FIBER**; 42 mg **SODIUM**; 0 mg **CHOL**

Rockin' Moroccan Snack Mix

MAKES 5 cups **PREP** 10 minutes
BAKE at 350° for 1 hour, 5 minutes

2	cans (15.5 ounces each) chickpeas, drained and rinsed
2	tablespoons packed brown sugar
1	teaspoon ground cumin
1	teaspoon cinnamon
1	teaspoon sweet paprika
1	teaspoon ground coriander
¾	teaspoon salt
½	teaspoon ground ginger
½	teaspoon ground allspice
⅛	teaspoon ground cayenne (optional)
2	tablespoons olive oil
1	cup whole unsalted almonds
¼	cup sesame seeds
1½	cups dried apricots, chopped
1	cup pitted dates, chopped

• Heat oven to 350°. Dry chickpeas in a single layer between paper towels.

• In a bowl, combine brown sugar, cumin, cinnamon, paprika, coriander, salt, ginger, allspice and, if using, cayenne. Toss chickpeas with half the spice mix and 1 tablespoon of the oil. Arrange on a sided baking sheet in a single layer and bake at 350° for 45 minutes.

• Toss almonds and sesame seeds with remaining spice mix and 1 tablespoon oil; mix into chickpeas on baking sheet. Bake another 20 minutes, or until chickpeas are slightly crispy and almonds are toasted. Cool slightly and toss with apricots and dates. Store in an airtight container.

PER ¼ CUP 189 **CAL**; 7 g **FAT** (1 g **SAT**); 6 g **PRO**; 27 g **CARB**; 6 g **FIBER**; 91 mg **SODIUM**; 0 mg **CHOL**

Almond-Avocado Pudding

MAKES 6 servings **PREP** 5 minutes

2	ripe avocados
¾	cup unsweetened vanilla almond milk
¼	cup honey
¼	cup sliced almonds, toasted

• Combine avocados, almond milk and honey in a blender. Puree until smooth. Spoon into 6 individual dessert bowls or glasses, and top with toasted almonds.

PER SERVING 178 **CAL**; 12 g **FAT** (2 g **SAT**); 2 g **PRO**; 18 g **CARB**; 5 g **FIBER**; 28 mg **SODIUM**; 0 mg **CHOL**

Parmesan Kale Chips

MAKES 4 servings (1 cup each) **PREP** 5 minutes
BAKE at 300° for 25 minutes

1	box (5 ounces) mixed baby kales or 10 cups kale leaves, tough stems removed, torn into small pieces
1	tablespoon olive oil
⅛	teaspoon salt
2	tablespoons grated Parmesan

• Heat oven to 300°. In a large bowl, toss kale with oil and salt. Transfer to 2 baking sheets in a single layer.

• Bake at 300° on the middle rack for 25 minutes or until kale is crispy. Gently remove chips from baking sheets with a metal spatula; toss with cheese. Store in an airtight container.

PER SERVING 58 **CAL**; 4 g **FAT** (1 g **SAT**); 2 g **PRO**; 4 g **CARB**; 1 g **FIBER**; 126 mg **SODIUM**; 2 mg **CHOL**

Peachy Keen Pops

MAKES 10 pops **PREP** 15 minutes
FREEZE 6 hours or overnight

1	envelope (0.25 ounce) unflavored gelatin
¼	cup peach juice
2	tablespoons agave nectar
1	bag (10 ounces) frozen peaches, thawed, or 2 cups peeled and sliced fresh peaches
4	containers (6 ounces each) low-fat peach yogurt
1	ice pop mold (10-pop capacity)
10	wooden Popsicle sticks

• Stir together gelatin and peach juice in a microwave-safe bowl. Microwave 1 minute on HIGH. Stir in agave and set aside for 5 minutes.

• Meanwhile, combine peaches and yogurt in the base of a blender. Puree until smooth. With blender running, add gelatin mixture in a thin stream.

• Pour mixture into ice pop molds, place sticks carefully into center and freeze 6 hours or overnight.

PER POP 79 **CAL**; 1 g **FAT** (1 g **SAT**); 4 g **PRO**; 14 g **CARB**; 0 g **FIBER**; 47 mg **SODIUM**; 5 mg **CHOL**

RISE & DINE

Jump-start your mornings with healthy breakfasts that cook while you sleep.

HONEY-BLUEBERRY
8-GRAIN HOT CEREAL

Set up the slow cooker before you tuck in for the night and wake up to a warm and satisfying start to your day.

Honey-Blueberry 8-Grain Hot Cereal

MAKES 8 servings **PREP** 10 minutes
SLOW COOK on LOW for 9 hours
COOK 5 minutes

- 4 **cups skim milk blended with 3 cups water**
- 2 **cups 8-grain hot cereal blend (such as Bob's Red Mill)**
- 2 **cups blueberries**
- 1 **teaspoon ground ginger**
- 1 **teaspoon salt**
- ½ **cup walnuts**
- ½ **cup honey**
- 8 **thin slices unsalted butter (about 2 tablespoon total)**

• Coat slow cooker bowl with nonstick cooking spray. Combine milk and water with cereal in prepared slow cooker bowl. Stir in ½ cup of the blueberries, the ginger and ¾ teaspoon of the salt. Cover and slow cook on LOW for 9 hours.

• In the morning, toast walnuts in a skillet over medium heat, 5 minutes. Stir remaining 1½ cups blueberries, remaining ¼ teaspoon salt and the honey into cereal mixture.

• Spoon half of the cereal into bowls; top each serving with a thin slice of butter and some of the walnuts. Serve warm; save remainder for another day.

PER SERVING 323 **CAL**; 11 g **FAT** (4 g **SAT**); 10 g **PRO**; 50 g **CARB**; 4 g **FIBER**; 276 mg **SODIUM**; 14 mg **CHOL**

Potato & Turkey Bacon Quiche

MAKES 6 servings **PREP** 15 minutes **COOK** 9 minutes **SLOW COOK** on LOW for 6 hours

- 1 **package (6 ounces) turkey bacon, diced**
- 1 **package (15 ounces) Alexia Oven Reds olive oil, Parmesan and garlic frozen potato wedges, cut into bite-size pieces**
- 1 **sweet red pepper, cored and diced**
- ½ **Vidalia onion, chopped**
- 6 **ounces (1½ cups) 50% reduced-fat cheddar cheese, shredded**
- 6 **large eggs**
- 1½ **cups skim milk**
- 2 **tablespoons minced chives, plus more for garnish**
- ¼ **teaspoon salt**
- ½ **teaspoon black pepper**
- 1 **cup Bisquick Heart Smart**

• Coat programmable slow cooker insert with nonstick cooking spray. Cook turkey bacon in a nonstick skillet over medium heat until just crisp, 9 minutes.

• In a large bowl, toss together potato wedges, turkey bacon, red pepper, onion and 1 cup of the cheese. In a medium bowl, whisk eggs, milk, chives, salt and pepper. Whisk in Bisquick.

• Pour potato mixture into slow cooker. Add egg mixture and top with remaining cheese. Cover and slow cook on LOW for 5½ to 6 hours (machine will switch to WARM after cooking). Cut into wedges and serve.

PER SERVING 296 **CAL**; 13 g **FAT** (4 g **SAT**); 19 g **PRO**; 28 g **CARB**; 2 g **FIBER**; 783 mg **SODIUM**; 189 mg **CHOL**

Oats and other whole grains are a natural for the slow cooker because they just get creamier as they cook.

Oatmeal-Banana Maple Parfaits

MAKES 6 servings **PREP** 15 minutes
SLOW COOK on LOW for 8 hours

½	**cup half-and-half**
1½	**cups steel-cut oats**
¾	**teaspoon salt**
7	**tablespoons maple syrup, plus more for drizzling**
1	**cup part-skim ricotta cheese**
2	**ripe bananas**
⅛	**teaspoon pumpkin pie spice**

• Pour 3 cups water into slow cooker insert. Place a slow cooker liner into slow cooker (on top of water). Combine half-and-half, 5½ cups water, the oats and salt into slow cooker liner.

• Cover and slow cook on LOW for 8 hours. Uncover and stir in 6 tablespoons of the maple syrup. Blend ricotta and remaining 1 tablespoon maple syrup.

• Begin layering: Spoon ½ cup oatmeal into 6 cups or bowls. Top each with a heaping tablespoon ricotta mixture. Peel and slice bananas. Spread about 4 banana slices onto each serving. Repeat layering with oatmeal, ricotta and banana slices. Drizzle each serving with a little maple syrup and sprinkle with pumpkin pie spice.

PER SERVING 320 **CAL**; 8 g **FAT** (4 g **SAT**); 12 g **PRO**; 54 g **CARB**; 5 g **FIBER**; 355 mg **SODIUM**; 23 mg **CHOL**

Apple-Cinnamon Wheat Berries

MAKES 6 servings **PREP** 15 minutes **SLOW COOK** on LOW for 9 hours

4	**cups unsweetened vanilla almond milk**
1½	**cups wheat berries**
1	**cup apple juice or water**
3	**Idared, Braeburn or Gala apples, peeled, cored and cut into 1-inch pieces**
⅓	**cup old-fashioned oats**
1	**teaspoon ground cinnamon**
¼	**teaspoon salt**
½	**cup packed dark brown sugar**
¼	**cup sliced almonds**
6	**tablespoons sweetened dried cranberries**

• Coat a 4- to 5½-quart slow cooker insert with nonstick cooking spray. Combine almond milk, wheat berries, juice, apples, oats, cinnamon and salt in prepared slow cooker.

• Cover and slow cook on LOW for 9 hours. Uncover and stir in brown sugar. Spoon into bowls and top with sliced almonds and cranberries. Serve warm.

PER SERVING 384 **CAL**; 6 g **FAT** (0 g **SAT**); 10 g **PRO**; 76 g **CARB**; 8 g **FIBER**; 233 mg **SODIUM**; 0 mg **CHOL**

OATMEAL-BANANA
MAPLE PARFAITS

POLENTA PIZZA,
PAGE 252

OCTOBER

260

265

269

SEASONAL SUPPERS

Easy ways to turn vitamin-packed veggies into healthy, delicious meals.

BLT PASTA,
PAGE 255

SESAME
CHICKEN
STIR-FRY,
PAGE 255

SQUASH & LENTIL STEW

Fall vegetables such as butternut squash, cabbage and cauliflower are hearty enough to be the main ingredient in many recipes.

Squash & Lentil Stew

MAKES 6 servings **PREP** 20 minutes
COOK 56 minutes

- 3   tablespoons olive oil
- 3   carrots, peeled and diced
- 2   ribs celery, trimmed and diced
- 1   medium onion, diced
- 1   medium butternut squash (about 2¾ pounds), peeled, seeded and diced (5½ cups)
- 2   tablespoons chili powder
- ½   teaspoon ground cumin
- 1   can (14.5 ounces) light and fat-free chicken broth or low-sodium vegetable broth
- 1   can (14.5 ounces) diced tomatoes in juice
- 1½   cups small brown or French green lentils, picked through
- ¾   teaspoon salt
- ⅓   cup cilantro leaves, chopped

• Heat oil in a large stockpot or Dutch oven over medium heat. Add carrots, celery and onion and cook 5 minutes. Add squash and season with chili powder and ground cumin. Cook 1 minute.

• Stir in broth, tomatoes, ½ cup water and lentils. Cover and simmer on medium-low heat for 40 minutes, stirring occasionally. Uncover and stir in salt. Simmer, uncovered, an additional 10 minutes. Stir in cilantro and serve.

PER SERVING 361 **CAL**; 8 g **FAT** (1 g **SAT**); 17 g **PRO**; 62 g **CARB**; 20 g **FIBER**; 795 mg **SODIUM**; 0 mg **CHOL**

MOO SHU PORK

Moo Shu Pork

MAKES 6 servings **PREP** 15 minutes **COOK** 14 minutes **MICROWAVE** 2 minutes

- 1   pound boneless pork chops, cut into thin strips
- 2   tablespoons low-sodium soy sauce
- 2   tablespoons vegetable oil
- 1   small head cabbage, cored and shredded (8 cups)
- 1   bag (8 ounces) shredded carrots
- 4   scallions, sliced
- ⅓   cup plus 2 tablespoons hoisin sauce
- 12   white whole wheat traditional tortillas

• Toss pork strips with 1 tablespoon of the soy sauce. Heat oil in a lidded 12-inch skillet over medium-high heat. Add pork and cook 3 to 4 minutes, until no longer pink. Remove to a bowl with a slotted spoon.

• Add cabbage, carrots and half the scallions to skillet. Cover and cook 3 minutes. Uncover and cook 5 minutes.

• Add pork back to skillet along with remaining 1 tablespoon soy sauce and ⅓ cup of the hoisin. Cook 2 minutes.

• Meanwhile, wrap tortillas in damp paper towels and microwave 2 minutes. Spread each with ½ teaspoon hoisin. Spoon moo shu mixture onto wraps and sprinkle with some of the remaining sliced scallions.

PER SERVING 333 **CAL**; 13 g **FAT** (2 g **SAT**); 25 g **PRO**; 37 g **CARB**; 16 g **FIBER**; 800 mg **SODIUM**; 42 mg **CHOL**

No one will miss the meat in these satisfying vegetarian dishes based on veggies, grains, tofu and cheese.

Veggie Paella

MAKES 6 servings   PREP 20 minutes
DRAIN overnight   COOK 25 minutes
BAKE at 400° for 20 minutes

1	package (14 ounces) extra-firm tofu, drained
4	tablespoons olive oil
¼	plus ⅛ teaspoon seasoned salt
1	head cauliflower, trimmed, cored and cut into florets
1	green pepper, cored and diced
1	medium onion, chopped
1	package (10 ounces) yellow rice (such as Vigo)
3	plum tomatoes, seeded and diced
1	cup frozen peas, thawed

• Cut tofu into ¾-inch cubes. Spread between layers of paper towels on a plate. Drain in refrigerator overnight.

• Heat oven to 400°. Toss tofu cubes with 1 tablespoon of the oil and ¼ teaspoon of the seasoned salt. Spread onto a foil-lined sheet and bake at 400° for 20 minutes.

• Meanwhile, heat remaining oil in a large, lidded skillet over medium heat. Add cauliflower, pepper and onion; sauté for 5 minutes. Sprinkle with remaining ⅛ teaspoon seasoned salt.

• Stir in rice mix, tomatoes and 2¼ cups water. Bring to a simmer. Cover and reduce heat to medium-low. Cook 18 to 20 minutes. Uncover and gently stir in baked tofu and peas. Heat through.

PER SERVING 380 CAL; 13 g FAT (2 g SAT); 16 g PRO; 53 g CARB; 6 g FIBER; 792 mg SODIUM; 0 mg CHOL

Polenta Pizza

MAKES 6 servings   PREP 15 minutes   COOK 12 minutes   BAKE at 425° for 15 minutes

2	cups plus 1 tablespoon instant polenta
1½	teaspoons salt
½	teaspoon garlic powder
6	tablespoons grated Parmesan
3	tablespoons olive oil
4	cloves garlic, sliced
1	bunch broccoli rabe (about 1 pound), tough stems removed, cut into 1-inch pieces, or broccoli florets
1	container (15 ounces) part-skim ricotta cheese

• Heat oven to 425°. Coat a 14-inch pizza pan with nonstick cooking spray. Dust with 1 tablespoon of the polenta.

• Bring 6 cups water to boiling. Add 1¼ teaspoons of the salt and the garlic powder. Slowly add polenta in a thin stream, whisking constantly. Reduce heat to medium and cook, stirring frequently, 5 minutes.

• Remove from heat and stir in 3 tablespoons of the Parmesan. Spread onto prepared pizza pan. Set aside.

• Heat oil in a large, lidded skillet over medium heat. Add garlic and cook 1 minute. Add broccoli rabe and ¼ cup water. Cover and cook 3 minutes. Uncover, increase heat to medium-high and cook an additional 3 minutes until just tender.

• Spread ricotta over polenta, leaving a 1-inch border. Scatter broccoli rabe and garlic over ricotta. Top with remaining 3 tablespoons Parmesan.

• Bake at 425° for 15 minutes until cheese is melted. Season with remaining ¼ teaspoon salt; cut into wedges and serve.

PER SERVING 407 CAL; 14 g FAT (5 g SAT); 17 g PRO; 52 g CARB; 2 g FIBER; 769 mg SODIUM; 26 mg CHOL

VEGGIE PAELLA

BLT PASTA

BLT Pasta

MAKES 6 servings PREP 15 minutes
COOK 22 minutes

- 8 ounces center-cut bacon (12 or 13 slices), diced
- 1 box (1 pound) penne pasta
- 4 tablespoons olive oil
- 1 medium onion, diced
- 1 bunch spinach (1 pound), trimmed, roughly chopped
- 1 bunch red chard, well cleaned, tough stems discarded, sliced
- 2 cups cherry tomatoes, halved
- ⅓ cup fresh basil, torn
- 3 tablespoons white balsamic vinegar
- ½ teaspoon each salt and pepper

• Bring a large pot of lightly salted water to boiling.

• Cook bacon in a large skillet for 10 minutes over medium heat until just crispy. Remove to a paper towel-lined plate. Reserve 2 tablespoons of the drippings in skillet.

• Meanwhile, cook penne in boiling water for 11 minutes. Drain.

• Add 2 tablespoons of the olive oil to skillet with bacon drippings. Return to medium heat. Add onion and cook 5 minutes. Add spinach and chard and cook 4 minutes until wilted. Stir in cherry tomatoes; cook 2 minutes.

• In a large bowl, toss penne, bacon, spinach mixture, basil, remaining 2 tablespoons olive oil, the vinegar, salt and pepper.

PER SERVING 477 CAL; 18 g FAT (4 g SAT); 17 g PRO; 60 g CARB; 4 g FIBER; 519 mg SODIUM; 15 mg CHOL

Sesame Chicken Stir-Fry

MAKES 6 servings PREP 20 minutes COOK 8 minutes

- 3 tablespoons vegetable oil
- 1½ pounds boneless, skinless chicken breasts, cut into thin strips
- ¾ teaspoon salt
- ½ teaspoon black pepper
- 1 head bok choy (about 2 pounds), trimmed and roughly chopped
- 1 sweet red pepper, cored and sliced
- 3 ribs celery, trimmed and sliced
- 1 cup low-sodium chicken broth
- 2 tablespoons low-sodium soy sauce
- 1 tablespoon cornstarch
- 2 teaspoons sugar
- ¼ teaspoon hot sauce
- 2 teaspoons sesame oil
- 2 teaspoons black or white sesame seeds
- 4 cups cooked brown rice

• Heat 2 tablespoons of the oil in a large skillet or wok. Season chicken with ¼ teaspoon each of the salt and pepper. Add chicken to skillet and stir-fry 3 minutes. Remove to a bowl with a slotted spoon.

• Add remaining tablespoon oil to skillet. Stir in bok choy, red pepper and celery. Stir-fry 4 minutes, seasoning with remaining ½ teaspoon salt and ¼ teaspoon pepper.

• Meanwhile, mix chicken broth, soy sauce, cornstarch, sugar and hot sauce in a small bowl. Stir into skillet. Cook 1 minute and stir in sesame oil and sesame seeds. Serve with rice.

PER SERVING 392 CAL; 12 g FAT (1 g SAT); 33 g PRO; 38 g CARB; 5 g FIBER; 781 mg SODIUM; 67 mg CHOL

HAPPY HAUNTING

Scare up some crowd-pleasing fun with ghoulishly good eats and treats.

RED DEVILED EGGS,
PAGE 260

Beeting Heart Skewers

MAKES 12 servings **PREP** 25 minutes

- 8 ounces fresh goat cheese, at room temperature
- 2 teaspoons finely chopped fresh rosemary
- ¼ teaspoon freshly cracked pepper
- 1 package (8 ounces) Melissa's peeled and steamed baby beets
- 1 can (14 ounces) whole hearts of palm
- 36 4-inch skewers
  Arugula (optional)

• Mix together goat cheese, rosemary and pepper. Roll into thirty-six ¾-inch balls. Slice both beets and hearts of palm into 36 pieces.

• Place 1 goat cheese ball, 1 piece of beet and 1 piece of hearts of palm on each skewer. If desired, arrange skewers on a bed of arugula.

PER SKEWER 23 CAL; 1 g FAT (1 g SAT); 2 g PRO; 1 g CARB; 0 g FIBER; 75 mg SODIUM; 3 mg CHOL

BAD-TO-THE-BONE RIBS

Bad-to-the-Bone Ribs

MAKES 8 servings **PREP** 10 minutes
REFRIGERATE overnight **BAKE** at 300°/400° for
3 hours, 45 minutes

2	**racks (5 to 6 pounds total) pork back ribs**
3	**tablespoons sweet paprika**
1	**tablespoon plus 1 teaspoon onion powder**
1½	**teaspoons salt**
¼	**teaspoon pepper**
1	**tablespoon unsalted butter**
1	**head garlic, cloves removed, peeled and minced**
1¼	**cups ketchup**
¼	**cup honey**
2	**tablespoons molasses**
2	**tablespoons Worcestershire sauce**
1	**tablespoon cider vinegar**
1	**tablespoon Dijon mustard**

• Pat ribs dry with paper towels. Combine paprika, 1 tablespoon of the onion powder, the salt and pepper in a small bowl. Rub onto both sides of ribs. Place meaty side up on a baking sheet fitted with a wire rack. Cover tightly with aluminum foil and refrigerate overnight.

• Heat oven to 300°. Transfer foil-wrapped ribs directly to oven and bake at 300° for 3 to 3½ hours or until fork-tender.

• Meanwhile, melt butter in a small pot over medium-low heat. Add garlic and cook 2 minutes or until softened. Stir in ketchup, honey, molasses, Worcestershire, vinegar, mustard and remaining 1 teaspoon onion powder. Simmer 15 minutes until sauce thickens. Cover and set aside (see Note).

• Remove ribs from oven. Increase temperature to 400°. Remove foil and brush ribs with 1 cup of the sauce. Return to oven, uncovered, and bake at 400° for 10 to 15 minutes until sauce is bubbly.

• Slice ribs and serve with remaining sauce alongside.

Note: Sauce can be made a day ahead and refrigerated. Yield is approximately 1⅔ cups.

PER RIB 272 **CAL**; 20 g **FAT** (8 g **SAT**); 14 g **PRO**; 8 g **CARB**; 0 g **FIBER**; 343 mg **SODIUM**; 69 mg **CHOL**

Black-as-Night Rice Salad

MAKES 14 servings **PREP** 15 minutes **COOK** 50 minutes **LET STAND** 10 minutes **COOL** 5 minutes

1	**bag (16 ounces) Lundberg Black Japonica rice**
1	**can (13.5 ounces) light coconut milk**
3⅓	**cups low-sodium chicken broth**
3	**mangoes, peeled, pitted and diced (about 4 cups)**
1	**cup unsweetened flaked coconut, toasted**
⅔	**cup sliced scallions**
½	**cup unsalted dry-roasted peanuts, roughly chopped**
2¼	**teaspoons salt**
¼	**teaspoon pepper**

• In a large, lidded pot combine rice, coconut milk and chicken broth. Cover and bring to a boil. Reduce heat to low and cook 50 minutes or until tender. Let stand 10 minutes covered.

• Transfer cooked rice to a bowl; cool 5 minutes. Stir in mangoes, coconut, scallions, peanuts, salt and pepper. Serve warm or at room temperature.

PER SERVING 230 **CAL**; 10 g **FAT** (5 g **SAT**); 6 g **PRO**; 34 g **CARB**; 4 g **FIBER**; 441 mg **SODIUM**; 0 mg **CHOL**

MAPLE-NUT-PUMPKIN
CANDIES

Red Deviled Eggs

MAKES 12 servings **PREP** 15 minutes
COOK 10 minutes

- **12** **eggs**
- **1** **cup (4 ounces) diced cured chorizo, casing removed**
- **1** **tablespoon tomato paste**
- **2** **teaspoons Dijon mustard**
- **¼** **cup sour cream**
- **¼** **cup light mayonnaise**
- **¼** **teaspoon plus ⅛ teaspoon ground cayenne pepper**
- **¼** **teaspoon salt**
  Smoked or sweet paprika, for garnish

- Place eggs in a lidded pot and cover with 1 inch of cold water; cover. Bring to a boil. Turn off heat and let stand 10 minutes. Remove to a bowl filled with ice water; cool completely.

- Meanwhile, cook diced chorizo in a skillet over medium heat for 7 minutes, until barely crisp. Set aside to cool slightly.

- Peel eggs; discard shells. Halve eggs lengthwise. Remove yolks to a bowl. Place whites cut-side up on a large platter.

- Using the back of fork, break up yolks in bowl. Transfer cooked chorizo and any of its fat to bowl, along with tomato paste, mustard, sour cream, mayonnaise, cayenne and salt. Mix until smooth.

- Spoon some of the yolk mixture into each egg white half. Garnish with a pinch of paprika.

PER DEVILED EGG 147 **CAL**; 11 g **FAT** (4 g **SAT**); 9 g **PRO**; 1 g **CARB**; 0 g **FIBER**; 358 mg **SODIUM**; 225 mg **CHOL**

Maple-Nut-Pumpkin Candies

MAKES 36 servings **PREP** 10 minutes **COOK** 12 minutes **COOL** 1 hour **REFRIGERATE** 1 hour

- **1** **cup light brown sugar, packed**
- **1** **cup granulated sugar**
- **¼** **cup maple syrup**
- **¼** **cup unsalted butter**
- **½** **cup solid-pack pumpkin**
- **½** **cup heavy cream**
- **1** **teaspoon pumpkin pie spice**
- **¼** **teaspoon salt**
- **1** **cup walnuts, toasted and chopped**

- Line an 8 x 8-inch metal baking pan with parchment paper. Spray paper with nonstick cooking spray.

- In a medium pot, combine sugars, maple syrup, butter, pumpkin, cream, pumpkin pie spice and salt over medium heat. Stir until butter is melted and all ingredients are combined. Bring to a simmer and cook 10 to 12 minutes or until temperature reaches 238° on a candy thermometer. Stir in walnuts.

- Pour mixture into lined baking pan. Cool 1 hour on the counter, then refrigerate an additional 1 hour. Slice into 36 squares.

PER PIECE 92 **CAL**; 4 g **FAT** (2 g **SAT**); 1 g **PRO**; 14 g **CARB**; 0 g **FIBER**; 20 mg **SODIUM**; 8 mg **CHOL**

• Rest a frozen cookie sandwich on a 2-pronged barbecue fork and dip it into chocolate; flip to coat well on both sides. Remove, again resting cookie sandwich on fork, tapping utensil lightly on side of bowl to remove excess chocolate. Repeat with each sandwich. Transfer cookies to parchment paper. Let stand 1 hour or until chocolate sets.

PER COOKIE SANDWICH 338 CAL; 19 g FAT (10 g SAT); 4 g PRO; 39 g CARB; 2 g FIBER; 32 mg SODIUM; 31 mg CHOL

Witches' Brew

MAKES 6 servings PREP 5 minutes

3 bottles (12 ounces each) chilled white beer (such as Blue Moon)
8 ounces PAMA pomegranate liqueur
1½ cups pomegranate juice (such as POM Wonderful)
  Pomegranate seeds (optional)

• Stir together beer, liqueur and juice in a pitcher. Serve in a glass over ice. Garnish with pomegranate seeds, if desired.

PER SERVING 214 CAL; 0 g FAT (0 g SAT); 2 g PRO; 27 g CARB; 0 g FIBER; 11 mg SODIUM; 0 mg CHOL

Howl-at-the-Moon Pies

MAKES 24 cookie sandwiches PREP 45 minutes
REFRIGERATE 40 minutes BAKE at 350° for 14 minutes FREEZE 30 minutes
LET STAND 1 hour

2 sticks unsalted butter, at room temperature
¾ cup light brown sugar, packed
1 egg
½ teaspoon vanilla extract
2½ cups all-purpose flour, plus more for rolling
½ teaspoon baking powder
¼ teaspoon salt
1 cup marshmallow creme
1 cup Jif Mocha Cappuccino or Chocolate Spread
20 ounces semisweet chocolate, chopped
1 tablespoon vegetable oil

• Heat oven to 350°. In the bowl of a stand mixer fitted with the paddle attachment, beat butter on medium-high until creamy, about 3 minutes. Add sugar and beat another 3 minutes on medium-high until mixture is fluffy. Add egg and vanilla; beat on medium until combined. Add flour, baking powder and salt; mix on low until just combined.

• Form dough into 2 disks. Wrap in 2 separate pieces of plastic wrap. Refrigerate 30 minutes.

• Sprinkle a large piece of parchment paper with flour. Roll out 1 disk until ⅛ inch thick. Using a 2½-inch round cookie cutter, cut out 24 cookies. Place rounds on baking sheets about 1 inch apart. Repeat with second disk for a total of 48 cookies. Refrigerate dough for 10 minutes.

• Bake cookies at 350° for 12 to 14 minutes or until lightly golden. Allow cookies to cool on baking sheet for 1 minute, then transfer to a wire rack to cool completely. (Baking might take 2 batches.)

• On 24 of the cookies, dollop 2 teaspoons of the marshmallow creme. On remaining 24 cookies, dollop 2 teaspoons of the Jif spread. Make 24 sandwich cookies using 1 marshmallow cookie and 1 Jif cookie. Freeze cookie sandwiches 30 minutes.

• Meanwhile, fill a small pot with 1 inch of water. Bring to a low simmer. Combine chocolate and oil in a metal bowl large enough to rest on top of pot. Stir until chocolate is melted.

ONE-POT WONDERS

Great taste, minimal mess—you have enough on your plate without worrying about dinner.

One-dish meals are easy on the cook in many ways. There's not much to clean up—and you know you're serving a nutritionally balanced meal.

Skillet Chicken, Chorizo & Rice

MAKES 4 servings PREP 15 minutes
COOK 10 minutes BAKE at 400° for 20 minutes

1	tablespoon vegetable oil
4	bone-in chicken thighs (about 6 ounces each)
¼	teaspoon salt
⅛	teaspoon black pepper
1	large onion, sliced
½	fennel bulb, sliced
4	ounces chorizo, chopped
3	cups cooked white rice
1	cup reduced-sodium chicken broth
1	can (15 ounces) pigeon peas (such as Goya), drained
	Chopped cilantro (optional)

• Heat oven to 400°. Heat oil in a large cast-iron skillet over medium-high heat. Season chicken with salt and pepper. Cook chicken, skin side down, for 3 minutes; turn and cook for 2 minutes. Remove chicken to a plate.

• Add onion, fennel and chorizo to skillet; cook for 5 minutes. Stir in rice, broth and pigeon peas. Arrange chicken thighs, skin side up, on top of rice mixture. Roast at 400° for 20 minutes or until chicken reaches 165°.

• To serve, garnish with chopped cilantro, if desired.

PER SERVING 561 CAL; 24 g FAT (7 g SAT); 35 g PRO; 50 g CARB; 7 g FIBER; 739 mg SODIUM; 100 mg CHOL

Sirloin & Cremini Teriyaki

MAKES 4 servings PREP 15 minutes SOAK 10 minutes COOK 14 minutes

7	ounces stir-fry rice noodles (such as Thai Kitchen, from a 14-ounce package)
2	tablespoons vegetable oil
2	pounds boneless beef sirloin, cut against the grain into ¼-inch slices
¼	teaspoon salt
2	red onions, sliced
2	sweet peppers, cored, seeded and sliced
8	ounces cremini mushrooms, sliced
2	cloves garlic, sliced
1	tablespoon cornstarch
1	cup reduced-sodium beef broth
¼	cup sesame teriyaki sauce (such as Soy Vay)
2	tablespoons rice vinegar

• Place noodles in a bowl. Boil 8 cups water in a large nonstick skillet and pour over noodles. Soak 10 minutes and drain.

• Heat 1 tablespoon of the oil in same skillet. Season beef with salt and sauté 2 minutes per side. Remove to a plate. Add remaining 1 tablespoon oil. Add onions, peppers, mushrooms and garlic; stir-fry for 8 minutes.

• Combine cornstarch and broth; add to skillet and simmer for 1 minute. Stir in beef, noodles, teriyaki sauce and vinegar; simmer for 1 minute until heated through.

PER SERVING 583 CAL; 17 g FAT (4 g SAT); 52 g PRO; 54 g CARB; 4 g FIBER; 970 mg SODIUM; 83 mg CHOL

Chicken Gumbo

MAKES 6 servings PREP 15 minutes
COOK 16 minutes

2	tablespoons vegetable oil
7	ounces kielbasa (from a 14-ounce package), sliced into coins
1¼	pounds boneless, skinless chicken breast, cut into 1-inch pieces
4	cloves garlic, chopped
1	can (14½ ounces) stewed tomatoes
2	cups reduced-sodium chicken broth
1	package (8 ounces) frozen okra, thawed
1	teaspoon dried oregano
¼	teaspoon salt
¼	teaspoon black pepper
1	cup instant rice
4	scallions, sliced

• Heat oil in a large pot over medium-high heat. Add kielbasa and cook for 5 minutes, stirring occasionally. Add chicken and garlic; cook for 5 more minutes, stirring.

• Add tomatoes, breaking apart with a wooden spoon, the chicken broth, okra, 1 cup water, oregano, salt and pepper. Simmer for 3 minutes; stir in rice and simmer for 3 additional minutes.

• To serve, spoon into individual bowls and garnish with scallions.

PER SERVING 348 CAL; 16 g FAT (5 g SAT); 27 g PRO; 24 g CARB; 3 g FIBER; 834 mg SODIUM; 74 mg CHOL

Skillet Red Bean Picadillo

MAKES 6 servings PREP 15 minutes COOK 10 minutes BAKE at 400° for 15 minutes

1	tablespoon vegetable oil
1	onion, chopped
1	green pepper, cored, seeded and chopped
1	sweet red pepper, cored, seeded and chopped
1	large zucchini, cut into small dice
2	cans (15 ounces each) red kidney beans, drained and rinsed
1	can (8 ounces) no-salt-added tomato sauce
1	teaspoon chili powder
1	teaspoon garlic salt
½	teaspoon ground cumin
½	teaspoon ground cinnamon
¼	cup pimiento-stuffed olives, chopped
¼	cup raisins
1	box (8½ ounces) cornbread mix
¼	cup chopped scallion
	Zest of 1 lime
	Cilantro for garnish

• Heat oil in a large oven-proof skillet over medium-high heat. Add onion, peppers and zucchini; cook for 5 minutes. Stir in beans, tomato sauce, chili powder, garlic salt, cumin and cinnamon. Simmer for 5 minutes. Stir in olives and raisins.

• Meanwhile, heat oven to 400°. Prepare cornbread mix following package directions. Stir in scallion and lime zest.

• Dollop heaping tablespoons of cornbread batter evenly over skillet. Bake at 400° for 15 minutes or until cornbread is cooked through.

• Allow to cool slightly before serving. Garnish with cilantro.

PER SERVING 397 CAL; 10 g FAT (3 g SAT); 13 g PRO; 67 g CARB; 12 g FIBER; 906 mg SODIUM; 39 mg CHOL

Caramelized Shallot, Capicola & Fontina Frittata

MAKES 4 servings **PREP** 15 minutes
COOK 10 minutes **BAKE** at 350° for 10 minutes

- **1** tablespoon unsalted butter
- **2** large shallots, finely sliced
- **2** ounces capicola ham, sliced into ribbons
- **6** eggs
- **¼** cup reduced-fat milk
- **⅛** teaspoon black pepper
- **⅛** teaspoon ground nutmeg
- **6** ounces Fontina cheese, cut into cubes
  Basil for garnish (optional)

• Heat oven to 350°.

• Melt butter in a 10-inch oven-proof nonstick skillet over medium-high heat. Add shallots and cook for 4 minutes, stirring occasionally. Add capicola and cook for 1 minute.

• Whisk together eggs, milk, pepper and nutmeg; stir in 4 ounces of the cheese and pour into skillet. Cook for 5 minutes, stirring once after 2 minutes.

• Place skillet in oven and bake at 350° for 5 minutes. Scatter remaining 2 ounces cheese on top and bake an additional 5 minutes until frittata is set.

• To serve, gently slide frittata onto a serving plate and garnish with basil, if desired.

PER SERVING 336 **CAL**; 25 g **FAT** (13 g **SAT**); 23 g **PRO**; 4 g **CARB**; 0 g **FIBER**; 638 mg **SODIUM**; 383 mg **CHOL**

Hearty Scallop & Corn Stew

MAKES 4 servings **PREP** 15 minutes **COOK** 18 minutes

- **6** slices bacon, cut into ¼-inch pieces
- **1** tablespoon olive oil
- **1½** pounds sea scallops
- **2** teaspoons Old Bay Seasoning
- **1** onion, chopped
- **2** cloves garlic, chopped
- **2** cups reduced-sodium vegetable broth
- **1** bag (1 pound) frozen corn, thawed
- **1** teaspoon fresh thyme leaves
- **¼** teaspoon black pepper
- **⅛** teaspoon salt
- **¼** pound angel hair pasta, broken into 2-inch pieces
- **2** large tomatoes, seeds removed, chopped

• Cook bacon in a medium saucepan over medium-high heat until crisp, about 4 minutes. Remove to a plate with a slotted spoon. Add olive oil to drippings in saucepan. Season scallops with 1 teaspoon of the Old Bay and add to saucepan. Sauté 2 minutes per side. Remove to a plate. Halve scallops, if desired.

• Add onion and garlic; cook for 5 minutes, stirring frequently. Add broth, 1½ cups water, remaining 1 teaspoon Old Bay, half the corn, the thyme, pepper and salt. Simmer for 3 minutes.

• Puree remaining corn and ¼ cup water in a blender and add to saucepan. Stir in scallops, angel hair and tomatoes. Simmer for 2 minutes or until pasta is tender (it will continue to absorb broth as it sits).

• Before serving, garnish each portion with some of the cooked bacon.

PER SERVING 459 **CAL**; 10 g **FAT** (2 g **SAT**); 39 g **PRO**; 33 g **CARB**; 5 g **FIBER**; 965 mg **SODIUM**; 67 mg **CHOL**

Wild Mushroom Risotto

MAKES 4 servings **PREP** 15 minutes
COOK 38 minutes

2	cups reduced-sodium beef broth
2	tablespoons olive oil
½	onion, chopped
½	pound sweet Italian sausage, casings removed, crumbled
½	pound mixed mushrooms, sliced
1¼	cups arborio rice
½	cup dry red wine
1	cup crushed tomatoes
⅛	teaspoon black pepper
1	bag (6 ounces) baby spinach
1	cup shredded Italian cheese blend, plus more for garnish (optional)

• In a large measuring cup, combine broth with 1 cup water. Set aside.

• Heat oil in a large pot over medium heat; add onion and cook for 3 minutes, stirring occasionally. Add crumbled sausage and mushrooms and cook for 5 minutes, stirring occasionally. Stir in rice and cook for 1 minute; add wine and cook 1 minute until liquid evaporates.

• Add ½ cup of the broth-water mixture. Stir frequently and when broth is almost absorbed add another ½ cup. Continue adding broth-water mixture in ½-cup increments, stirring until rice is tender, about 28 minutes.

• Stir in crushed tomatoes and black pepper. Gradually wilt in spinach.

• Remove risotto from heat and stir in cheese. Spoon into a large warm bowl and serve immediately. Garnish with additional cheese, if desired.

PER SERVING 545 **CAL**; 22 g **FAT** (8 g **SAT**); 22 g **PRO**; 65 g **CARB**; 5 g **FIBER**; 996 mg **SODIUM**; 36 mg **CHOL**

Spinach & Roasted Red Pepper Lasagna

MAKES 10 servings **PREP** 15 minutes **SOAK** 10 minutes **BAKE** at 400° for 45 minutes **COOL** 15 minutes

2	cups light Alfredo sauce
2	cups marinara sauce
12	Delverde instant lasagna noodles with spinach (1.1 pound package) or 6 instant lasagna noodles with spinach and 6 instant lasagna noodles with tomato
2	packages (10 ounces each) frozen spinach, thawed and squeezed dry
1	container (15 ounces) part-skim ricotta cheese
¼	teaspoon salt
½	cup jarred sliced roasted red peppers, drained
2	cups shredded part-skim mozzarella cheese
½	cup grated Parmesan

• Heat oven to 400°. Coat a 13 x 9 x 2-inch baking dish with nonstick cooking spray. In a medium bowl combine Alfredo and marinara sauces. Soak lasagna noodles in warm water for 10 minutes. Set aside.

• Spoon ½ cup of the sauce into bottom of prepared baking dish. Cover with 3 noodles, overlapping and alternating spinach and tomato, if using both varieties. Cover with 1 cup of the sauce; spread ricotta evenly over sauce. Cover with another 3 noodles and 1 cup sauce. Season spinach with salt and evenly distribute over sauce; scatter red pepper slices over spinach. Continue layering with 3 noodles, 1 cup sauce and mozzarella. Top with 3 remaining noodles and remaining sauce.

• Cover with foil and bake at 400° for 30 minutes. Uncover and sprinkle with Parmesan; bake, uncovered, for 15 minutes or until cheese is golden brown. Cool 15 minutes before serving.

PER SERVING 349 **CAL**; 15 g **FAT** (8 g **SAT**); 20 g **PRO**; 37 g **CARB**; 4 g **FIBER**; 903 mg **SODIUM**; 39 mg **CHOL**

Rigatoni with Red Clam Sauce

MAKES 6 servings **PREP** 15 minutes
COOK 18 minutes

- **1** **pound rigatoni**
- **4** **cans (6½ ounces each) minced clams**
- **2** **tablespoons olive oil**
- **4** **cloves garlic, sliced**
- **1** **can (28 ounces) crushed tomatoes**
- **4** **cherry peppers, sliced**
- **½** **teaspoon salt**
- **½** **teaspoon sugar**
- **¼** **teaspoon black pepper**
- **¼** **cup parsley, chopped**
- **2** **tablespoons lemon juice**
- **1** **lemon, cut into wedges**

• In a large pot, cook rigatoni 2 minutes less than package directions, about 10 minutes. Drain, reserving 1 cup of the cooking water.

• Drain clams, reserving ½ cup of the juice.

• In the same pot that pasta was cooked in, heat olive oil over medium-high heat; add garlic and cook for 1 minute until lightly browned. Stir in reserved clam juice, tomatoes, cherry peppers, salt, sugar and pepper; simmer for 4 minutes. Add clams and simmer for 2 minutes. Stir in cooked pasta and cook for 1 minute or until pasta is tender, adding some of the reserved cooking water if needed.

• Stir in parsley and lemon juice. Serve with lemon wedges.

PER SERVING 440 **CAL**; 7 g **FAT** (1 g **SAT**);
26 g **PRO**; 69 g **CARB**; 5 g **FIBER**; 923 mg **SODIUM**;
36 mg **CHOL**

Sunday Roast with Carrots & New Potatoes

MAKES 6 servings **PREP** 15 minutes **ROAST** at 450° for 50 minutes

- **2½** **pounds beef eye round roast**
- **2** **tablespoons vegetable oil**
- **1¼** **teaspoons salt**
- **¼** **plus ⅛ teaspoon black pepper**
- **1½** **pounds new potatoes, about 1-inch diameter, scrubbed**
- **1** **pound peeled small carrots**
- **⅓** **cup dry red wine**
- **2** **cups reduced-sodium beef broth**
- **1** **tablespoon all-purpose flour**
- **2** **teaspoons chopped fresh tarragon**
- **2** **teaspoons chopped fresh chervil or marjoram**

• Heat oven to 450°. Rub roast with 1 tablespoon of the oil and season with ¼ teaspoon each of the salt and pepper. Place in a large flame-proof roasting pan.

• Place potatoes and carrots in a large bowl and toss with ½ teaspoon of the salt and remaining ⅛ teaspoon pepper.

Arrange potatoes and carrots around meat and roast at 450° for 50 minutes or until internal temperature of meat registers 130° on an instant-read thermometer. Stir vegetables once after 25 minutes.

• Remove roast and vegetables to a serving platter and cover for 10 minutes. Place roasting pan on stovetop over medium-high heat. Add wine and scrape up browned bits from bottom of pan. Combine broth and flour and stir into pan; add ¼ teaspoon of the salt and simmer for 1 minute until thickened. Stir in tarragon and chervil.

• Thinly slice meat and sprinkle with remaining ¼ teaspoon salt. Serve with vegetables and herb gravy.

PER SERVING 414 **CAL**; 11 g **FAT** (3 g **SAT**);
46 g **PRO**; 29 g **CARB**; 4 g **FIBER**; 799 mg **SODIUM**;
77 mg **CHOL**

SUPPER SANDWICHES

Our satisfying slow cooker dinners are real bread winners.

OPEN-FACED TURKEY

Open-Faced Turkey

MAKES 6 servings PREP 15 minutes
SLOW COOK on HIGH for 5 hours or on LOW for 7 hours

- **1   bone-in turkey breast half (3½ pounds), skin removed**
- **¼   teaspoon salt**
- **¼   teaspoon pepper**
- **1   box (32 ounces) low-sodium chicken broth**
- **1   bay leaf**
- **3   sprigs fresh thyme**
- **2   teaspoons fresh oregano, chopped**
- **1   packet mashed potato granules (from a 6.5-ounce box)**
- **1   envelope (0.87 ounces) turkey gravy mix (such as McCormick)**
- **6   slices hearty white bread**

• Place turkey breast half in slow cooker insert. Season with salt and pepper. Pour broth around turkey; add bay leaf, thyme and oregano. Cover and cook on HIGH for 5 hours or on LOW for 7 hours.

• Using a large spatula, carefully remove turkey from slow cooker to a cutting board. Remove and discard bones; strain broth from slow cooker into a bowl.

• Place mashed potato granules in a medium bowl. Ladle 1½ cups of the strained broth over granules. Whisk to blend, then cover and set aside.

• Meanwhile, combine gravy mix and 1 cup cold water in small saucepan. Bring to a simmer; cook 1 minute.

• Cut turkey crosswise into slices. Place 1 piece of bread on a plate. Spread with ⅓ cup mashed potatoes and some of the turkey, and top with a little gravy. Repeat to make 6 sandwiches and serve.

PER SERVING 419 CAL; 3 g FAT (1 g SAT); 56 g PRO; 37 g CARB; 2 g FIBER; 761 mg SODIUM; 140 mg CHOL

Sweet Chili Rolls

MAKES 8 servings PREP 15 minutes SLOW COOK on HIGH for 6 hours or on LOW for 8 hours

- **2   tablespoons chili powder**
- **2   tablespoons sugar**
- **1   tablespoon cornstarch**
- **¾   cup ketchup**
- **1   tablespoon Dijon mustard**
- **1   can (15 ounces) pinto beans, drained and rinsed**
- **½   Vidalia onion, chopped**
- **2   cloves garlic, minced**
- **1   package (20.8 ounces) ground turkey**
- **¼   teaspoon salt**
- **8   soft potato sandwich rolls**
- **1   cup shredded sharp cheddar cheese**

• Blend chili powder, sugar and cornstarch in a bowl. Add ketchup and mustard and stir to combine.

• Pour ketchup mixture into slow cooker and stir in 1 cup water, beans, onion and garlic. Crumble in half the turkey and gently stir to combine. Repeat with remaining turkey. Cover and slow cook on HIGH for 6 hours or on LOW for 8 hours.

• Uncover and add salt. Spoon ½ cup of the mixture onto a roll. Top with 2 tablespoons shredded cheese. Repeat, reserving any leftover mixture for another meal.

PER SERVING 383 CAL; 13 g FAT (5 g SAT); 24 g PRO; 42 g CARB; 5 g FIBER; 856 mg SODIUM; 73 mg CHOL

BBQ Pulled Chicken

MAKES 12 servings **PREP** 5 minutes **SLOW COOK** on HIGH for 6 hours or on LOW for 8 hours

- **1**   **can (15 ounces) tomato sauce**
- **¾**   **cup cider vinegar**
- **1**   **small onion, finely chopped**
- **¼**   **cup plus 2 tablespoons packed dark brown sugar**
- **3**   **tablespoons molasses**
- **½**   **teaspoon salt**
- **½**   **teaspoon black pepper**
- **1½**   **pounds boneless, skinless chicken breasts**
- **1½**   **pounds boneless, skinless chicken thighs**
- **1**   **tablespoon cornstarch**
- **12**   **seeded hamburger buns**
     Jarred sliced mild jalapeño peppers (optional)

• Whisk together tomato sauce, vinegar, onion, brown sugar, molasses, salt and pepper in slow cooker insert. Add chicken breasts and thighs. Cover and cook on HIGH for 6 hours or on LOW for 8 hours.

• Uncover and remove chicken from sauce to a bowl. Pour sauce into a medium pot. In a small bowl, blend cornstarch and 1 tablespoon water. Stir into sauce in pot. Bring to a boil; boil 1 minute until thickened.

• Meanwhile, with 2 forks, roughly shred chicken. Pour sauce over chicken and gently stir to combine. Spoon shredded chicken mixture onto rolls and top with sliced jalapeños, if desired.

PER SERVING 312 **CAL**; 6 g **FAT** (1 g **SAT**); 29 g **PRO**; 35 g **CARB**; 2 g **FIBER**; 616 mg **SODIUM**; 88 mg **CHOL**

The Cuban

MAKES 6 servings **PREP** 15 minutes
SLOW COOK on HIGH for 6 hours or on LOW for
8 hours **GRILL** 4 minutes per batch

1	**pork loin roast (2 pounds)**
1	**envelope (from a 1.41-ounce package) Sazón Goya with annatto**
¼	**teaspoon black pepper**
12	**teaspoons yellow mustard**
6	**kaiser rolls, split**
¼	**pound thinly sliced ham**
6	**slices Swiss cheese (about 5 ounces)**
12	**slices pickles**

• Coat slow cooker bowl with nonstick cooking spray. Rub pork loin roast with Sazón Goya and pepper. Place in prepared slow cooker bowl and pour ¾ cup water around roast. Cover and cook on HIGH for 6 hours or on LOW for 8 hours.

• Heat a panini press or an indoor grill to medium-high. Remove roast from slow cooker to a cutting board. Spread 1 teaspoon mustard onto 1 side of each roll. Gently break roast apart into large shreds, dividing evenly among rolls.

• Top each sandwich with some ham, a slice of cheese and 2 pickle slices. Spread rolls with remaining 6 teaspoons mustard (1 teaspoon per roll). Close sandwiches and grill in panini press (or weighed down on indoor grill) for 3 to 4 minutes (2 sandwiches per batch). Serve warm.

PER SERVING 497 **CAL**; 17 g **FAT** (7 g **SAT**); 49 g **PRO**; 33 g **CARB**; 2 g **FIBER**; 913 mg **SODIUM**; 125 mg **CHOL**

French Dip

MAKES 6 servings **PREP** 15 minutes **SLOW COOK** on HIGH for 6 hours or on LOW for 8 hours
BROIL 3 minutes

1	**bottom round beef rump roast (3 pounds)**
½	**teaspoon garlic salt**
½	**teaspoon black pepper**
3	**medium onions, sliced**
1	**can (14.5 ounces) reduced-sodium beef broth**
3	**tablespoons Worcestershire sauce**
6	**hoagie rolls**
½	**cup light mayonnaise**
1	**tablespoon horseradish**

• Coat slow cooker bowl with nonstick cooking spray. Rub roast with garlic salt and pepper. Place onions in bottom of prepared slow cooker. Add beef broth and Worcestershire sauce; place roast on top of onions. Cover and cook on HIGH for 6 hours or on LOW for 8 hours.

• Heat broiler. Toast cut side of rolls for 2 to 3 minutes.

• Carefully remove roast to a cutting board. Strain liquid from slow cooker into a bowl, reserving onions. Cut roast horizontally in half, then crosswise into slices. In a small bowl, blend mayonnaise and horseradish. Spread 1½ tablespoons mayo blend on each roll. Top with beef and some of the reserved onions. Serve each sandwich with ⅓ cup of the liquid (jus) for dipping.

PER SERVING 401 **CAL**; 15 g **FAT** (4 g **SAT**); 14 g **PRO**; 54 g **CARB**; 4 g **FIBER**; 897 mg **SODIUM**; 15 mg **CHOL**

CRANBERRY TART,
PAGE 299

NOVEMBER

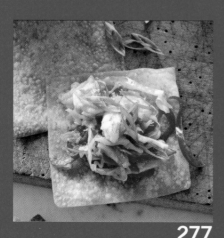

277

289

301

LIGHT FANTASTIC

Satisfying 350-calorie family suppers.

FIVE-SPICE TURKEY BURGERS, PAGE 278

FARFALLE ALFREDO WITH
OYSTER MUSHROOMS,
PAGE 281

20-MINUTE
ANCHO BEEF STEW

**SWEET & SPICY CHICKEN &
CAULIFLOWER CURRY**

AUTUMN ROOT
VEGETABLE CHILI

Autumn Root Vegetable Chili

MAKES 4 servings **PREP** 25 minutes
COOK 33 minutes

1	tablespoon vegetable oil
1	small onion, chopped
3	cloves garlic, sliced
1	butternut squash (about 1½ pounds), peeled, seeded and cut into ½-inch cubes
½	pound parsnips, peeled and cut into ¼-inch-thick half moons
½	pound white turnips, peeled and cut into ¼-inch-thick half moons
½	pound carrots, peeled and cut into ¼-inch-thick half moons
1	green pepper, cored, seeded and diced
2	cans (14½ ounces each) fire-roasted diced tomatoes
¼	cup chili powder
1	teaspoon dried oregano
1	teaspoon ground cumin
1	can (15 ounces) kidney beans, drained and rinsed
½	cup cilantro, chopped
4	scallions, chopped
	Lime wedges for garnish

• Heat oil in a large saucepan over medium-high heat. Add onion and garlic; cook 3 minutes, stirring occasionally.

• Add squash, parsnips, turnips and carrots. Cook 5 minutes, stirring occasionally. Add green pepper, tomatoes, chili powder, oregano and cumin. Simmer on medium heat, partially covered, for 25 minutes, stirring occasionally. Add beans and heat through. Stir in cilantro.

• Sprinkle each portion with some of the scallions and place lime wedges on the side.

PER SERVING 344 **CAL**; 6 g **FAT** (1 g **SAT**); 12 g **PRO**; 67 g **CARB**; 21 g **FIBER**; 759 mg **SODIUM**; 0 mg **CHOL**

Farfalle Alfredo with Oyster Mushrooms

MAKES 8 servings **PREP** 15 minutes **COOK** 13 minutes

1	pound farfalle (bow ties)
½	pound string beans, cut into 1-inch pieces
1	onion, chopped
½	pound oyster mushrooms, sliced
6	ounces Neufchâtel cheese
1	cup fat-free milk
½	teaspoon salt
½	teaspoon garlic powder
½	teaspoon black pepper
½	cup sliced roasted red peppers
¾	cup grated Parmesan cheese
½	cup basil leaves

• Cook farfalle for about 12 minutes, following package directions. Add string beans during last 3 minutes of cooking time. Drain and return to pot.

• Meanwhile, heat a nonstick skillet over medium heat. Coat with nonstick cooking spray. Add onion and mushrooms; cook 10 minutes, stirring occasionally. Break Neufchâtel into pieces and add to skillet, stirring for about 1 minute until it starts to melt.

• Add milk, salt, garlic powder and pepper to skillet. Simmer on medium-low heat for 2 minutes. Add roasted peppers to sauce; toss sauce with pasta. Stir in ½ cup of the Parmesan.

• Spoon pasta into a large bowl; garnish with remaining ¼ cup Parmesan and the basil.

PER SERVING 350 **CAL**; 9 g **FAT** (6 g **SAT**); 17 g **PRO**; 51 g **CARB**; 4 g **FIBER**; 510 mg **SODIUM**; 27 mg **CHOL**

SIDE SHOW

10 dishes that ramp up your Thanksgiving menu.

Herb-Roasted Potatoes

MAKES 8 servings **PREP** 15 minutes **ROAST** at 425° for 35 minutes

- **3 pounds 2-inches round red-skinned potatoes, scrubbed and dried**
- **2 tablespoons olive oil**
- **1 teaspoon salt**
- **¼ teaspoon pepper**
- **Fresh rosemary and thyme sprigs**

• Heat oven to 425°.

• Halve potatoes and toss in a large bowl with olive oil, salt and pepper. Pluck a piece of rosemary or thyme smaller than the width of the potato and press onto the cut side. Place cut sides down on a large, light-colored, heavy-bottomed baking pan about 1 inch apart.

• Roast at 425° for 35 minutes, or until potatoes are fork-tender and cut sides are browned.

PER SERVING 149 **CAL**; 4 g **FAT** (1 g **SAT**); 3 g **PRO**; 27 g **CARB**; 3 g **FIBER**; 301 mg **SODIUM**; 0 mg **CHOL**

Maple-Glazed Delicata Squash

MAKES 6 servings **PREP** 15 minutes **COOK** 15 minutes **BAKE** at 400° for 40 minutes

½ cup maple syrup
¼ cup packed fresh sage leaves
2½ pounds delicata squash, ends trimmed, halved lengthwise, seeded and sliced into 1-inch half moons
1 tablespoon olive oil
½ teaspoon salt

• Heat oven to 400°. In a small lidded pot, combine maple syrup and sage. Bring to a simmer; reduce heat to low, cover and cook 15 minutes. Set aside, covered.

• Meanwhile, in a bowl, toss squash slices with olive oil and salt. Transfer to a foil-lined baking sheet in a single layer; bake at 400° for 20 minutes. Pour maple syrup-sage mixture evenly on top of squash; bake 20 minutes more until squash is browned and tender.

PER SERVING 155 **CAL**; 3 g **FAT** (0 g **SAT**); 2 g **PRO**; 35 g **CARB**; 5 g **FIBER**; 203 mg **SODIUM**; 0 mg **CHOL**

SHAVED BRUSSELS
SPROUTS SALAD

Shaved Brussels Sprouts Salad

MAKES 8 servings **PREP** 15 minutes

- **6** **cups fresh Brussels sprouts**
- **½** **cup toasted unsalted pistachios, roughly chopped**
- **⅓** **cup parsley, chopped**
- **2** **ounces Pecorino Romano cheese, shaved (about 1 cup)**
- **2** **tablespoons olive oil**
- **3** **tablespoons lemon juice**
- **1** **teaspoon lemon zest**
- **1** **teaspoon salt**
   Freshly cracked pepper

• Slice Brussels sprouts in a food processor fitted with the slicing blade. Transfer to a large bowl and toss with pistachios, parsley, cheese, oil, lemon juice, lemon zest, salt and freshly cracked pepper.

PER SERVING 134 **CAL**; 9 g **FAT** (2 g **SAT**); 7 g **PRO**; 9 g **CARB**; 3 g **FIBER**; 430 mg **SODIUM**; 7 mg **CHOL**

Caramelized Broccoli

MAKES 6 servings **PREP** 15 minutes **COOK** 9 minutes

- **2** **tablespoons plus 1 teaspoon olive oil**
- **8** **cups small broccoli florets**
- **1** **cup diced sweet onion**
- **½** **cup walnuts, roughly chopped**
- **2** **tablespoons balsamic vinegar**
- **½** **cup raisins**
- **¾** **teaspoon salt**
- **⅛** **teaspoon pepper**

• Heat 2 tablespoons of the olive oil in a large skillet over medium-high heat. Add broccoli florets and onion; cook 5 minutes. Stir in walnuts; cook 2 minutes. Add balsamic vinegar and raisins; cook 2 more minutes. Remove from heat and stir in salt, pepper and remaining 1 teaspoon olive oil.

PER SERVING 191 **CAL**; 11 g **FAT** (1 g **SAT**); 5 g **PRO**; 22 g **CARB**; 4 g **FIBER**; 324 mg **SODIUM**; 0 mg **CHOL**

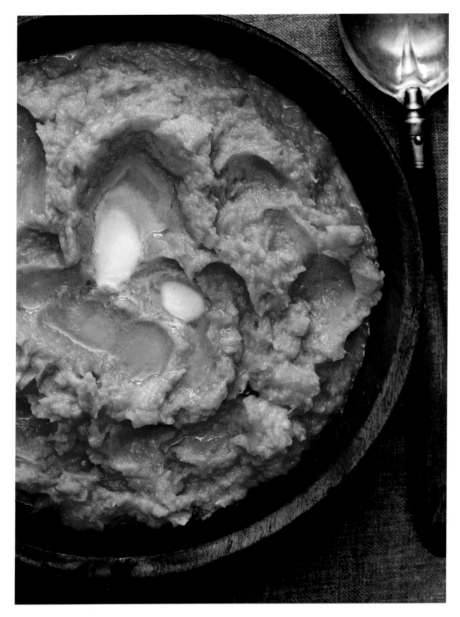

The turkey may be what everyone talks about before the big feast, but it's the side dishes that make it memorable. Choose a selection that creates a balance of sweet and savory flavors, creamy and crisp textures, and temperatures.

Cranberry-Clementine Sauce

MAKES 8 servings **PREP** 10 minutes
COOK 15 minutes

- **1** **bag (12 ounces) whole cranberries**
- **¾** **to 1 cup sugar**
- **½** **cup clementine juice (from approximately 5 clementines)**
- **1** **teaspoon clementine zest**
- **4** **clementines, peeled and segments separated**

• In a medium pot, combine cranberries, sugar (¾ cup for a tart sauce, 1 cup if more sweetness is desired), juice, ¼ cup water and zest. Bring to a simmer over medium heat. Reduce heat to medium-low and cook 10 minutes, until cranberries burst. Stir in clementine segments and cook 5 more minutes. Cool, cover and refrigerate until serving. (Dish can be made up to 2 days prior to serving.)

PER SERVING 89 **CAL**; 0 g **FAT** (0 g **SAT**); 1 g **PRO**; 25 g **CARB**; 3 g **FIBER**; 1 mg **SODIUM**; 0 mg **CHOL**

Sweet Potato-Parsnip Mash

MAKES 8 servings **PREP** 15 minutes **COOK** 15 minutes

- **1** **pound parsnips, peeled and cut into 1-inch pieces**
- **2** **pounds sweet potatoes, peeled and cut into 1-inch pieces**
- **½** **cup 2% milk**
- **¼** **cup packed brown sugar**
- **2** **tablespoons unsalted butter**
- **¾** **teaspoon salt**
- **¼** **teaspoon ground allspice**

• Combine parsnips and sweet potatoes in a medium pot; cover with 1 inch of cold water. Bring to a boil, then reduce heat to medium and simmer for 10 to 15 minutes, or until vegetables are tender and parsnips have lost their bitterness.

• Drain cooked vegetables and immediately return to pot over low heat. Mash with milk, brown sugar, butter, salt and allspice.

PER SERVING 188 **CAL**; 3 g **FAT** (2 g **SAT**); 3 g **PRO**; 38 g **CARB**; 6 g **FIBER**; 264 mg **SODIUM**; 9 mg **CHOL**

CRANBERRY-CLEMENTINE SAUCE

GREEN BEANS, HAZELNUTS & SHALLOTS

Green Beans, Hazelnuts & Shallots

MAKES 8 servings **PREP** 15 minutes
COOK 8 minutes

- 1½ **pounds green beans, trimmed**
- 2 **tablespoons unsalted butter**
- 2 **large shallots, thinly sliced**
- ½ **cup hazelnuts, roughly chopped**
- ½ **teaspoon salt**
- ⅛ **teaspoon pepper**

• Bring a large pot of lightly salted water to boiling. Add beans, return to a boil and cook 3 to 4 minutes, until crisp-tender. Remove to a bowl filled with ice water to cool. Drain and set aside.

• In a sauté pan, melt butter over medium heat. Add shallots and hazelnuts; cook 3 to 4 minutes until shallots are softened. Stir in cooked beans, salt and pepper. Stir until beans are warmed through.

PER SERVING 125 **CAL**; 8 g **FAT** (2 g **SAT**); 4 g **PRO**; 13 g **CARB**; 4 g **FIBER**; 151 mg **SODIUM**; 8 mg **CHOL**

Garlicky Swiss Chard

MAKES 8 servings **PREP** 15 minutes
COOK 12 minutes

- 2 **pounds Swiss chard (red or rainbow)**
- 2 **tablespoons olive oil**
- 6 **cloves garlic, sliced**
- ¼ **teaspoon red pepper flakes**
- 1 **teaspoon salt**

• Remove stems from chard and slice into 1-inch pieces. Wash and place in a bowl. Roughly chop leaves, wash and place in a separate bowl.

• In a large lidded pot, heat olive oil over medium heat. Add garlic and red pepper flakes to pan. Cook 1 to 2 minutes, being careful not to burn garlic. Stir in chard stems; increase heat to medium-high and cook 4 minutes. Add chard leaves and place lid on pot for 2 minutes. Remove lid and stir with tongs. Replace lid for 2 more minutes. Remove lid, stir and cook for 2 more minutes, uncovered. Stir in salt.

• Transfer cooked chard to a serving dish, allowing excess liquid to drip back into pot.

PER SERVING 55 **CAL**; 4 g **FAT** (1 g **SAT**); 2 g **PRO**; 5 g **CARB**; 2 g **FIBER**; 533 mg **SODIUM**; 0 mg **CHOL**

Instead of dressing or stuffing, give a savory bread pudding a try. Add bacon and cheddar cheese to the mix and it's sure to be a hit.

Bacon Bread Pudding

MAKES 8 servings **PREP** 10 minutes
LET STAND 10 minutes **BAKE** at 350° for
50 minutes **COOL** 10 minutes

6	ounces bacon (about 6 slices), diced
4	eggs
2	cups whole milk
6	ounces sharp white cheddar cheese, shredded (1½ cups)
½	cup sliced scallions
½	teaspoon salt
¼	teaspoon pepper
1	loaf brioche or challah bread (about 1 pound), cubed into 1-inch pieces (about 12 cups)

• Heat oven to 350°. In a skillet over medium heat, cook bacon 5 to 7 minutes, until crispy. Remove with a slotted spoon; set aside.

• In a large bowl, whisk together eggs and milk. Stir in cooked bacon, cheese, scallions, salt and pepper. Stir in bread cubes, coating well with egg mixture. Set aside for 10 minutes, stirring every once in a while to coat with egg mixture.

• Transfer bread-egg mixture to a 2-quart baking dish. Cover with foil. Bake at 350° for 35 minutes. Remove foil and bake another 10 to 15 minutes, until browned and eggs are set (a knife inserted in bread pudding will come out clean). Allow bread pudding to cool 10 minutes before serving.

PER SERVING 348 **CAL**; 17 g **FAT** (8 g **SAT**); 18 g **PRO**; 31 g **CARB**; 0 g **FIBER**; 755 mg **SODIUM**; 202 mg **CHOL**

Curried Carrot Soufflé

MAKES 6 servings **PREP** 10 minutes **COOK** 12 minutes **BAKE** at 350° for 55 minutes

2	pounds carrots, peeled and cut into ½-inch pieces
½	cup sugar
4	tablespoons unsalted butter, melted
3	eggs, beaten
3	tablespoons all-purpose flour
1	tablespoon curry powder
1	teaspoon baking powder
¾	teaspoon salt

• Heat oven to 350°. In a large sided sauté pan, add carrots. Cover with 1 inch of water and bring to a boil. Reduce heat to medium and cook 12 minutes or until carrots are softened. Drain.

• Place carrots in a food processor; process for 30 seconds. Add sugar, butter, eggs, flour, curry powder, baking powder and salt. Process mixture until smooth. Transfer mixture to a buttered 1½-quart soufflé dish; gently smooth top. Bake at 350° on center rack for 50 to 55 minutes, until carrot mixture is puffed and set. Serve immediately.

PER SERVING 218 **CAL**; 10 g **FAT** (6 g **SAT**); 6 g **PRO**; 29 g **CARB**; 4 g **FIBER**; 510 mg **SODIUM**; 126 mg **CHOL**

BACON BREAD PUDDING

THE SWEET LIFE

Family and friends may just rush through dinner to dig into these delicious desserts.

MAPLE CAKE, PAGE 299

CRANBERRY TART, PAGE 299

Coconut-Chocolate Pecan Pie

MAKES 12 servings PREP 15 minutes
BAKE at 350° for 1 hour, 10 minutes COOL 2 hours

1	cup sweetened flake coconut, plus more for garnish (optional)
1	refrigerated piecrust (from a 15.5-ounce package)
1	cup light corn syrup
¾	cup sugar
3	eggs
1	teaspoon vanilla extract
2	cups pecan halves
½	cup mini chocolate chips
	Whipped cream (optional)

• Heat oven to 350°. Spread coconut onto a baking sheet. Bake at 350° for 10 minutes until lightly toasted. Cool.

• Meanwhile, coat a 9-inch deep-dish pie plate with nonstick cooking spray. Roll piecrust slightly and fit into prepared dish, fluting edge.

• In a bowl, whisk corn syrup, sugar, eggs and vanilla. Stir in pecans. Spread coconut into piecrust; top with chocolate chips. Carefully pour pecan mixture into crust.

• Bake at 350° for 1 hour, covering crust with foil if browning too quickly. Cool at least 2 hours, then refrigerate until serving. Garnish with whipped cream and toasted coconut, if desired.

PER SERVING 423 CAL; 24 g FAT (8 g SAT); 5 g PRO; 52 g CARB; 2 g FIBER; 121 mg SODIUM; 56 mg CHOL

Eggnog Cheesecake

MAKES 12 servings PREP 15 minutes BAKE at 350° for 55 minutes

12	cinnamon graham cracker boards, crushed
6	tablespoons unsalted butter, melted
2	tablespoons plus ⅔ cup sugar
3	packages (8 ounces each) cream cheese, softened
¼	cup cornstarch
½	teaspoon ground cinnamon
¼	teaspoon ground nutmeg
1	egg plus 2 egg yolks
½	cup milk
1½	teaspoons rum flavoring

• Heat oven to 350°. Combine graham crackers, butter and 2 tablespoons of the sugar. Press into bottom and 1 inch up side of a 9-inch springform pan. Bake at 350° for 10 minutes. Cool slightly.

• In a bowl, beat cream cheese until smooth. In a small bowl, blend remaining ⅔ cup sugar, the cornstarch, cinnamon and nutmeg. On low speed, beat into cream cheese. Increase speed to medium; beat in egg, then yolks. Beat in milk and rum flavoring.

• Pour filling into crust, spreading level. Bake at 350° for 45 minutes, or until just set in center. While warm, run a thin spatula between pan and crust. Cool to room temp and refrigerate until serving.

PER SERVING 320 CAL; 27 g FAT (16 g SAT); 5 g PRO; 16 g CARB; 0 g FIBER; 199 mg SODIUM; 128 mg CHOL

Apple Turnovers

MAKES 8 servings PREP 15 minutes
COOK 5 minutes BAKE at 400° for 15 minutes

2	medium Fuji apples (about 1 pound), peeled, cored and diced
1	tablespoon all-purpose flour
2	tablespoon unsalted butter
¼	cup golden raisins
2	tablespoons sugar
1	tablespoon fresh lemon juice
⅛	teaspoon ground ginger
1	egg, separated
1	package (17.3 ounces) frozen puff pastry sheets, thawed

• Heat oven to 400°. Toss diced apples with flour. Melt butter in a large nonstick skillet over medium heat. Add apples, golden raisins, sugar, lemon juice and ginger. Cook, stirring, 4 to 5 minutes or until apples are tender. Remove from heat and let cool. Stir in egg yolk.

• Unfold 1 pastry sheet on a lightly floured surface. Roll out slightly to measure 11 inches square. With pizza cutter or sharp knife, cut pastry into 4 equal squares.

• Spoon ¼ cup of the apple mixture into center of 1 square. Brush edges with egg white. Fold in half diagonally to form a triangle. Pinch edges to seal, and transfer to an ungreased baking sheet. Repeat.

• Bake at 400° for 14 to 15 minutes, until puffed and nicely browned on top. While turnovers bake, repeat rolling, filling and folding with remaining pastry sheet, filling and egg white.

• Remove turnovers from pans to wire rack, cool 10 minutes. Best if served same day as baking; reheat in 350° oven for 5 minutes.

PER SERVING 331 CAL; 20 g FAT (6 g SAT); 6 g PRO; 32 g CARB; 2 g FIBER; 309 mg SODIUM; 34 mg CHOL

Pumpkin Custard Squares

MAKES 12 servings PREP 15 minutes COOK 4 minutes BAKE at 350° for 50 minutes

CRUST

2	cups crushed gingersnaps (36 cookies)
6	tablespoons unsalted butter, melted
1	tablespoon granulated sugar

FILLING

2	tablespoons cornstarch
2	tablespoons granulated sugar
1	can (12 ounces) evaporated milk, or ¾ cup milk
1	egg
1	can (15 ounces) solid-pack pumpkin (not pie mix)
⅔	cup packed dark brown sugar
1	teaspoon pumpkin pie spice
¼	teaspoon salt
	Whipped cream (optional)

• Heat oven to 350°. Line a 9 x 9 x 2-inch pan with nonstick foil.

• For crust, in a bowl, combine cookie crumbs, melted butter and sugar. Stir until combined. Press into bottom of prepared pan. Refrigerate while making filling.

• For filling, in a saucepan, whisk cornstarch and sugar. Stir in milk and egg. Cook, stirring constantly, over medium heat until smooth, steaming and slightly thickened, about 4 minutes.

• In a large bowl, blend pumpkin, brown sugar, pumpkin pie spice and salt. Whisk in milk mixture. Pour over crust; transfer to oven. Bake at 350° for 50 minutes or until center is set. Cool completely on a wire rack; refrigerate until serving. Use foil to lift bar from pan. Slice into squares. Garnish with whipped cream, if desired.

PER SERVING 215 CAL; 9 g FAT (5 g SAT); 4 g PRO; 31 g CARB; 2 g FIBER; 142 mg SODIUM; 37 mg CHOL

APPLE TURNOVERS

Maple Cake

MAKES 16 servings   PREP 20 minutes
BAKE at 350° for 30 minutes

CAKE

3	**cups self-rising cake flour (such as Presto)**
1	**teaspoon ground cinnamon**
½	**teaspoon ground ginger**
½	**teaspoon baking soda**
¼	**teaspoon ground nutmeg**
½	**cup (1 stick) unsalted butter, softened**
⅔	**cup packed light brown sugar**
½	**cup maple syrup**
2	**eggs**
⅔	**cup sour cream blended with ½ cup milk**
½	**teaspoon maple flavoring**

FROSTING

1	**cup (2 sticks) unsalted butter, softened**
1	**package (8 ounces) cream cheese, softened**
1	**box (16 ounces) confectioners' sugar**
1	**to 2 tablespoons milk**
¼	**teaspoon maple flavoring**
¾	**cup finely chopped walnuts (optional)**
	Cinnamon sticks (optional)

• Heat oven to 350°. For cake, coat a 13 x 9 x 2-inch baking pan with nonstick cooking spray. Line bottom with wax paper. Coat paper with spray.

• In a medium bowl, whisk together flour, cinnamon, ginger, baking soda and nutmeg. In a large bowl, beat butter until creamy. Beat in brown sugar and maple syrup. Beat in eggs (mixture will look slightly curdled). On low speed, beat in half the flour mixture, then the sour cream mixture and ending with the remaining flour mixture. Stir in maple flavoring. Transfer to prepared pan and spread level. Bake at 350° for 30 minutes, or until toothpick inserted in center of cake tests clean. Cool in pan for 5 minutes on wire rack. Remove from pan and remove wax paper. Cool completely.

• Meanwhile, make Frosting. Beat together butter and cream cheese in a large bowl. Sift in confectioners' sugar. Add milk and maple flavoring. Beat on low speed until smooth and good spreading consistency.

• Cut cake in half crosswise, then split each half horizontally to create 4 thin layers. Place 1 layer on a platter. Spread with ⅔ cup of the frosting. Sprinkle with ¼ cup of the walnuts, if desired. Repeat twice. Top final layer with cinnamon sticks or additional walnuts, if desired.

PER SERVING 517 CAL; 28 g FAT (16 g SAT); 6 g PRO; 63 g CARB; 1 g FIBER; 405 mg SODIUM; 95 mg CHOL

Cranberry Tart

MAKES 12 servings   PREP 10 minutes
COOK 10 minutes   BAKE at 425° for 18 minutes, at 375° for 20 minutes

1	**prepared piecrust**
2	**logs (4 ounces each) cinnamon-cranberry goat cheese**
6	**tablespoons plus 1 cup sugar**
1	**egg**
2	**tablespoons milk**
1	**bag (12 ounces) cranberries**
1	**cup cranberry juice**
½	**teaspoon lemon zest**
1	**tablespoon lemon juice**

• Heat oven to 425°. Fit piecrust into a 9- or 9½-inch removable-bottom tart pan. Line with a double layer of nonstick foil, pressing against side of crust. Bake at 425° for 18 minutes. Remove crust from oven, reduce heat to 375° and remove foil.

• Meanwhile, blend goat cheese, 6 tablespoons of the sugar, the egg and milk in a bowl. Pour into crust. Bake at 375° for 20 minutes or until set.

• While cheese layer bakes, make topping. Combine remaining 1 cup sugar, the cranberries, cranberry juice, lemon zest and lemon juice in a saucepan. Bring to a boil and cook for 10 minutes over medium heat, stirring occasionally. Remove from heat and pour over baked goat cheese layer. Cool until set.

PER SERVING 251 CAL; 9 g FAT (5 g SAT); 5 g PRO; 38 g CARB; 1 g FIBER; 144 mg SODIUM; 30 mg CHOL

SEASONAL TREATS

These pretty pumpkins are simple but so impressive.

Mini Pumpkin Cakes

MAKES 12 mini pumpkin cakes **PREP** 20 minutes **BAKE** at 350° for 20 minutes **DECORATE** 1 hour

1 **box (15.25 ounces) spice or devil's food cake mix**

3 **large eggs**

½ **cup vegetable oil**

1 **cup buttermilk**

1 **can (16 ounces) vanilla or chocolate frosting**

Orange paste food coloring (optional)

Honey wheat pretzel twists, Kit Kat bars or Twix bars for stems

⅓ **cup corn syrup**

Assorted colored sugars or sprinkles

• Heat oven to 350°. Grease and flour two 12-cup mini Bundt cupcake pans. Prepare cake mix according to package directions with eggs and oil, but use buttermilk in place of water. Spoon batter into prepared pans, filling halfway full (about 2 tablespoons batter in each).

• Bake at 350° for 15 to 20 minutes or until golden brown and a toothpick inserted in center comes out clean. Transfer to a wire rack; cool in pans for 5 minutes. Invert and cool completely. Use a small serrated knife to trim domed top from each cake to make level.

• Tint vanilla frosting orange, if desired. Spread a small amount of frosting on top of trimmed side of a cake. Place another trimmed cake, cut side down, on top of frosting to make a small pumpkin shape. Repeat to make 12 mini cakes.

• For frosted cakes, spread some of the frosting all over a mini cake to cover. Use a small spatula to spread frosting in ridges, starting from bottom to top. Add a trimmed candy bar piece on top as the stem.

• For sugared cakes, microwave corn syrup for 3 to 5 seconds. Brush over an assembled cake, then roll cake in colored sugar to coat lightly. Add a candy or pretzel stem on top.

• For glazed cakes, microwave ¼ cup of the frosting for 5 to 7 seconds until smooth but not too thin. Spoon a little on top of a mini cake, allowing it to drip down the side. Add sprinkles while frosting is still wet. Add a trimmed candy or pretzel piece on top as stem.

• Repeat recipe with the other flavor of cake mix, if desired.

PER CAKE (AVG) 476 **CAL**; 22 g **FAT** (5 g **SAT**); 4 g **PRO**; 68 g **CARB**; 0 g **FIBER**; 360 mg **SODIUM**; 54 mg **CHOL**

PASSPORT TO FLAVOR

Slow cooker suppers from around the globe.

CREAMY TURKEY RAGU

Use America's favorite kitchen appliance to prepare delicious dishes inspired by the cuisines of Italy, Morocco, Poland, France and Indonesia.

Creamy Turkey Ragu

MAKES 6 servings **PREP** 15 minutes
SLOW COOK on HIGH for 6 hours or on LOW for 8 hours

- 1   **can (28 ounces) crushed tomatoes**
- 1   **large onion, chopped**
- 1   **large carrot, peeled and diced**
- 4   **cloves garlic, chopped**
- 1   **teaspoon dried oregano**
- 1   **teaspoon sugar**
- 1   **teaspoon salt**
- ½   **teaspoon red pepper flakes**
- 1   **package (20.4 ounces) lean ground turkey**
- ⅔   **cup Philadelphia reduced-fat Italian & Herb Cooking Creme**
- 1   **box (14.5 ounces) Barilla Plus Rotini, cooked following package directions**
      Fresh basil for garnish (optional)

• Coat slow cooker bowl with nonstick cooking spray. Stir in tomatoes, onion, carrot, garlic, oregano, sugar, salt and red pepper flakes. Crumble in ground turkey and stir to combine.

• Cover and cook on HIGH for 6 hours or LOW for 8 hours.

• Stir in Cooking Creme until evenly incorporated into sauce. Stir half of sauce into cooked pasta; serve remaining sauce on the side. Garnish with basil, if desired.

PER SERVING 489 **CAL**; 9 g **FAT** (4 g **SAT**); 46 g **PRO**; 56 g **CARB**; 5 g **FIBER**; 792 mg **SODIUM**; 73 mg **CHOL**

Chicken Tagine

MAKES 4 servings **PREP** 10 minutes **SLOW COOK** on HIGH for 2½ hours or on LOW for 5 hours

- 1¾   **pounds boneless, skinless chicken thighs, trimmed and cut into 1-inch pieces**
- 2   **large onions, thinly sliced**
- ½   **cup dried apricots, coarsely chopped**
- ⅓   **cup raisins**
- 1¼   **cups low-sodium chicken broth**
- 2   **tablespoons tomato paste**
- 2   **tablespoons lemon juice**
- 2   **tablespoons flour**
- 1½   **teaspoons ground cumin**
- 1½   **teaspoons ground ginger**
- 1   **teaspoon ground cinnamon**
- ½   **teaspoon black pepper**
- 2   **cups cooked couscous**

• Place chicken, onions, apricots and raisins in slow cooker bowl.

• In a small bowl, whisk together chicken broth, tomato paste, lemon juice, flour, cumin, ginger, cinnamon and black pepper. Pour over chicken in slow cooker. Cover and cook on HIGH for 2½ hours or LOW for 5 hours.

• Uncover and spoon over cooked couscous.

PER SERVING 482 **CAL**; 11 g **FAT** (3 g **SAT**); 45 g **PRO**; 54 g **CARB**; 5 g **FIBER**; 345 mg **SODIUM**; 195 mg **CHOL**

Sweet & Sour Stuffed Cabbage Rolls

MAKES 6 servings **PREP** 20 minutes **COOK** 15 minutes **SLOW COOK** 5 hours on LOW

1	small head green cabbage, cored
1	tablespoon vegetable oil
1	medium onion, finely chopped
2	cloves garlic, minced
1	teaspoon cinnamon
¼	teaspoon nutmeg
2	cans (8 ounces each) tomato sauce
2	tablespoons packed light brown sugar
2	tablespoons red wine vinegar
2	slices reduced-calorie wheat bread
⅓	cup skim milk
1	pound lean ground beef
¼	teaspoon salt
¼	teaspoon black pepper
6	cups cooked egg noodles

• Bring a large pot of salted water to a boil. Boil cabbage 12 to 15 minutes, removing 9 leaves as they become pliable. Drain well, then remove tough stem from leaves; cut leaves in half. Remove remaining cabbage from water and shred. Place shredded cabbage in bottom of slow cooker.

• Meanwhile, heat oil in a large nonstick skillet over medium heat; cook onion 5 minutes. Add garlic, cinnamon and nutmeg; cook 1 minute. Remove half of onion mixture; set aside. Stir tomato sauce, sugar and vinegar into skillet and remove from heat.

• Pulse bread and milk in food processor until a paste is formed. Add reserved onion mixture, beef, salt and pepper to food processor and pulse until well combined.

• With stem ends of cabbage leaves facing you, place 2 heaping tablespoons of meat mixture in center of each leaf and roll up. Place rolls, seam sides down, in slow cooker. Pour sauce over top. Cover; cook on LOW for 5 hours. Serve with noodles.

PER SERVING 368 **CAL**; 9 g **FAT** (2 g **SAT**); 25 g **PRO**; 47 g **CARB**; 5 g **FIBER**; 603 mg **SODIUM**; 91 mg **CHOL**

Cassoulet

MAKES 8 servings   PREP 15 minutes
SLOW COOK on HIGH for 4 hours or on LOW
for 7½ hours

- **1** onion, chopped
- **2** cloves garlic, crushed
- **1** can (14.5 ounces) diced tomatoes, drained
- **1½** cups low-sodium chicken broth
- **1** cup white wine
- **2** pounds chicken thighs, skin and excess fat removed
- **1** pound boneless pork shoulder, trimmed and cut into 1-inch pieces
- **1** tablespoon tomato paste
- **2** sprigs fresh thyme
- **1** bay leaf
- **1** cup bread crumbs
- **2** cans (15 ounces each) cannellini beans, drained and rinsed
- **½** pound kielbasa, halved lengthwise and cut into ½-inch slices
- **½** teaspoon fresh thyme, chopped
- **½** teaspoon salt
- **½** teaspoon black pepper

• In a 5- to 6-quart slow cooker, combine onion, garlic, tomatoes, broth, wine, chicken, pork, tomato paste, thyme sprigs and bay leaf. Cook on HIGH for 4 hours or LOW for 7½ hours.

• Stir in ¾ cup of the bread crumbs, the beans, kielbasa, chopped thyme, salt and pepper; remove thyme sprigs and bay leaf and discard. Sprinkle each serving with ½ tablespoon bread crumbs and serve.

PER SERVING 498 CAL; 19 g FAT (7 g SAT); 44 g PRO; 31 g CARB; 6 g FIBER; 945 mg SODIUM; 153 mg CHOL

Indonesian Beef

MAKES 6 servings   PREP 15 minutes   COOK 6 minutes   SLOW COOK on HIGH for 6 hours or on LOW for 8 hours

- **2** tablespoons vegetable oil
- **2** pounds beef chuck, cut into 2-inch chunks
- **½** teaspoon salt
- **¼** teaspoon black pepper
- **1** large onion, peeled and thinly sliced
- **¾** pound small potatoes, about 2 inches in diameter, quartered
- **¼** pound peeled baby carrots
- **1** can (13.6 ounces) light coconut milk
- **2** tablespoons curry powder
- **1** tablespoon reduced-sodium soy sauce
- **½** teaspoon ground ginger
- **½** teaspoon garlic powder
- **¼** teaspoon cayenne pepper
- **3** large pitas or flatbreads, cut into wedges
  Chopped parsley, low-fat plain yogurt and lime wedges (optional)

• Coat slow cooker bowl with nonstick cooking spray.

• Heat oil in a large nonstick skillet over medium-high heat. Season beef with ¼ teaspoon each of the salt and pepper and add to skillet. Sauté 3 minutes per side.

• Transfer beef to slow cooker. Layer in onion, potatoes and carrots. In a medium bowl, whisk together coconut milk, curry, soy sauce, ginger, garlic powder and cayenne. Pour over beef and vegetables in slow cooker.

• Cover and cook on HIGH for 6 hours or LOW for 8 hours. Gently stir in remaining ¼ teaspoon salt. Serve over flatbread wedges with parsley, yogurt and lime, if desired.

PER SERVING 517 CAL; 17 g FAT (7 g SAT); 41 g PRO; 50 g CARB; 4 g FIBER; 589 mg SODIUM; 67 mg CHOL

ROSEMARY SHORTBREAD,
PAGE 319

DECEMBER

311

323

325

HOMEMADE WITH LOVE

Marshmallows, cake pops, cookie mix and other goodies to give this season.

MARBLED WALNUT FUDGE,
PAGE 316

Peppermint Bark

MAKES 2 pounds (4 small tins) at $1.96 each
PREP 10 minutes **MICROWAVE** 2 minutes
REFRIGERATE 1 hour

- **2** **bags (12 ounces each) white chocolate chips**
- **1** **cup peppermint candies, unwrapped**

- Line a 15 x 10 x 1-inch baking pan with foil. Coat with nonstick cooking spray. Place chips in a large glass bowl. Microwave at 60% power for 1 minute. Stir. Repeat, stirring until smooth.

- Place candies in a quart-size resealable plastic bag. Place bag inside a gallon-size resealable bag. Crush with a meat mallet or heavy saucepan.

- Fold half the crushed candies into melted chocolate. Pour onto prepared pan, spreading almost to edge of pan. Sprinkle top with remaining crushed candies. Refrigerate until firm, about 1 hour. Break apart into bite-size pieces.

PER SERVING 143 **CAL**; 7 g **FAT** (4 g **SAT**); 1 g **PRO**; 20 g **CARB**; 0 g **FIBER**; 22 mg **SODIUM**; 3 mg **CHOL**

**CHOCOLATE-PEPPERMINT
CAKE POPS**

Chocolate-Peppermint Cake Pops

MAKES 48 pops at 23¢ each **PREP** 15 minutes
BAKE at 350° for 35 minutes **CHILL** 2½ hours
DECORATE at least 1 hour

1	box (18.25 ounces) chocolate cake mix
2	large eggs
⅓	cup vegetable oil
1	cup canned chocolate frosting
1½	bags (14 ounces each) super white candy coating disks
4	drops peppermint oil (optional)
6	ounces red candy coating disks
	Assorted red and white holiday decorations, nonpareils and colored sugars

• Heat oven to 350°. Coat a 13 x 9 x 2-inch baking pan with nonstick cooking spray. In a large bowl, combine cake mix, 1⅓ cups water, eggs and oil. Prepare according to package directions. Pour into prepared pan; bake at 350° for 32 to 35 minutes. Cool completely in pan on a wire rack.

• Finely crumble cake into a large bowl. Stir in frosting and press together with the back of a spoon. Shape mixture into 1¼-inch balls and place on a baking sheet. Refrigerate for 2 hours or freeze for 20 minutes.

• Once cake balls are chilled, melt candy according to package directions, adding peppermint oil to white candy disks. Remove a few balls from the refrigerator or freezer. Dip a lollipop stick about ½ inch into melted candy. Press a cake ball onto stick, being careful not to press stick too far. Dip ball into desired coating and gently tap so that excess coating drips back into bowl. Garnish with red drizzle, holiday decorations, nonpareils or colored sugar. Transfer decorated pops to a wax paper-lined sheet. Repeat, reheating candy melts as needed. Refrigerate for 30 minutes, then store at room temperature up to 2 weeks.

PER POP 142 **CAL**; 7 g **FAT** (3 g **SAT**); 2 g **PRO**; 17 g **CARB**; 0 g **FIBER**; 122 mg **SODIUM**; 9 mg **CHOL**

Chunky Salsa

MAKES 10 cups at $1.53 each **PREP** 35 minutes **COOK** 15 minutes

3	pounds plum tomatoes, cored, seeded and diced
1	package (20 ounces) frozen corn kernels, thawed
2	medium onions, chopped
6	cloves garlic, roughly chopped
2	jalapeño chiles, seeded and minced
½	cup cilantro, chopped
1	can (5.5 ounces; about ⅔ cup) tomato juice
1	teaspoon salt
½	teaspoon black pepper
1	can (15 ounces) black beans, drained and rinsed

• Combine tomatoes, corn, onions, garlic, jalapeños, cilantro, tomato juice, salt and pepper in an 8-quart pot. Bring to a simmer over high heat.

• Reduce heat to medium and simmer for 10 minutes. Stir in beans and cook 5 minutes. Cool and spoon into jars. To give as a gift, pair with tortilla chips and include a chip-and-dip bowl, if desired. Refrigerate with this note: Use within 2 weeks.

PER CUP 126 **CAL**; 1 g **FAT** (0 g **SAT**); 6 g **PRO**; 26 g **CARB**; 6 g **FIBER**; 418 mg **SODIUM**; 0 mg **CHOL**

Layered Chocolate Cookie Mix

MAKES 1 jar at $7.33 each; 3½ dozen baked cookies
PREP 20 minutes

1	2-quart jar
2¾	cups all-purpose flour
1¼	teaspoons baking powder
½	teaspoon baking soda
¼	teaspoon salt
½	cup unsweetened cocoa powder
1¼	cups packed light brown sugar
¾	cup granulated sugar
1	cup red M&M's candies
1	cup semisweet chocolate chips
1	cup white chocolate chips

• In a medium bowl, combine 1¾ cups of the flour, the baking powder, baking soda and salt. In small bowl, blend cocoa and remaining 1 cup flour.

• Begin layering: Spoon half the flour-cocoa mixture into jar. Press down to flatten (a small spice jar works well). Spoon half the plain flour mixture over cocoa layer; compact. Repeat. Top with brown sugar layer and granulated sugar layer, compacting each. Spoon M&M's over sugar.

• Toss together both kinds of chips in a small bowl and add to jar. Attach a note with baking instructions: In large bowl, combine 1 cup (2 sticks) cooled, melted unsalted butter with 3 eggs, ⅓ cup milk and 2 teaspoons vanilla extract. Stir in contents of jar just until mixed. Drop dough by heaping tablespoon onto baking sheets. Bake at 350° for 13 minutes or until firm. Cool on sheet on wire rack for 1 minute. Remove directly to rack to cool completely.

PER COOKIE 178 **CAL**; 9 g **FAT** (5 g **SAT**); 2 g **PRO**; 25 g **CARB**; 1 g **FIBER**; 58 mg **SODIUM**; 29 mg **CHOL**

Steak Rub

MAKES 1 jar (11 teaspoons) at $1.50 each
PREP 5 minutes

• Blend 1 tablespoon kosher salt, 2 teaspoons smoked paprika, 2 teaspoons dried oregano, 1½ teaspoons dried minced onion, 1 teaspoon dried minced garlic, ½ teaspoon ground cumin and ½ teaspoon red pepper flakes in a small bowl. Spoon into a small jar and attach these instructions: Rub 1 teaspoon spice mix onto both sides of a 1½-pound steak. Grill or broil as desired.

Pork Rub

MAKES 1 jar (9 teaspoons) at $1.51 each
PREP 5 minutes

• Blend 1 tablespoon kosher salt, 2 teaspoons crumbled dried rosemary, 1 teaspoon crushed fennel seeds, 1 teaspoon dried minced onion, 1 teaspoon dried minced garlic, 1 teaspoon coarsely ground peppercorn medley and ½ teaspoon dried orange peel in a small bowl. Spoon into a small jar and attach these instructions: Rub 1 teaspoon spice mix onto both sides of 1-pound pork chops. Grill or broil as desired.

Chicken and Fish Rub

MAKES 1 jar (10 teaspoons) at $1.14 each
PREP 5 minutes

• Blend 1 tablespoon kosher salt, 2 teaspoons dried minced garlic, 2 teaspoons dried parsley, 1 teaspoon dried thyme, 1 teaspoon dried tarragon and 1 teaspoon coarsely ground peppercorn medley in a small bowl. Spoon into a small jar and attach these instructions: Rub 1 to 2 teaspoons spice mix onto 1-pound skinless chicken or fish fillets. Grill or broil as desired.

happy
holidays

MARSHMALLOWS

Marshmallows

MAKES 8 servings (6 marshmallows) at 28¢ each
PREP 5 minutes   **COOK** 7 minutes
BEAT 12 minutes   **LET STAND** 3 hours

- ½   **cup confectioners' sugar**
- ⅓   **cup cornstarch**
- 2   **envelopes (0.25 ounce each) unflavored gelatin**
- 1¼   **cups granulated sugar**
- ⅔   **cup light corn syrup**
- ⅛   **teaspoon salt**
- ¼   **teaspoon cherry or lime extract or flavoring (optional)**
       Red or green food coloring (optional)

• Sift confectioners' sugar and cornstarch into a small bowl. Line a 9 x 9 x 2-inch pan with foil. Coat with nonstick cooking spray. Sift 2 tablespoons of the confectioners' sugar mixture into pan, tilting to coat sides. Leave any excess in pan.

• Place ⅔ cup water in a large bowl and sprinkle with gelatin. Soften for 5 minutes.

• Meanwhile, combine granulated sugar, corn syrup and salt in medium heavy-bottomed saucepan. Cook over medium heat until sugar is dissolved, stirring occasionally, about 7 minutes. Strain into bowl with gelatin.

• Beat on high with an electric mixer until light and fluffy, about 12 minutes, adding flavoring and food coloring, if desired (cherry and red for pink ones, lime and green for green). Spread into prepared pan and smooth top. Dust with 2 tablespoons of the confectioners' sugar mixture. Let stand 2 hours until set.

• Lift marshmallow from pan with foil. With a wet knife, cut into 4 squares. Cut each square into 12 pieces. Spread remaining confectioners' sugar mixture onto sheet pan. Toss marshmallows in sugar mixture; let stand 1 hour. Store in an airtight container at room temperature.

PER SERVING 207 **CAL**; 0 g **FAT** (0 g **SAT**); 2 g **PRO**; 56 g **CARB**; 0 g **FIBER**; 57 mg **SODIUM**; 0 mg **CHOL**

Cranberry-Poppy Seed Biscuits

MAKES three 2¾-cup bags at $1.55 each   **PREP** 10 minutes

- 6   **cups all-purpose flour**
- 1½   **cups sweetened dried cranberries, coarsely chopped**
- 6   **tablespoons sugar**
- 4   **tablespoons baking powder**
- 2   **tablespoons poppy seeds**
- 1   **teaspoon salt**
- 3   **½-pound lined tin-tie coffee bags**

• In a large bowl, combine flour, cranberries, sugar, baking powder, poppy seeds and salt. Whisk until combined.

• Spoon an equal amount of mixture into each bag. To give as a gift: Package with a biscuit cutter, honey and a honey wand.

• Attach these instructions: Mix ⅓ cup shortening or unsalted butter (cut up) into biscuit mix with fingers. Add ¾ cup milk and stir just until blended. On a floured surface, pat into a 1-inch-thick circle. Cut into biscuits and transfer to a baking sheet. Gather dough scraps together and cut out more biscuits. Bake at 425° for 14 minutes. Serve with honey.

PER BISCUIT 236 **CAL**; 9 g **FAT** (5 g **SAT**); 4 g **PRO**; 34 g **CARB**; 1 g **FIBER**; 308 mg **SODIUM**; 22 mg **CHOL**

Whether it's something healthful (like homemade granola) or indulgent (like fudge), a handmade gift from the kitchen is always appreciated.

Mixed Berry Granola

MAKES about 6 cups at $1.98 per cup
PREP 10 minutes **COOK** 3 minutes
BAKE at 325° for 30 minutes

- ⅓   **cup honey**
- 2   **tablespoons unsalted butter**
- ¼   **teaspoon salt**
- 2   **cups rolled oats**
- 1   **cup pecans, coarsely chopped**
- ½   **cup flax seeds**
- 1   **bag (6 ounces) dried mixed berries and cherries**

• Heat oven to 325°. In a small saucepan, combine honey, butter and salt. Place over low heat and cook until butter is melted, 3 minutes, stirring to blend.

• In a large bowl, combine oats, pecans and flax seeds. Pour honey mixture over oat mixture. Toss to coat. Pour into rimmed baking sheet. Bake at 325° for 30 minutes, stirring halfway through.

• Transfer oat mixture to large bowl and toss with dried fruit. Cool completely and package in jars or cellophane bags.

PER ½-CUP SERVING 115 **CAL**; 6 g **FAT** (1 g **SAT**); 3 g **PRO**; 15 g **CARB**; 3 g **FIBER**; 27 mg **SODIUM**; 3 mg **CHOL**

Marbled Walnut Fudge

MAKES 4 dozen pieces at $4.01 per dozen **PREP** 5 minutes **COOK** 7 minutes
REFRIGERATE 3 hours or overnight

- 18   **ounces (3 cups) white chocolate chips**
- 2   **cans (14 ounces each) sweetened condensed milk**
- 1   **bag (12 ounces) semisweet chocolate chips**
- ½   **teaspoon baking soda**
- 1   **cup finely chopped walnuts**
- ½   **teaspoon vanilla extract**

• Line a 13 x 9 x 2-inch pan with nonstick foil. Combine white chocolate chips and 1 can of the condensed milk in a medium saucepan. Combine semisweet chips and remaining condensed milk in a different saucepan. Add ¼ teaspoon baking soda to each pan. Heat both over medium-low heat until chocolates are melted and smooth, about 5 to 7 minutes, stirring frequently.

• Remove pans from heat and stir ½ cup chopped walnuts into each. Add vanilla to semisweet chocolate mixture. Spoon alternate mounds of chocolate mixtures into prepared pan. Swirl together with a knife. Refrigerate for 3 hours or until firm, then lift from pan with foil and cut into squares.

PER PIECE 183 **CAL**; 9 g **FAT** (5 g **SAT**); 3 g **PRO**; 24 g **CARB**; 1 g **FIBER**; 50 mg **SODIUM**; 7 mg **CHOL**

MIXED BERRY
GRANOLA

mixed berry
GRANOLA

CHOCOLATE-COVERED
PRETZELS

Even the simplest gift—such as sweet and salty pretzels that take less than 30 minutes to make—is a special way to spread cheer.

Chocolate-Covered Pretzels

MAKES 36 pretzels at 34¢ each
PREP 15 minutes **MICROWAVE** 6 minutes

- 1 bag (12 ounces) white chocolate chips
- 8 ounces red candy coating melts
- 1 bag (12 ounces) semisweet chocolate chips
- 36 pretzel rods
  Assorted colored sugars and nonpareils

• Microwave white chocolate chips in a glass bowl at 60% power for 1 minute. Stir. Repeat, stirring until smooth. Place red candy melts in 2 small glass bowls and microwave as with white chocolate. Transfer to a pastry bag, snipping off a small opening at the tip.

• Microwave semisweet chocolate in a glass bowl on high for 1 minute. Stir. Repeat, stirring until smooth.

• Spoon white or semisweet chocolate over ¾ of each pretzel rod. Tap off excess and sprinkle with colored sugar or place on wax paper-lined sheet. Let dry. Drizzle with candy melts and decorate with sugars and nonpareils. (If candy melts harden, microwave for 20 seconds.)

PER PRETZEL 165 **CAL**; 8 g **FAT** (5 g **SAT**); 2 g **PRO**; 23 g **CARB**; 1 g **FIBER**; 137 mg **SODIUM**; 1 mg **CHOL**

Rosemary Shortbread

MAKES 24 cookies **PREP** 15 minutes **REFRIGERATE** 45 minutes **BAKE** at 350° for 12 minutes

- 2½ cups all-purpose flour
- 2 tablespoons chopped fresh rosemary
- ¾ teaspoon salt
- 1 cup (2 sticks) unsalted butter, softened
- ⅔ cup confectioners' sugar

• In a bowl, whisk together flour, rosemary and salt. In a stand mixer, beat butter and sugar on medium until well blended. Reduce speed to low and slowly add flour mixture; blend until the mixture resembles coarse crumbs. Gather dough into two balls, wrap both tightly in plastic wrap and refrigerate for 30 minutes.

• Heat oven to 350°. Remove one dough ball and roll out to ¼-inch thickness on parchment paper. Punch out cookies using a 3½-inch tree-shaped cookie cutter. Transfer cutouts to a cookie sheet about 2 inches apart; refrigerate for 15 minutes. Repeat with second dough ball. Bake at 350° for 10 to 12 minutes. (Do not allow cookies to brown.) Transfer cookies to a cooling rack.

PER COOKIE 127 **CAL**; 8 g **FAT** (5 g **SAT**); 1 g **PRO**; 13 g **CARB**; 0 g **FIBER**; 74 mg **SODIUM**; 20 mg **CHOL**

BIG NIGHT

A memorable menu for a sumptuous 5-course feast.

SUN-DRIED TOMATO
TAPENADE, PAGE 323

WHITE BEAN
SPREAD, PAGE 323

RADICCHIO, APPLE &
CELERY ROOT SALAD,
PAGE 325

POTATO-PEAR SOUP,
PAGE 325

RED RICE WITH ROASTED
BUTTERNUT SQUASH

CHESTNUT-AND-DATE-
STUFFED PORK ROAST

Chestnut-and-Date-Stuffed Pork Roast

MAKES 8 servings PREP 20 minutes
COOK 18 minutes ROAST at 375° for 45 minutes
LET REST 10 minutes

- 2½ pounds boneless pork roast
- 2 teaspoons garam masala
- 1½ teaspoons salt
- 2 tablespoons unsalted butter
- ½ Vidalia onion, diced
- 1¾ cups low-sodium chicken broth
- 1 cup dried pitted dates, finely chopped
- 1 cup peeled and cooked chestnuts, finely chopped
- ½ cup plain bread crumbs
- ¼ teaspoon pepper
- 1 tablespoon canola oil
- 1 tablespoon all-purpose flour

• Heat oven to 375°. Using a sharp knife, butterfly the top third of the roast from long end to long end, opening it like a book. Butterfly the remaining two-thirds of the roast in half, opening it the same way to create a flat piece of pork.

• Mix together garam masala and ½ teaspoon of the salt. Rub mixture onto the entire fat side of the roast. Turn over and set aside.

• Melt 1 tablespoon of the butter in a large, oven-safe sauté pan (not nonstick) over medium heat. Add onion; cook 5 minutes until softened. Pour in ½ cup of the chicken broth and the dates. Bring to a simmer; cook 2 minutes. Remove mixture to a bowl. Stir in chestnuts, bread crumbs, ½ teaspoon of the salt and the pepper.

• Distribute stuffing on the nonrubbed side of the pork, pressing down and leaving a 1-inch border on long ends and a 2-inch border on short ends. Roll tightly from one short end to the other. Tie 4 or 5 pieces of butcher string around pork to secure it.

• In the same pan, heat canola oil over medium-high heat. Sear pork on one side for 2 minutes. Repeat twice, carefully turning each time. Turn pork once more and transfer pan to oven. Roast at 375° for 45 minutes or until internal temperature reaches 145°.

• Remove pork to a cutting board to rest for 10 minutes. Being careful of the hot handle, melt remaining 1 tablespoon butter over medium heat. Whisk in flour; cook for 2 minutes. Whisk in remaining 1¼ cups chicken broth. Bring to a simmer and cook until thickened, 2 to 3 minutes. Stir in remaining ½ teaspoon salt.

• Slice pork and serve with pan sauce.

PER SERVING 344 CAL; 10 g FAT (3 g SAT); 33 g PRO; 30 g CARB; 3 g FIBER; 567 mg SODIUM; 78 mg CHOL

Red Rice with Roasted Butternut Squash

MAKES 8 servings PREP 10 minutes
COOK 50 minutes LET STAND 10 minutes
ROAST at 450° for 20 minutes

- 1½ cups red rice
- 2 cups low-sodium chicken broth
- 2 tablespoons unsalted butter
- 1½ pounds butternut squash, peeled, seeded and diced into ½-inch pieces (about 3 cups)
- 1 tablespoon olive oil
- 1¼ teaspoons salt
- ½ teaspoon black pepper
- ⅔ cup unsalted pepitas (hulled pumpkin seeds)
- ⅓ cup parsley, chopped

• Heat oven to 450°. In a large lidded pot, combine rice, broth, 1 cup water and 1 tablespoon of the butter. Bring to a boil; reduce heat to a simmer, cover and cook 50 minutes. Remove from heat and let stand 10 minutes, covered.

• Meanwhile, toss butternut squash with oil, ¼ teaspoon of the salt and ¼ teaspoon of the pepper. Roast at 450° for 10 minutes. Flip and roast for another 10 minutes or until browned.

• Transfer hot cooked rice to a large bowl. Stir in remaining 1 tablespoon butter, ½ cup of the pepitas, the parsley, remaining 1 teaspoon of the salt and remaining ¼ teaspoon of the pepper. Gently stir in cooked squash. Garnish with remaining pepitas.

PER SERVING 324 CAL; 13 g FAT (4 g SAT); 11 g PRO; 45 g CARB; 3 g FIBER; 389 mg SODIUM; 8 mg CHOL

White Bean Spread

MAKES 8 servings PREP 5 minutes

- 2 cans (15 ounces each) cannellini beans, drained and rinsed
- 2 tablespoons extra virgin olive oil
- 2 tablespoons lemon juice
- 1 teaspoon chopped fresh thyme
- ¾ teaspoon salt
- ¼ teaspoon pepper

• Combine beans, oil, lemon juice, thyme, salt and pepper in a food processor. Process until smooth.

PER SERVING 115 CAL; 4 g FAT (0 g SAT); 4 g PRO; 15 g CARB; 4 g FIBER; 351 mg SODIUM; 0 mg CHOL

Sun-Dried Tomato Tapenade

MAKES 8 servings PREP 5 minutes

- 1 jar (8.5 ounces) sun-dried tomatoes packed in oil
- ¼ cup walnuts, toasted
- 1 tablespoon chopped parsley
- ¼ teaspoon salt
- ⅛ teaspoon pepper

• Combine sun-dried tomatoes (include oil), walnuts, parsley, salt and pepper in a food processor. Pulse until finely chopped.

PER TABLESPOON 42 CAL; 3 g FAT (0 g SAT); 1 g PRO; 4 g CARB; 1 g FIBER; 77 mg SODIUM; 0 mg CHOL

BLOOD ORANGE
PANNA COTTA

Blood Orange Panna Cotta

MAKES 8 servings **PREP** 10 minutes
LET STAND 5 minutes **COOK** 4 minutes
CHILL at least 6 hours

- **1** envelope unflavored gelatin (0.25 ounce)
- **¾** cup blood orange juice (such as Tropicana Trop50 Red Orange)
- **2** containers (6 ounces each) Chobani 0% Blood Orange yogurt
- **1½** cups whole milk
- **1** cup heavy cream
- **⅔** cup sugar
- **½** teaspoon vanilla extract
- **2** blood or navel oranges, zested, pith removed, cut into segments
  Fresh mint (optional)

• In a small bowl, sprinkle gelatin over ½ cup of the blood orange juice. Let stand until softened, about 5 minutes.

• In a large bowl, whisk yogurt until smooth; set aside. Bring milk, heavy cream and ⅓ cup of the sugar to a low simmer. Turn off heat. Stir in vanilla and juice-gelatin mixture; mix until gelatin is dissolved. Pour into bowl with yogurt and whisk until smooth.

• Coat eight 6-ounce ramekins with nonstick cooking spray. Pour mixture evenly among ramekins. Cover with plastic wrap and refrigerate for at least 6 hours or up to 2 days.

• In a small pot or pan, bring remaining ⅓ cup sugar, remaining ¼ cup blood orange juice and the orange zest to a simmer. Cook until sugar is dissolved and mixture has a syrupy consistency, about 4 minutes. Cool and refrigerate in a covered container until using.

• To serve, carefully run a paring knife around edge of each ramekin. Turn upside down onto a plate (shake if it doesn't immediately fall out). Place an orange segment on top, drizzle with blood orange syrup and, if desired, garnish with mint.

PER SERVING 234 **CAL**; 13 g **FAT** (8 g **SAT**); 7 g **PRO**; 26 g **CARB**; 1 g **FIBER**; 54 mg **SODIUM**; 45 mg **CHOL**

Potato-Pear Soup

MAKES 8 servings **PREP** 15 minutes
COOK 32 minutes

- **2** tablespoons unsalted butter
- **2** leeks (white and light green parts), cleaned and thinly sliced
- **4** cups low-sodium chicken broth
- **2** pounds russet potatoes, peeled and cut into 1-inch cubes
- **2** pounds Bartlett pears, peeled, cored and cut into 1-inch cubes
- **¼** cup packed light brown sugar
- **2** teaspoons salt
  Crème fraîche or sour cream (optional)
  Sliced chives (optional)

• Melt butter over medium heat in a large lidded pot. Add leeks and cook 7 minutes, until softened. Add chicken broth, potatoes and pears. Bring to a boil. Reduce heat to medium-low, cover and cook 25 minutes.

• Using a handheld blender (or a countertop blender, in batches), puree soup until smooth. (If using countertop blender, return mixture to pot.) While still hot, stir in brown sugar and salt.

• Ladle soup into 8 bowls. Garnish with a dollop of crème fraîche and sliced chives, if desired.

PER SERVING 213 **CAL**; 3 g **FAT** (2 g **SAT**); 4 g **PRO**; 46 g **CARB**; 5 g **FIBER**; 622 mg **SODIUM**; 8 mg **CHOL**

Radicchio, Apple & Celery Root Salad

MAKES 8 servings **PREP** 25 minutes

- **½** cup buttermilk
- **⅓** cup light mayonnaise
- **4** ounces Roquefort cheese, crumbled (about 1 cup)
- **¼** teaspoon onion powder
- **½** teaspoon salt
- **⅛** teaspoon pepper
- **2** medium heads radicchio, cored and thinly sliced (about 8 cups)
- **½** pound celery root, peeled and sliced into matchsticks
- **2** Granny Smith apples, cored and thinly sliced
- **1** tablespoon fresh lemon juice

• Whisk together buttermilk and mayonnaise until smooth. Stir in Roquefort, onion powder, ¼ teaspoon of the salt and the pepper. Cover and refrigerate until using.

• Toss together radicchio, celery root, apples, lemon juice and remaining ¼ teaspoon of the salt. Drizzle half the dressing on top of salad and serve remaining dressing on the side.

PER SERVING 136 **CAL**; 8 g **FAT** (3 g **SAT**); 5 g **PRO**; 14 g **CARB**; 2 g **FIBER**; 476 mg **SODIUM**; 15 mg **CHOL**

INDEX

Q

QUESADILLAS
Chicken Quesadillas, 163
Smoky Chicken Quesadillas, 133
QUICHE
Caramelized Onion Quiche, 103
Potato & Turkey Bacon Quiche, 243
Quick Ratatouille, 130
QUINOA
Chicken-Apple Sausage Quinoa, 134
Grilled Tuna with Red Quinoa Risotto, 40
PB&J Bites, 240

R

Radicchio, Apple & Celery Root Salad, 325
Radicchio & Shaved Fennel, 122
Raita, 211
Raspberry Pavlova, 190
Raspberry Smoothie, 192
Ratatouille, Quick, 130
Real Barbecued Chicken, 156
Red Deviled Eggs, 260
Red Rice with Roasted Butternut Squash, 323
Red Slaw Dogs, 160
RICE
Apricot-Lime Glazed Shrimp, 182
Black-as-Night Rice Salad, 259
Chicken Gumbo, 264
Coconut Shrimp Curry, 137
Lemony Vegetable Risotto, 177
Red Rice with Roasted Butternut Squash, 323
Sausage & Mushroom Risotto, 106
Skillet Chicken, Chorizo & Rice, 263
Veggie Paella, 252
Wild Mushroom Risotto, 266
Wild Rice Salad with Apricots, Fennel & Feta, 148
Rigatoni with Creamy Pepper Sauce, 73
Rigatoni with Red Clam Sauce, 267
RISOTTO
Grilled Tuna with Red Quinoa Risotto, 40
Lemony Vegetable Risotto, 177
Sausage & Mushroom Risotto, 106
Wild Mushroom Risotto, 266
Roasted Beet, Apple & White Bean Salad, 103
Roasted Cauliflower, 42
Roasted Cherry Tomato Bisque, 51
Roasted Salmon & Brussels Sprouts with Bacon Orzo, 69
Roasted Salmon & Easy Romesco Sauce, 15

Rockin' Moroccan Snack Mix, 241
Rosemary Shortbread, 319
Rotini with Sautéed Chicken Sausage & Vegetables, 225
Rubs, Trio of, 312

S

SALADS
Arugula-Carrot Salad, 122
Avocado Chopped Salad, 155
Bean, Corn & Turkey Salad, 221
Beef & Chickpea Toss, 219
Black-as-Night Rice Salad, 259
Blueberry-Blue Cheese Salad, 188
Broccoli-Carrot Slaw, 43
Chicken & Shaved Squash Salad, 202
Coleslaw, 140
Fajita Salad, 219
Flank Steak with Tomato, Cucumber & Watermelon Salad, 201
Greek Shrimp & Feta, 220
Grilled Peaches, Beans & Arugula with Warm Bacon Dressing, 150
Grilled Sausage & Pepper Pasta Salad, 163
Grilled Steak Salad with Chimichurri Dressing, 147
Grilled Tofu Salad, 121
Grilled Tuna Salad with Garden Dressing, 181
Layered Shrimp & Avocado Salad, 220
Miso-Glazed Salmon Salad, 151
Radicchio, Apple & Celery Root Salad, 325
Radicchio & Shaved Fennel, 122
Roasted Beet, Apple & White Bean Salad, 103
Shaved Brussels Sprouts Salad, 285
Shrimp Spinach Salad, 220
Shrimp Taco Bowl, 220
Steak Salad with Maple Balsamic, 134
Sundried Tomato Pesto Turkey Salad, 221
Thai Salad with Chicken, 218
Wheat Berry & Edamame Salad, 125
Wild Rice Salad with Apricots, Fennel & Feta, 148
SALMON
Juicy Salmon Burgers, 217
Miso-Glazed Salmon Salad, 151
Pecan Salmon & Smashed Potatoes, 42
Roasted Salmon & Brussels Sprouts with Bacon Orzo, 69
Roasted Salmon & Easy Romesco Sauce, 15
Salmon Cakes with Old Bay Aïoli, 102
Smoked Salmon Breakfast Pizza, 89

SALSA
Chunky Salsa, 311
Strawberry Salsa, 189
Saltimbocca Sandwiches, 208
SANDWICHES. SEE ALSO BURGERS
Asian Beef & Lentil Sloppy Joes, 227
BBQ Pulled Chicken, 270
Carolina Pulled-Pork Sandwiches, 140
Chicken Gyros, 218
Chicken Shawarma, 212
Cornmeal-Crusted Catfish Po'Boys, 39
The Cuban, 271
French Dip, 271
Honey-Dijon Chicken & Spinach Wraps, 218
Muffaletta, 219
Open-Faced Turkey, 269
Pulled Buffalo Chicken Sliders, 95
Saltimbocca Sandwiches, 208
Sweet Chili Rolls, 269
Turkey Pita Club, 221
Veggie Gyros, 218
Veggie Muffaletta, 219
Wasabi Beef Pockets, 219
SAUCES
Cranberry-Clementine Sauce, 286
Hot Fudge Sauce, 58
Spicy Yogurt Sauce, 105
Strawberry-Ancho Chile Sauce, 167
SAUSAGES. SEE ALSO PORK SAUSAGES
Breakfast Strata, 86
Cheddar-Apple Sausage Mac, 23
Chicken-Apple Sausage Quinoa, 134
Creole Sausage & Shrimp, 98
Orecchiette with Roasted Red Pepper Sauce, 203
Rotini with Sautéed Chicken Sausage & Vegetables, 225
Stuffed Shells, 237
SCALLOPS
Hearty Scallop & Corn Stew, 265
Honey-Sesame Scallops, 39
SEAFOOD. SEE ALSO FISH; SHELLFISH
Seafood Chowder, 52
Sesame Chicken Stir-Fry, 255
SHALLOTS
Caramelized Shallot, Capicola & Fontina Frittata, 265
Green Beans, Hazelnuts & Shallots, 289
Shaved Brussels Sprouts Salad, 285
SHELLFISH. SEE ALSO SHRIMP
Hearty Scallop & Corn Stew, 265
Honey-Sesame Scallops, 39

IN-A-PINCH SUBSTITUTIONS

It can happen to the best of us: Halfway through a recipe,
you find you're completely out of a key ingredient. Here's what to do:

Recipe Calls For:	You May Substitute:
1 square unsweetened chocolate	3 tbsp. unsweetened cocoa powder + 1 tbsp. butter/margarine
1 cup cake flour	1 cup less 2 tbsp. all-purpose flour
2 tbsp. flour (for thickening)	1 tbsp. cornstarch
1 tsp. baking powder	¼ tsp. baking soda + ½ tsp. cream of tartar + ¼ tsp. cornstarch
1 cup corn syrup	1 cup sugar + ¼ cup additional liquid used in recipe
1 cup milk	½ cup evaporated milk + ½ cup water
1 cup buttermilk or sour milk	1 tbsp. vinegar or lemon juice + enough milk to make 1 cup
1 cup sour cream (for baking)	1 cup plain yogurt
1 cup firmly packed brown sugar	1 cup sugar + 2 tbsp. molasses
1 tsp. lemon juice	¼ tsp. vinegar (not balsamic)
¼ cup chopped onion	1 tbsp. instant minced
1 clove garlic	¼ tsp. garlic powder
2 cups tomato sauce	¾ cup tomato paste + 1 cup water
1 tbsp. prepared mustard	1 tsp. dry mustard + 1 tbsp. water

HOW TO KNOW WHAT YOU NEED

Making a shopping list based on a recipe can be tricky if you don't know
how many tomatoes yields 3 cups chopped. Our handy translations:

When the Recipe Calls For:	You Need:
4 cups shredded cabbage	1 small cabbage
1 cup grated raw carrot	1 large carrot
2½ cups sliced carrots	1 pound raw carrots
4 cups cooked cut fresh green beans	1 pound beans
1 cup chopped onion	1 large onion
4 cups sliced raw potatoes	4 medium-size potatoes
1 cup chopped sweet pepper	1 large pepper
1 cup chopped tomato	1 large tomato
2 cups canned tomatoes	16-oz. can
4 cups sliced apples	4 medium-size apples
1 cup mashed banana	3 medium-size bananas
1 tsp. grated lemon rind	1 medium-size lemon
2 tbsp. lemon juice	1 medium-size lemon
4 tsp. grated orange rind	1 medium-size orange
1 cup orange juice	3 medium-size oranges
4 cups sliced peaches	8 medium-size peaches
2 cups sliced strawberries	1 pint
1 cup soft bread crumbs	2 slices fresh bread
1 cup bread cubes	2 slices fresh bread
2 cups shredded Swiss or cheddar cheese	8 oz. cheese
1 cup egg whites	6 or 7 large eggs
1 egg white	2 tsp. egg white powder + 2 tbsp. water
4 cups chopped walnuts or pecans	1 pound shelled